PANAMA
AT THE CROSSROADS

Economic Development and Political
Change in the Twentieth Century

ANDREW ZIMBALIST AND JOHN WEEKS

UNIVERSITY OF CALIFORNIA PRESS
BERKELEY   LOS ANGELES   OXFORD

University of California Press
Berkeley and Los Angeles, California

University of California Press, Ltd.
Oxford, England

© 1991 by
The Regents of the University of California

Library of Congress Cataloging-in-Publication Data

Zimbalist, Andrew S.
   Panama at the crossroads : economic development and political
change in the twentieth century / Andrew Zimbalist and John Weeks.
     p. cm.
   Includes bibliographical references and index.
   ISBN 0-520-07311-8 (alk. paper)
   1. Panama—Economic conditions. 2. Panama—Politics and
government. I. Weeks, John. II. Title.
HC147.Z44 1991
338.97287'009'04—dc20   90-50923
                                                 CIP

Printed in the United States of America

1 2 3 4 5 6 7 8 9

To our fathers,
Samuel Zimbalist
and
Alden Weeks

Contents

List of Tables

Acknowledgments

As in the case of all books, this one benefited from the support, comments, and suggestions of many people. We would like particularly to thank Willy Cochez, Richard Wanio, and Roberto Méndez, our invaluable contacts in Panama and endless sources of information. Many other Panamanians also extended themselves and were extremely helpful: Nicky Barletta, Paul Smith, Ron Holloman, Luis Moreno, Marco Gandásegui, Eddie Vallarino, Ricardo Arias Calderón, Pepe Galán, Miguel Bernal, Eduardo Jaén, Catín Vásquez, Roberto Arosemena, Alejandro Cordero, and Leonel Méndez. In the United States many colleagues provided insights, useful critiques, and support: Lowell Gundmundson, Manuel Pastor, Elizabeth Dore, Lydia Nettler, Mustafa Topiwalla, Carmen Diana Deere, Walter LaFeber, Stephen Gudeman, and Blake Friscia. Suji Im and Yan Zhang offered excellent research assistance. The editors at the University of California Press were patient and perceptive. Our families, Jeffrey, Michael, Lydia, Matthew, Rachel, and Liz, put up with our extended absences and our distractions with understanding and good humor (most of the time). Our sincere gratitude goes to all.

Chapter One

Power in Panama

Apparently Mao Tse-tung once said, "Political power grows out of the barrel of a gun." As a half-truth, its repetition evokes an aura of profundity; yet political power derives from the control of weapons only under rare circumstances. Quite the contrary is the general rule: control of the instruments of force derives from holding effective political power. Particularly in Panama in the 1980s, however, the line of causality suggested by Mao's quotation seemed valid, for the government of Manuel Noriega appeared to develop little popular support and to rule by the dubious legitimacy of armed force. At the risk of cliché, it should be said that the basis of Noreiga's rule was considerably more complex than his willingness to use force with ruthless disregard of the niceties of legal procedure. The government of Noriega represented but the most extreme manifestation of an autocratic state, derived from a society in which the relationship between ruler and ruled had developed its own peculiar characteristics.

In the more important areas of South America and Meso-America, political power in the colonial period frequently involved the elite's direct control over labor and land (e.g., Peru and Mexico). Of course, formal political power was usually held by a group of urban bureaucrats or professionals. However, in these agrarian societies wealth came primarily from the surplus production of the laboring population, extracted through various forms of coerced labor. The systems of coerced labor provided the basis of the increasing commercialization of agriculture during the eighteenth and nineteenth centuries. For example, in the Central American territories of Guatemala and El Salvador, the development of coffee production after independence relied upon the mechanisms of forced labor initiated under colonial rule. Toward the end of the nineteenth century "vagrancy" laws and debt peonage, not formally abolished until the 1930s and continuing in practice, replaced the older mechanisms. This legalized servitude was then replaced by the *colono* system, in which a peasant family was tied to a particular estate through the grant of a small parcel of land; this system, persistent as a major source of field labor for coffee into the 1970s, still has not disappeared.[1]

Essentially the coercive labor system involved recruiting and binding labor to the land through extra-economic means. Neither the lure of wages nor the disciplining threat of unemployment primarily brought workers to the estates of the landlords; rather a direct repression of the freedom of movement and choice of alternative livelihoods forced their compliance. Certainly, the degree of effectiveness of coercion varied, but qualifications and specifics do not alter the general conclusion that this was coerced, not free, labor. As a consequence, forced labor systems had to be maintained through direct political control over the laboring population. At one end of this direct control was the police power of the state, which pursued and apprehended defectors from the fields and ensured that the peasantry made no organized attempt to alter the conditions of its servitude. On a day-to-day basis, freedom was repressed, and the peasant population was dominated through various mechanisms that united the landlords' entrepreneurial and political control functions. For example, it was not unusual for the landlord also to serve as the civil authority over the peasants laboring on the estate. Although these systems had their benign aspects as well as elements of flexibility, they existed to control labor and depress levels of payment.

This synthesis of economic and political power between peasant and landlord gave rise to the infamous oligarchy in Spanish America. Although the term "oligarchy" is elusive and used loosely, most who employ it mean more than merely "wealthy and powerful." The oligarchy in Latin America was, and in some countries remains, a landed class whose control over producers is direct, though certainly not total. It represented a form of paternalist domination different from that of urban capitalists over factory workers. Oligarchic peasant-landlord relations allowed despotic, repressive regimes. These regimes were necessarily despotic because the landlords displayed direct political domination over the peasants. Such a system precludes political participation because the operation of production relations requires the repression of political rights.

Coerced labor systems provide the vehicle for the oligarchy's consolidation of political power, which lies in its control over the access to land; in an underdeveloped agrarian society this usually implies domination over the majority of the population. Were an elite unable to control access to land, even mild forms of coerced labor would be difficult to enforce. Therefore, these labor systems form the basis of political stability, insofar as they can be maintained through ongoing repression. The oligarchy uses these labor systems to command loyalty, raise armies, tax peasants, and resist pressures for internal reform. In Central America, political power, growing largely out of the landlord's domination over the peasantry, provided the underlying stability of despotic regimes into the twentieth century. With urbanization and industrialization, this direct control broke down. But political control became increasingly indirect, mediated through a political arena formally characterized by augmenting degrees of mass participation.

Particularly in Central America, this dominance of the propertied classes manifested itself through a state whose primary purpose was to facilitate the continuation and renovation of the relations of production in agriculture. The laws, ideology, and political administration insured that the operation of civil society was consistent with the manner in which private wealth was accumulated. At the same time, the relations of production provided the vehicle for displaying the oligarchy's political influence, minimizing the state's use of force to maintain the political order. The power of the dominant classes did not arise from their economic wealth as such; they controlled the political arena, not because their incomes were great, but because they dominated a nexus of human relations centered around the process of production.

Political Power in Panama
to the Eve of Secession

Panama never had a landed oligarchy of the type described above;[2] indeed, the development of an indigenous class of large-scale agriculturalists, in grazing and sugar growing, developed relatively recently and postdated the Second World War. The absence of a landed oligarchy, with an organic link to the population by which political influence could be exercised, and the emergence of strong merchant interests help account for the nature of Panamanian society.[3] But prior to pursuing the implications of this point, it is necessary to trace briefly the postconquest history of the isthmus.

After the taking of Portobelo by the British in 1739, Panama was administered from the Spanish Viceroyalty of Nueva Granada. With the victory of the independence forces against the Spanish crown, the isthmian territory became part of Gran Colombia, which included the present countries of Ecuador, Colombia, and Venezuela.[4] Gran Colombia soon fragmented, and Panama remained a province of the reduced Colombian state.

From the beginning of the Spanish Empire in the New World, the importance of Panama lay in its geography—the shortest land bridge between the oceans. Until the 1730s, Panama had one of only three mainland ports (the others were Callao and Vera Cruz) through which trade between Spain and the New World was authorized. Borne by humans and pack animals, the wealth extracted from the Pacific and inland provinces of South America came through Panama. Around this trade developed a prosperous merchant class that, to the extent of the province of Panama's minimal autonomy, represented the local ruling class. In Mexico and Peru, and on a smaller scale in Guatemala, the importance of the merchant class derived from the power of the landed oligarchy, which asserted direct control over the mass of the population.[5] During certain periods merchant interests also dominated in parts of the Hispanic Caribbean and in Costa Rica and Nicaragua for Central America.[6] However, in Panama merchant dominance was never significantly mitigated by a landed class. In this regard, Panama was extreme but not unique.

If one views Panama in this early period as part of the larger administrative unit (Nueva Granada), then the isthmian merchant class is reduced to relatively little importance. Yet two reasons make it valid to focus upon Panama as a separate geographical unit for analysis even in the sixteenth and seventeenth centuries. First, soon after the conquest, Panama began to assume an ethnic diversity that gave it a character more Caribbean than South or Central American. Second, its merchant class enjoyed a degree of autonomy because of its great geographical distance from the ruling classes that presided over the production and extraction of material wealth.

During the first two centuries after the conquest, the isthmus lacked any significant productive activity in the hinterland that produced a surplus product upon which a rural ruling class could be based. There was little settlement of the interior of the isthmus during the colonial period, and no mineral wealth of note was found.[7] The reason for the lack of settlement in Panama, just as in other sparsely populated areas of the Spanish Empire in the New World, was simple: the absence of a substantial indigenous population that could be recruited into coerced labor for mining and plantation agriculture. Although there were *encomiendas* in Panama, the largest apparently had no more than thirty or forty workers, and the system was abolished, at least formally, by the mid-seventeenth century.

Although estimates vary widely on the size of the indigenous population at the time of the Spanish conquest, ranging from one hundred thousand to more than one million, virtually all analyses of the Panamanian economy in the sixteenth and seventeenth centuries refer to the absence of a substantial indigenous labor force.[8] Despite the considerable size of the indigenous population at the beginning of the sixteenth century, the population was apparently quickly and substantially reduced by initial skirmishes with the colonizers—rampant disease, the ravages of the encomienda system, and, most important, the brutality of Governor Pedro Arias Dávila (known as Pedrarias). According to one account, "he [Pedrarias] probably killed or enslaved—or both—as many as two million Indians."[9] The claim of a local labor shortage receives additional support from the need to import large numbers of slaves to exploit the small gold deposits during the first decades of the 1500s, the termination of the encomienda system in the Nata area in 1558, the small size of the encomienda to the west,[10] and the complete disappearance of the system by 1650. Largely for lack of a substantial indigenous population, a landed oligarchy failed to emerge; and, in consequence of the geography of the isthmus, a merchant class emerged instead as the dominant political force.

By the eighteenth century this merchant class had fallen upon hard times. The British destruction of the forts at Portobelo in 1739 coincided with the end of the royal monopoly of trade and accelerated the decline of the isthmus as a trading route. With less trade, members of the poorer classes abandoned the urban areas to seek livelihoods in the hinterland, joining descendants of the black slaves who had been thrown onto the land when the gold mines closed. These settlers did not generate a wealthy landed class; on the contrary, for the most part they remained poor and largely subsistence producers. Along with the peasants was a small sector of medium-sized, surplus-producing peasant holdings, usually involved in cattle raising. But the ranchers were not important in numbers or political influence. The class structure of Panama underwent important changes during the colonial period and then under Colombian rule, but this situation remained until the time of Panamanian secession from Colombia: generally, an urban merchant class held political power, and a subsistence peasantry sparsely settled the countryside.

In the colonial period the profits of the merchant class had been based upon the transshipment of commodities by human and animal power. Many of these laborers were black, either those brought to the isthmus as slaves or former slaves who had escaped from Caribbean islands. At the end of the eighteenth century urban Panama had a black majority, differentiated from the Creole merchants by both class and ethnicity. In the 1840s regular steamship service revived the depressed fortunes of the Panama crossing, though further north there was competition from Vanderbilt's route up the San Juan River and across Lake Nicaragua. New York capitalists ensured the cost advantage of the Panama route by constructing a railroad; begun in 1851 and completed in 1855, it reduced transshipment time from several days to several hours. This railroad not only brought great benefits to the Panamanian merchants but also characterized them permanently: their relationship to trade through the isthmus became secondary to foreign, increasingly North American, domination over the means of transport.

The impetus to Panamanian commerce brought by the railroad was short-lived, lasting only fifteen years until the Golden Spike was driven to complete the first rail line across the North American continent in 1869. The Panamanian railroad, though, did have the lasting effect of opening up the interior of the isthmus to large-scale agricultural production. But this was almost exclusively conducted by foreign capital; Minor C. Keith established the first banana plantations in the Bocas del Toro area near the Costa Rican border.

The first attempt to construct a canal across the isthmus is an oft-told tale.[11] Initiated in 1878 by Ferdinand de Lesseps, who had designed the Suez Canal, the sea-level canal was bold in its technical conception, but the de Lesseps attempt had to be abandoned for lack of financing.[12]

On the eve of separation from Colombia, the class structure of Panama had assumed the basic characteristics that would carry through the twentieth century. First, among the domestic classes on the isthmus political power was concentrated in the hands of an urban merchant class; although located at strategic points in the chain of commerce, the class did not control the key aspect of Panama's economic structure—transport. Second, the merchant class monopolized political power on the isthmus, but it held virtually no direct economic control over the population it dominated.

At the time of separation from Colombia, the vast majority of Panamanians carried on their productive activities with little reference to the politically dominant class. The importance of this economic nonrelation between the politically dominant and politically impotent is best appreciated by contrast. In Mexico, Peru, Bolivia, and Colombia itself, the vast majority of the rural population labored in some subservient relationship to a landlord class, which via repression and patronage asserted its direct control over producers. The Panamanian countryside by contrast was largely self-sufficient in its poverty, except for a politically unimportant commercial sector. Although there was commercial agriculture, the small units were involved in grazing, which hired little labor. In any event, the commercial agriculturalists who directly controlled labor were not part of the political elite.[13]

As stated above, the urban merchant class in Panama found itself in the anomalous position of dominating the population of the isthmus politically without exercising much direct economic control over that same population. Although the merchants controlled the markets through which the rural population bought and sold, these primarily subsistence producers were only marginally integrated into commerce. In consequence, at the end of the nineteenth century its power base was narrow because it directly touched the livelihoods of only a small portion of the population and shallow because political power depended upon the acquiescence of urban and rural masses.[14] In this context, the urban ruling class had only political means of control, which might have been effective had a political ideology bound the lower-class Panamanians to the urban elite, an ideology that would have allowed the facade of political participation. But until the emergence of the Arias brothers as a political force in the 1930s, no such ideology existed. And even if such an ideology had emerged in the nineteenth century, the merchant class would have been loath to allow mass political participation.

The ethnic divisions on the isthmus accentuated the fragile nature of the commercial class's political control. As early as the sixteenth century, Panama had a significant black population, initially the result of slavery in the gold mines. Moreover, urban Panama was predominantly black by the end of the eighteenth century, and more black labor was recruited for constructing the railroad and attempting de Lesseps's canal. After separation from Colombia, Panama's black population was further increased during the construction of the U.S.-financed canal, whose labor force was perhaps 75 percent black. Thus, the urban class structure between rich and poor was also divided between criollo and black, and the commercial elite lived in trepidation of a Haitian-type revolution breaking out on the isthmus. In 1856, a riot in Panama City of the black lower class fueled such fears. In the late nineteenth century emergence of the Negro Liberal party further intensified the commercial class's fears that it was besieged by a black majority over which it had limited political control; the commercial class saw its fears fulfilled in 1885 when Pedro Prestan led an unsuccessful Negro Liberal revolt against the ruling Conservatives. Nevertheless, the essentially narrow political base of the merchant class lay not in ethnic differences but in the narrow economic base of its control.

Elsewhere in Meso-America other regimes feared the transition to mass political participation, but those situations were less precarious than that of the Panamanian ruling elite. In Guatemala and El Salvador mass participation, even in form, was despotically opposed. But regimes in those countries, as elsewhere in earlier Spanish America, were firmly grounded in coercive labor systems, which placed the mass of the peasantry under their domination. Given this despotic base, the Central American oligarchy was able to resist the pressure for democratic reform into the 1970s. In other words, for these despotic regimes coercive control over the population was both the system to be maintained and the vehicle for preserving that system. This helps explain the extraordinary degree of violence in Guatemala and El Salvador in the 1970s and 1980s. In Panama, the elite's resistance to reform and its fear of the potential power of the masses derived from the fact that the elite only effectively controlled the masses through the police power of the state itself. The fact that merchants were powerful was not unique to Panama; on the contrary, this has been common enough in Latin America. The Panamanian case was somewhat unusual, however, because the power of merchants was not augmented by a powerful landed class.

The control by Panama's merchant class over politics was *formal,* derived from a monopolization of the political sphere itself. To establish *effective* control over the political sphere, the commercial ruling class would have had to convert itself into either a landed oligarchy dominating the access to peasant livelihood or an industrial capitalist class controlling the means by which workers gained employment. Although both conversions occurred in individual cases prior to the eve of separation from Colombia,[15] the extent of this transformation was not sufficient to alter the basic weakness of the commercial class vis-à-vis the mass of the population.

That is, control is more effective when it joins the economic with the political and subordinates classes that depend on the ruling class for their livelihood. Furthermore, a common economic project tends to unify the elite and, hence, stabilize the nature of political contestation. We make this argument specifically for Panama, though it is also relevant to other societies dominated by a commercial class. The degree to which it applies to other countries and the particular manner in which it manifests itself can only be determined through concrete analysis.

Political Power in Panama after Separation from Colombia

The commercial elite vacillated over the issue of independence in the nineteenth century. On the one hand, it resented the restrictions placed upon it by the central government in Bogota; on the other, it feared that an independent Panama would be dominated by the lower-class majority over which it had limited control.[16] During the Colombian civil war of 1840–1841 the merchants had declared the independence of Panama, but they had lacked the force of arms to maintain this status once the central government had consolidated its power. Certainly there was discontent, particularly during the presidency of Conservative Rafael Nuñez in the 1880s,[17] and again during the "War of 1,000 Days" from 1899 to 1902. It is not surprising that a secessionist cause would blossom when the central government was in disarray; but also it is suggestive of the weakness and therefore vacillation of the commercial elite that only in such moments did its nationalism assume active form.

The conflicting forces, acting on the commercial elite with regard to secession, were resolved through the action of the administration of Theodore Roosevelt. Following the unanimous rejection of a canal deal by the Colombian legislature, in an intervention violating the Bidlack-Mallarino Treaty that guaranteed Colombian sovereignty over the isthmus, the U.S. government first encouraged a show of insurrection in Panama and then prevented a landing of Colombian troops that would certainly have crushed the mock uprising. With the events of 1903, Panama's status changed from a province of Colombia to a protectorate of the United States. Formal subservience to the U.S. government, while perhaps offensive to national pride, helped resolve the central political difficulty of the commercial ruling class: political control of a population over which it had little direct economic dominion. It is a misrepresentation of history to suggest that the U.S. government created the country of Panama out of whole cloth. However, had the U.S. government not intervened in support of a separate Panama, it is doubtful whether the commercial elite would have taken the risky step of pursuing independence on its own. And had the U.S. government concluded a canal agreement with Colombia, which it almost did,[18] certainly there would have been no independent Panama early in this century or perhaps even now.

After formal independence the direct hold of the ruling commercial class over the laboring population grew, if anything, weaker. While plantations and large cattle ranches expanded in the interior, this development was offset by the construction and subsequent operation of the lock canal. In 1910, ninety thousand people lived in the Canal Zone,[19] and the U.S.-owned and -controlled waterway was the largest employer in Panama. In 1920, the population of the Zone fell to its lowest point (less than thirty thousand), but it stayed between forty and fifty-five thousand from 1930 to the time of the Torrijos-Carter Treaties in 1977. Because the Canal Zone was in practice U.S. territory, beyond the reach of any Panamanian government, the Panamanian population in the Zone was largely free from even political and economic control of the Panamanian ruling class.

Thus, the defining characteristics of Panama's dominant class in the nineteenth century—moderate wealth and partial political power with little control over economic life—became more apparent in the early twentieth century. These characteristics made the postindependence ruling groups politically vulnerable and more prone to turn to representatives of the U.S. government in Panama to protect their rule over the lower classes and even to settle disputes among themselves. Again, this tendency certainly prevailed elsewhere in Latin America, but it assumed an extreme form in Panama. The role for the U.S. government as de facto viceroy of the isthmus was legally enshrined in the 1904 Panamanian constitution, which granted Washington the unilateral and, in practice, unrestricted right of intervention in the hastily created country.

The U.S. government's heavy-handed role as colonial governor in Panama should not be interpreted as arising solely from security interests with regard to the Canal or fawning cooperation of a U.S.-installed government.[20] The new government of Panama also had security interests that the U.S. military presence served, as embarrassing as that presence might be for national pride. During the first ten years after formal independence Panama had no army,[21] the police force numbered eleven hundred at most, and serious threats to the government's rule required the intervention of U.S. troops. The role of the U.S. troops in maintaining order casts in a different light the notorious Article 136 of the first constitution; the article granted unilateral right of armed intervention throughout the country. The Conservative party, which held the presidency until 1912, strongly supported Article 136 at the constitutional convention. Setting aside considerations of national pride, one can see the advantage to the urban ruling class of this concession to the U.S. government. The presence of U.S. troops avoided the need for a substantial standing army, the leaders of which might have political ambitions of their own. Furthermore, as long as the Panamanian government fully cooperated with its U.S. viceroy, any intervention would serve the interests of both parties.

Immediately after formal independence the personnel who assumed the high posts of government in Panama were intimately involved with the interests of the United States and the success of a canal venture; indeed, they could be described as virtual American agents. In 1894, the de Lesseps venture had been reorganized as the New Panama Canal Company (NPCC), a corporate creation primarily designed to maintain claim to the dormant canal concession. Through this concession the Spooner Amendment authorized the U.S. government to purchase the Canal. Manuel Amador Guerrero, head of the junta that declared Panama's independence, served as the medical officer for the NPCC-owned railroad, and another junta member, Jose Agustin Arango, was an attorney for the railroad. In Washington Philippe Bunau-Varilla, former engineer for the de Lesseps enterprise and financial backer in the NPCC, negotiated the new canal treaty for the insurrectionary junta. Perhaps because these Conservatives had such close ties to the canal effort and had supported so faithfully Article 136, the U.S. government arranged their holding the presidency for the first ten years after independence.

Panamanian nationalists refer to the 1903 agreement as "the Treaty no Panamanian signed." Indeed, no Panamanian even read the treaty before it was signed. Bunau-Varilla, neither Panamanian nor diplomat, used the plenipotentiary powers assigned him reluctantly by the junta to sign the treaty with the U.S. government. To be sure, the junta was suspicious of Bunau-Varilla and tried to nullify his powers, but Bunau-Varilla prevailed by arguing that if the treaty was not signed immediately the U.S. would withdraw its support for an independent Panamanian state. To assure U.S. cooperation, Bunau-Varilla sweetened the deal that had been offered in the rejected Colombian Treaty: he widened the Canal Zone from six to ten miles, gave the U.S. jurisdiction over the entire zone "as if sovereign," and changed the lease from ninety-nine years to "in perpetuity."[22] The treaty was signed by Bunau-Varilla and John Hay on November 18, 1903.

The personal gain that may have motivated the Conservative politicians to cooperate so fully with the U.S. government should not obscure the underlying and more basic causality, for the Liberals would hardly have behaved differently; in fact, they behaved the same when they gained the presidency in 1912.[23] Fundamentally, the commercial class, which dominated both the Conservative and the Liberal parties, lacked the economic basis upon which to construct stable political power. Lacking this, the relationship with the United States served as a surrogate for maintaining the authority of the state. In the second half of the 1910s a more broadly based Liberal party developed, led by Belisario Porras, but the limited command it held over the Panamanian masses would be demonstrated in subsequent elections.

By 1930 the Liberal and Conservative parties, either separately or in coalition, had lost the ability to perpetuate their rule through elections. Always paper-thin and requiring U.S. patronage, the political facade of the commercial and business classes collapsed before the onslaught of middle-class nationalists, led by Harmodio and Arnulfo Arias. Elections were acutely problematical for the Panamanian ruling class because it lacked either the repressive force or sustaining ideology to manage them. The U.S. government actually disarmed the Panamanian police in 1915–1916 and then left it in an ambiguous relation to the Panamanian state by appointing an American commander. Absent U.S. cooperation, the Panamanian government lacked the effective means to control the election process and, as an ultimate sanction, to nullify it. If one defining characteristic of a modern state is the effective and unilateral control (if not monopoly) over armed force, then Panama did not qualify until the 1930s, at the earliest.

The Arias brothers rose to power through the Acción Comunal, an organization of professionals and bureaucrats who particularly objected to the flagrant discriminatory hiring practices and wage differentials in the Canal Zone. These middle-class grievances were accompanied by an ideology of racism that attracted the portion of the lower classes that identified with a Latin cultural heritage. The racism of the Acción Comunal exceeded rhetoric and was codified in the new constitution of 1941, ratified by plebiscite under the presidency of Arnulfo Arias.[24]

The alternating and increasingly cozy rule of Liberal and Conservative presidents ended dramatically in January 1931 when armed members of Acción Comunal, led by Arnulfo Arias, seized the presidential palace and deposed President Florencio Arosemena. The key to this successful venture was Washington's decision to let the coup stand in exchange for a pledge from the Arias brothers that U.S. interests would not be threatened. In 1932 Harmodio Arias won the presidential election, and in 1940 Arnulfo swept to victory, devastating the parties of the commercial and business classes. With the victory of Arnulfo it was clear that, when combined with U.S. viceroyalty powers, the commercial elite could contain and even tame

Arias; but it had no hope of retaining direct control of the state through open elections.

However, another route to power for the commercial class had opened up during the 1930s. It is ironic that Harmodio Arias in the 1930s created an effective internal security force because for the next fifty years the Panamanian armed forces would prevent his brother Arnulfo from achieving the presidency and then remove him from office when he actually achieved it. Harmodio Arias eliminated the position of a U.S. superintendent of police and appointed José Antonio Remón Cantera to command the security force.[25] With initial U.S. acquiescence and later encouragement, the police force developed into a unit that could enforce the will of the state. In October 1941, in its first major venture into politics, the police overthrew the elected government of Arnulfo Arias,[26] encouraged and aided in so doing by the U.S. authorities in the Canal Zone. By banning Arias from active political life and suspending the electoral rules, the commercial and business classes held direct state power during the 1940s.[27] As soon as Arias was again allowed to contest an election he again won the presidency with a strong majority and assumed the office in November 1949. Arias's second term also proved brief, for the National Police deposed him again in 1951.

After the second Arias presidency the commercial and business classes, with a cohesive military arm to enforce their will, moved more decisively. The 1953 electoral reform law in effect reduced the field of political parties to lineal descendants of the old Liberals and Conservatives, though Arias would live to contest and win three more presidential elections—1964, 1968, and 1984.[28] After Arias's 1968 electoral victory, he lost office for a third time through a military coup.

The period from the coup of 1941 to that of 1968 is important for understanding the nature of Panamanian society in the late twentieth century. Instructive of the changes that occurred during these years are the consequences of each *golpe del estado*. In 1941, the military quickly yielded to a restoration of the traditional ruling groups, leaving the commercial and business classes to sort out state power themselves. In 1968, the military took power for itself, and the old order of upper-class parties was swept aside.[29]

During the less than eight years between the first two Arias administrations, the commercial and business classes went through six presidents; three served during 1949, and they, along with Arias himself, made four sitting chief executives during the year.[30] Between the second and third Arias presidencies the facade of power holding was much more stable. After the interim president who finished the term of the assassinated José Antonio Remón, three consecutive presidents reached office through election and served their full terms.[31] More apparent than real, this era of stability was achieved by banning Arias from politics and developing a series of intricate, shifting, and unsustainable coalitions within the commercial and business classes.[32] Furthermore, the coalitions proved successful only through the support of the military leadership, which had risen to the prominence of political intermediation. The exiguous economic base of the traditional elites, described above, both instigated this political instability and invited the military to become more involved in economic affairs.

Political Power under Military Rule

After the Second World War the military in virtually every country of Latin America became a major force in politics. In most countries military rule itself emerged either in response to the failure of the parties of both the oligarchy and the newly emergent capitalists to contain the pressure from the parties of the left for social and economic reform or in response to an armed insurrection to achieve the same ends. Obvious examples are Guatemala (1954), Brazil (1964), and Chile, Uruguay, and Argentina in the 1970s, with Peru (1968) an exception to this rule. In the case of Panama, the rise of the military in political importance and its seizure of power in 1968 were not the result of a threat from the left or the masses, but a response to the weakness of the traditional, urban-based ruling class. In countries elsewhere in the hemisphere military coups also reflected the specific weakness of the ruling groups: the inability to contain the forces of reform. In Panama, unlike Chile, for example, there were no threatening forces of reform to contain. The urban-based elite lost political power to the military; it did not shift power when it could no longer rule in a constitutional manner. In a sense, the urban-based elite fell from political power as a result of its own dead weight, lacking the cohesion and strength to rule.

In most countries of Latin America military rule served as the vehicle for the dominant social classes to reassert or solidify power, but in Panama the coup of 1968 further weakened the political role of the country's traditional commercial and business elites. A year after the coup, when Omar Torrijos had asserted his leadership of the military, the weakness of the commercial and business classes was demonstrated; they plotted with sympathetic officers of the National Guard to launch a countercoup. With the aid of loyal officers (among them Manuel Noriega), Torrijos successfully thwarted the attempt at a civilian restoration.[33] While representatives of the traditional ruling class would remain influential and hold key posts during the Torrijos era, gone, perhaps permanently, was the *ancien régime* of politics dominated by a civilian upper class and unmediated by effective political representation of popular classes.[34]

Torrijos ruled in a new way; he pursued an economic strategy of private accumulation to the benefit of international capital and its associated domestic groups, and at the same time he sought the support of the masses through a series of populist economic reforms that included extending the rights of organized labor and modestly redistributing agricultural land. But, most important among Torrijos's populist causes, he determined to renegotiate the U.S. agreement over the Canal, with the nonnegotiable requirement that the Panamanian government would assume control of the waterway.

To this point we have not placed much stress upon the politics of the Canal in determining the political economy of Panama. To have done so would have detracted from our argument that the nature of governance in Panama derived largely from the narrow economic base of the traditional ruling class as well as the U.S. military and colonial presence. Our effort has been to uncover the constellation of internal socioeconomic and political forces that predisposed Panama to embrace an externally oriented development pattern determined by its geography. Panama's crossroads geography in itself is insufficient to explain the economy's overwhelming orientation to international service, decidedly neglecting domestic agricultural and industrial production. In short, geography and domestic forces together reinforced the economy's lopsided development.

The Canal was the natural pillar upon which the unmitigated, geography-centered development strategy would be built. Once the strategy was chosen, of course, the Canal and its foreign control were dominant in Panama's economic and political evolution. Since 1903 the offenses to national pride associated with the U.S. occupation of the Canal Zone emerged as a theme in virtually every Panamanian election and seethed in the background.[35] Torrijos made sovereignty over the Canal the keystone of the government program through which he hoped to acquire the loyalty of the masses. In June 1967, the Robles government and the administration of Lyndon Johnson announced agreement on the texts of three new treaties to cover the existing Canal's administration and defense and the construction of a new sea-level waterway. However, these treaties did not clearly revoke U.S. control, and in September 1970 Torrijos announced that the three drafts remained unacceptable to his government.

For seven years the Canal issue never strayed far from the political center stage in Panama, an issue that could be brought out to rally the population and demonstrate the nationalism of the regime. As real as the Canal question was both to the Panamanian people and Torrijos himself,[36] it was a control mechanism for a weak regime with limited links to the mass of the population. Like the commercial class before it, the military suffered from a narrow political base and no initial economic base, unless one counts the growing importance of contraband and the drug trade. To stay in power without employing brute force, the military regime was required to continuously deliver benefits to the population and/or forge political support through nationalist appeals. By the end of the 1970s, the state of the economy precluded the former, and the signing of the Torrijos-Carter Treaties undermined the latter.

Since the seizure of state power by Acción Comunal in 1931, the commercial and business classes had been unable to rule the country effectively; for almost forty years they muddled through with ad hoc responses to the political challenge of Arias. A common interpretation of the events of the 1980s is that the severe instability of the country arose from the collapse of the political coalition constructed by Omar Torrijos. Certainly this coalition did collapse, but the crisis of governance in Panama had much deeper roots, and the period of stability under Torrijos merely interrupted and unsustainably postponed a fifty-year deterioration of the ability of any group to rule Panama.

The fundamental problem of political control in Panama became, if anything, more acute after the coup of 1968. The three major contributors to the country's economic growth during the Torrijos period (which we treat in detail in later chapters) were the Canal, an international banking enclave in Panama City, and a duty-free trade zone in Colon. Each of these projects continued the four-hundred-year-old tradition in Panama in which the economic base of the country was divorced from the classes that held political power. The banks of the International Financial Center were foreign-owned and employed relatively few lower-class Panamanians. The Colon Free Trade Zone provided a modest amount of employment for unskilled workers, but again the companies in the Zone were the property of foreign capital. Although Torrijos put together a broad coalition, with representatives of the commercial and business elites holding key posts in the government, as with all previous governments, it was a coalition with a narrow economic base whose national elements did not control the relations of production where most Panamanians worked.

With the Canal issue apparently resolved, the ideological hold of the regime over the Panamanian population was already on the wane when Torrijos died in a mysterious plane crash in 1981. The command of the state over the political arena progressively deteriorated and came to a head in the late 1980s when virtually all normal functioning of government authority broke down. It is always tempting to treat dramatic contemporary events as culminations of past trends, as if historical tendencies had awaited the current moment to express themselves in most virulent form. And it is difficult to resist this temptation in the case of Panama, for the Noriega regime seemed to revive the underlying instability of the Panamanian political system. While many regimes in Latin America have appeared to rule by brute force, few in fact have stayed in power on this basis alone. But the Noriega regime was an exception that proved the rule that political power does not grow out of the barrel of gun.

In the second half of the nineteenth century, Marx coined the term "exceptional regime" to refer to the reign of Napoleon III. He used this term to refer to a regime whose relationship to the dominant classes in society was ambiguous. Given the regime's lack of close correspondence to the dominant classes, the state assumed an autonomy in action: its policies could not be interpreted as the expression of any particular class interests. The Torrijos and Noriega periods bore many elements of such an "exceptional regime." Never secure in their power and always reliant upon external patrons, the domestic commercial and business classes lost state power at the end of the 1960s. Furthermore, their ability to regain power grew weaker. At the same time, no other class or coalition of classes (such as the workers and peasants) offered a serious alternative. In this vacuum ruled Torrijos and after him Noriega. At the outset illusions of nationalism filled the vacuum; ultimately armed force alone ruled.

Some look at Panama and see an avenue between the oceans, others a conduit and haven for flight capital. Behind these stereotypes lies the country of Panama with all its complexities. In this chapter we have sought to dispel stereotypes and have touched briefly upon the complexities. In the following four chapters, having provided the historical context of Panama's development, we move from political economy to the analysis of economic relations.

Chapter Two

An Overview of Panama's Economic Development

In this chapter we consider the evolution of Panama's international service economy. As argued in chapter 1, the structural foundations of the economy, based on Panama's geography and relative labor scarcity, were laid in the sixteenth century. The commercial orientation was fortified with the completion of the cross-isthmian railroad in 1855 and the Canal in 1914. Although the U.S.-owned Canal and the trade-focused policies of the Panamanian government did little to promote either industrialization or agricultural development during the twentieth century, a growing nationalist movement along with the effects of the Great Depression and World War II brought incremental change to the Panamanian state and its policies. The greatest apparent change came in 1969 with the military government of Omar Torrijos. During his twelve-plus years in power, Torrijos redefined Panama's political agenda and transformed the institutions of government, allowing inter alia for the emergence of Manuel Noriega. Although Torrijos initiated many progressive reforms, their positive effect was not long lasting, and the international service character of Panama's economy only deepened.

Panama's international service economy can be considered a special case of the externally oriented strategy of development. Generally, this strategy finds the engine for economic growth in promoting exports and wooing the foreign sector. The success of the strategy theoretically hinges on the growth of the export sector and the linkages between the export activity and the domestic economy. In Panama's case the links are attenuated as well as distorted by the nature of Panama's international services. After charting the growth of and overwhelming dependence upon the service sector in Panama, we turn, at the end of this chapter, to begin our consideration of the distortions it engenders.

From Colonization to Statehood

On September 25, 1513, Vasco Nuñez de Balboa fixed Panama's destiny as a transit economy when he saw the Pacific Ocean from a peak along the Atlantic Coast of Panama. Among the territories of the Western Hemisphere, Panama provides the shortest distance between the two oceans. In 1534, Balboa's successor as governor, Pedrarias, commissioned a survey to determine the feasibility of building a canal between Panama City and the Atlantic port town of Nombre de Dios.[1] Instead of a canal, the Spanish linked the oceans with a narrow "Royal Road" of stone on which silver and gold from the western regions of South America were transported by mule to be sold at the fairs of Portobelo, successor to Nombre de Dios as Panama's Atlantic port, or shipped on to Spain.

Portobelo was to remain one of the three mainland ports in the Americas permitted by royal charter to carry on trade with Spain. Despite the plunderings of Francis Drake and other pirates, Panama City and Portobelo became two of the richest towns in the New World. Following the destruction of Portobelo by a British fleet in 1739, however, Spain ended Portobelo's monopoly and incorporated Panama into the Viceroyalty of Nueva Granada (encompassing the territory today of Colombia, Ecuador, and Venezuela). Portobelo's famous trade fairs ended; both legal commerce and contraband diminished to a trickle, and with them the lucrative provisioning of Panama's military garrisons stopped. Merchants dispersed to either the countryside or other ports outside Panama.

Panama's commercial star did not rise again for more than one hundred years when the Panama Railroad Company was organized by a group of New York financiers in 1847.[2] Construction, begun in 1851, was completed four years later at the cost of nine thousand workers' lives.[3] Eager gold rushers, who flooded the town of Colon on the Atlantic side of the railroad, waited, sometimes for weeks, to cross the isthmus. Again, merchants and purveyors flourished.

Between 1855 and 1869, 600,000 travellers used the railroad, and some $750 million worth of gold from California was transported over the railroad back to the East Coast of the United States. The forty-eight-mile railroad's limitations, however, soon revealed themselves when capacity was reached and the inefficiency inherent in loading and unloading cargo at each port became evident. The completion of the first rail line across North America in 1869 effectively undermined the isthmus route.

In the late 1870s, Ferdinand de Lesseps, builder of the Suez Canal, formed a French company to build a sea-level canal across Panama. After bringing thousands of Antilleans to the isthmus and stimulating the local economy, de Lesseps's company went bankrupt in 1889.[4] As described in Chapter 1, the canal project was resumed—this time as a lock canal—with the signing of the Panama Canal treaty of 1903. Initiated in 1907, work on the Canal was completed in 1914. Tens of thousands more Antilleans were imported to work on the construction.[5]

From Statehood to 1960

The Canal treaty of 1903, which no Panamanian read or signed, granted the United States rights in perpetuity "as if it were sovereign" over a ten-mile (wide) by fifty-mile (long) strip of land—the Canal Zone. The treaty also gave the United States the right in perpetuity to occupy and control land outside the Zone deemed necessary for effectively operating the Canal. For these and other rights the United States made Panama a lump-sum compensation of $10 million and agreed to pay an annual rent of $250,000, the latter amount equal to the annuity paid to Colombia for railroad rights alone prior to 1903. The United States also bought the uncompleted Canal from Bunau-Varilla's Panama Canal Company for $40 million and, following the death of Theodore Roosevelt, agreed in 1921 to compensate Colombia for Canal rights with a payment of $25 million.

Other provisions of the treaty ensured that the operation of the Canal would have minimal linkages to the rest of Panama's economy. Panamanians working in the Canal Zone and residing in Panama could not be taxed by the Panamanian government. Furthermore, they could make purchases at the Zone's commissaries, and Panamanian businesses were prohibited from selling inside the Zone. Further

still, the Zone controlled its own tariff and immigration polici
lowing U.S. goods to enter the Zone and eventually the rest of Panama duty-free.

The egregious giveaway of the treaty became an instant and constant political problem for Panama's leaders. The political problem
was compounded by the massive unemployment that followed the
completion of the Canal and the economic slowdown following
World War I.[6] Modest government efforts to confront this problem
through public works projects engendered large deficits that led to
the humiliation of U.S. government agents assuming control of fiscal
policy in 1919.[7] Social unrest erupted in the late 1910s and 1920s,
and the United States intervened twice with troops to quell the protests. Popular political movements and parties emerged, leading eventually to the succession of Harmodio Arias to the presidency in
1932.[8] Arias's nationalism and quasi-populism, combined with the
economic ravages wreaked on Panama by the worldwide depression,
led to Panama's first policy efforts, albeit meager, at building a domestic industrial base.

The tariff law of 1934 provided for some protection for eighteen
fledgling manufactured goods. But protectionism developed slowly.
The tariff law of 1937 made six previously duty-free imports taxable
and raised the tariff on fifteen commodities, but it also lowered or
eliminated the duty on eighty-one goods (U.S. Tariff Commission
1946, 7–9). The 1937 law appears to have been a quid pro quo for
the minor revision of the Canal treaty signed by Harmodio Arias and
President Roosevelt in 1936. This revision, known in Panama as *"El
Tratado de Carne y Cerveza,"* conceded to Panamanian merchants
the right to sell meat and beer in the Canal Zone. Overall, the impulse of these tariff measures for industrial development in the 1930s
was sufficiently minimal to lead the eminent Panamanian historian
Ricaurte Soler to conclude: "In contrast to other Latin American nations, in the case of Panama no significant process of import substitution followed the world crisis of 1929."[9]

However, the policies of the 1930s opened the door for Panama's
merchants and, hence, Panama's industry to enter the Zone market.
With the boom in Canal traffic during World War II and the dis-
ruption to normal trade routes, the demand for provisioning the
Canal's ships and their crews increased sharply. This time manufacturing was spurred, and a domestic political lobby on behalf of

TABLE 2.1. *Annual Rates of Real Growth: GDP and Industry*
(in percentages)

	1950–1960	1960–1973	1973–1981
GDP, growth rate	4.8	7.8	3.7
Industry, growth rate	8.8	9.8	0.3
Industrial share (at end of period)	13.1	16.7	12.9

Source. Calculated by the authors from *Panamá en cifras*, various years.

further protectionism was strengthened. Together with Panama's serious economic recession and unemployment after the war, these emergent economic interests were able to push the government gradually to adopt moderate import substitution policies in the 1950s.[10]

The first such measure, Law No. 12 of 1950, stated that the proper duty of the government was to protect and offer incentives to particular economic sectors to promote the development of the country. This step was extended by Law No. 19 of 1952, which gave the Oficina de Regulación de Precios power to fix import quotas. Law No. 25 of 1957 provided a comprehensive schedule of import tariffs and duties, marking the first significant application of industrial protectionism in Panama. The basic structure created by this law remained in effect until the International Monetary Fund (IMF)/World Bank–inspired Law of Industrial Incentives of March 1986. Also in the 1950s, the Remón-Eisenhower Treaty of 1955 restricted Panamanian employees in the Canal Zone from using the Zone's commissaries and import privileges, curbed many of the Zone's light manufacturing, agricultural, and service activities, and created a single wage scale for Panamanian and U.S. workers in the Zone. Each provision stimulated the development of Panama's internal market and, along with foreign investment, contributed to almost two decades (through 1973) of sustained industrial growth via import substitution. Industry's share in Panama's Gross Domestic Product (GDP) increased from 9.1 percent in 1950 to 16.7 percent in 1973 (see Table 2.1).

Despite the rapid growth rates of industry, the manufacturing sector remained small, and, with the exception of the refining of Venezuelan crude oil (begun by Texaco in 1962), it was overwhelmingly concentrated in traditional and light industrial activities. In 1975, for instance, fewer than 10 percent of industrial establishments employed more than one hundred people, nearly 50 percent of manufacturing value added was generated in the food and beverages branches, and manufacturing accounted for only 6 percent of Panama's merchandise exports. Diminutive though it was, the manufacturing sector still relied heavily on foreign capital for much of its investment. According to figures in a study by Programa Regional para Empleo en América Latina y el Caribe of the International Labour Office (PREALC), the stock of direct foreign investment in Panamanian manufacturing came to $5.7 million in 1960 and to $56 million in 1970, 12.9 percent and 32.9 percent of the estimated total capital stock in manufacturing, respectively.[11]

The frailty of Panama's industrial sector is suggested by its sudden stagnation in the mid-1970s following the collapse of Panama City's building boom. After peaking at 12.8 percent of GDP in 1975, the manufacturing share fell steadily to 8.2 percent in 1986. Interpreters of the Panamanian political economy commonly attribute the country's late and weak industrial development to political control by a merchant class until the military coup of 1968. For instance, according to the 1981 area handbook study of Panama published by the U.S. government: "At formation of the republic in 1903, a few white merchant families comprised the political and economic elite that dominated most governments until 1968" (Nyrop, 96). And in his history of the Panamanian economy, Robert Looney (4–5) concludes: "Also because of the political influence wielded by commercial interests, Panama has developed a mercantilist mentality. . . . Before 1968, the country had developed under a series of governments with a laissez-faire approach to government's role in the economy."

Although it is true that the thrust of government policy was to promote mercantile interests, the claim of unequivocal commercial control over the state is overly schematic and synchronic and genuinely misleading regarding the specifics of economic policy. The government began to formulate interventionist policies in the 1930s, and public involvement in education and social security also developed at this time, extending into the early 1940s; the 1950s witnessed additional interventionist policies. But whether each president directly represented merchant interests is somewhat beside the point. On the one hand, Acción Comunal was not rooted in the merchant class, yet once in office its policy choices were circumscribed by the institutions

of the transit economy. On the other hand, when the traditional political parties of the "oligarchy" ruled, their policy choices were limited by the exigencies of widespread penury and the need for political
stability. Consequently, a certain continuity in Panama's development strategy was rooted in its economic structure and proved
relatively independent of the immediate class interests of the gov-
erning party.

Some analysts have pointed to Panama's comparatively low tariff
rates prior to 1968 as evidence of merchant class domination, the
principal cause of weak industrial growth. This view is problematic
for two reasons. First, tariff rates are incomplete indicators of protection. Since the early 1950s, Panama's system of protectionism relied
heavily on import quotas, as opposed to tariffs. By the early 1980s,
there were quotas on some 470 different imported products (Panzer,
24). In many cases, quotas and tariffs were applied to the same product. Quotas were often imposed at the discretion of the relevant government body, usually the Oficina de Regulación de Precios, pursuant
to the request of a politically important local manufacturer (more recently, often with ties to the Defense Forces).[12] Furthermore, nominal
tariffs were supplemented by general import levies and hefty servic-
ing fees. Second, the basic tariff structure did not change significantly
after 1968 under Torrijos.[13] In short, there is no compelling evidence
either that Panama's lack of industrial growth was attributable simply to inadequate protectionism or that 1968 marked a turning point.
Many other factors, which we return to consider, were at play. The
central point is that the overriding project of the Panamanian state
was not industrialization, either before or after 1968. Neither a cohesive development strategy nor a coherent, stable set of policies ever
promoted industrial growth. When industrial growth occurred, it did
so primarily as a reflex in service of the needs of the Canal Zone.

The principal dynamic of Panama's transit economy has continued
to be as an export or service platform for transnational corporations.
Before stagnation in Canal traffic set in during the early 1970s, the
Canal directly or indirectly supported approximately 33 percent of
Panama's labor force, generated 33 percent of Panama's GDP, and
accounted for about 45 percent of foreign exchange earnings. The
Canal also spurred, together with Panama's geographical location
and tax benefits, the emergence of other international service opera-

tions, such as the Colon Free Zone (opened in 1953), and the host of institutions initiated in the early 1970s as part of Torrijos's development plan.

Torrijos's economic team, headed by Nicolás Barletta, formulated a development strategy based upon the perceived comparative advantage of Panama as an international service or transit economy. The expansion of the Colon Free Zone, the development of the offshore banking center, the modernization and expansion of the Canal, the transisthmian oil pipeline, and other related projects were part of the Barletta plan.[14] To the Barletta strategy, Torrijos added his own policies oriented toward social reform and the development of the internal market. The two-pronged approach had political logic, but it was carried out with little coordination and in an environment made unstable by the negotiations around the new Canal treaty, not signed until late 1977. In the end, Torrijos's effort to develop everything at once broke the fiscal budget and brought heavy foreign debt.[15] The ultimate impact of Torrijos's policies on Panama's economic structure was to deepen its dependence on services (as shown in Table 2.2). The service sector grew from 59.6 percent of GDP in 1950 to 77.4 percent in 1985, and, with the crisis of 1987–1988, to 80.1 percent in 1988.[16]

The intractable debt inherited by Torrijos's successors swayed the policy pendulum further away from developing the internal market and toward the promotion of new exports and international services. The political instability of the 1980s, aggravated by pervasive military interference in the economy and the post-June 1987 political and economic crisis, led to acute economic and social conditions.[17] Below we consider economic policies and performance during the 1960s and 1970s in more detail.

The 1960s

During the 1960s the policies and structural changes of the previous decade continued. The annual rate of real GDP growth increased 60 percent during the 1960s (7.7 percent) over the rate during the 1950s (4.8 percent). Whereas the manufacturing growth that outpaced export growth during the 1950s reflected the typical inward-oriented growth pattern, this relationship was reversed during the 1960s.

TABLE 2.2. *Sectoral Shares in GDP, 1950–1988*
(in percentages)

	1950	1955	1960	1965	1968	1970	1975	1980	1985	1988
Manufacturing	8.7	9.8	12.7	15.4	15.9	12.5	12.8	10.0	9.0	7.7
Agriculture	27.5	29.5	22.2	23.9	22.7	14.6	11.2	9.0	9.2	10.1
Construction	3.9	4.3	5.3	5.3	5.9	6.7	8.2	7.3	4.7	2.1
Services	59.6	56.1	59.4	55.1	55.2	66.0	67.6	73.5	77.4	80.1

Sources. Panamá en cifras; ECLA, *Statistical Yearbook for Latin America and the Caribbean*, various years. Figures for 1988 are preliminary, from CEPAL, *Panamá: la situación económica a principios de 1989*, 33.

Note. There is a discontinuity in the series in 1970. Post-1969 is valued in market prices, including net indirect taxes and subsidies, and pre-1970 is valued at factor cost. The valuation in market prices makes the service share increase by 7.2 percentage points in 1970. Figures for 1988 are preliminary. Rounding errors cause the sum to diverge from 100.0.

Manufacturing, however, was still a leading sector through 1968; its share in GDP grew from 12.7 percent in 1960 to a peak of 15.9 percent in 1968.[18]

Export expansion was led by rapid growth in Canal services, re-exports from the Colon Free Zone, Panama's traditional export, bananas, two other primary exports, shrimp and sugar, and by the emergence of refined petroleum exports. Increased banana exports were propelled by advances in pest-control techniques, the development of more resistant strains, and gradually rising prices. Shrimp and sugar were promoted by new investments, and refined petroleum exports began after Texaco opened its Atlantic Coast refinery in 1962. In value terms, banana exports grew from $23.5 million in 1960 to $108.2 million in 1970, an annual growth rate of 13.1 percent. In 1970, bananas represented 57.1 percent of Panama's merchandise exports. Refined petroleum exports grew from zero in 1961, to $13.8 million in 1962, to $21.5 million in 1970 (19.9 percent of merchandise exports). Only a small share of this latter figure, however, reflects net exports because Panama must import all its crude oil. Shrimp exports grew from $5.1 million in 1960 to $10.2 million in 1970 (9.4 percent of goods exports)—a growth rate of 7.4 percent; and sugar exports grew from $0.4 million to $5.0 million (4.6 percent of exports) during the decade—a growth rate of 28.7 percent.

A rapid increase in investment fueled this growth. Direct foreign investment, which accounted for 19.2 percent of total investment in Panama during the 1950s, almost doubled during the 1960s, from $17.3 million in 1960 to $33.4 million in 1970.[19] Domestic investment, however, increased more rapidly, and foreign investment's share in gross capital formation declined from 26.5 percent in 1960 to 12.4 percent in 1970. Overall, gross capital formation increased from 15.2 percent of GDP in 1960 to 26.5 percent in 1970.

An *increasing* government role in the economy accompanied the growth of the 1960s. Inspired by the reform-minded exhortations of the Alliance for Progress, domestic political pressures, and the need for a more modern infrastructure, the Panamanian government increased its share in GDP from 15.1 percent in 1960 to 20.4 percent in 1970 and its share in total investment from 14.5 percent to 25.3 percent during this decade. At the same time public investment spending grew by 7.2 times while private investment grew by 3.2 times. There were also important qualitative changes: the

TABLE 2.3.   *Key Proportions of the Panamanian Economy, 1956–1985*
(in percentages)

	I/GDP	Public I/Total I	G/GDP	DFI/Total I
1956–1960	14.2	18.6	15.1	23.2
1961–1965	18.7	25.3	15.1	15.1
1966–1970	23.7	18.3	17.3	7.3
1971–1975	29.1	32.6	23.9	5.3
1976–1980	23.7	47.9	24.2	0.5
1981–1985	19.5	31.3	26.4	6.4

Sources. *Panamá en cifras*, various years; IMF, *Balance of Payments Yearbook*, various years.

establishment of IRHE and IDAAN, the state-owned electric and wa-
ter/sewerage companies, in 1961; agrarian reform legislation in
1962; a major tax reform in 1964 making individual and corporate
income taxes more progressive and improving collection; a sharp increase in the number of import quotas after 1965; and increasing efforts at formulating medium-term development plans.

The 1960s also brought increased inequality. While Panama's
population grew by 3.4 percent a year (from 1.08 million to 1.43 million), the concentration of land ownership and the expansion of the
urban-based economy resulted in faster urban population growth
(4.3 percent) and an increasing urban share (41.5 to 47.6 percent).[20]
Panama's Canal-centered development was also reflected in sharp regional inequality. In 1970, per capita income in the provinces of the
Canal was $881 in Panama and $794 in Colon, while in the outlying
provinces of Bocas del Toro and Darien it was $402 and $145,
respectively.[21] Although employment expanded rapidly during the
decade, wages lagged behind productivity, and the real minimum
wage was constant from 1960 to 1968. By the early 1970s Panama
had one of the most unequal income distributions in Latin America:
the highest 20 percent of households earned 61.8 percent of household income, and the lowest 20 percent earned 2.0 percent.[22]

Torrijos and the 1970s

On October 1, 1968, Arnulfo Arias assumed the presidency for the
third time. His tenure was brief. On October 11 he was removed

from the presidency by the National Guard. The coup was supported by a broad group of officers, but Commander Omar Torrijos and Chief of Staff Boris Martínez emerged as the apparent leaders of the new government. In early March 1969, on national television Martínez announced a program to implement the agrarian reform legislation of 1962 and stated that the National Guard would no longer suppress demonstrations by Panamanians, but Martínez's moment in history was brief. Within a few days, he and three of his top supporters were sent into exile, with Torrijos assuming control of the government. In December 1969, this control was consolidated following an aborted countercoup attempt, allegedly supported by the CIA.[23] Torrijos was able to put down this insurrection despite being in Mexico at the time, thanks to strategic support from then Lieutenant Manuel Noriega in Chiriqui province.

The government of Omar Torrijos, which was to last until his death in a mysterious plane crash in July 1981, made an important mark on Panama and has been the subject of endless debates among interpreters of Panamanian development. For some, Torrijos was a popular, nationalist hero who represented a definitive break with previous oligarchic governments.[24] This view is sustained by the agrarian reform, prolabor legislation of 1972, health and educational reforms, development of state enterprises in agriculture, industry, and services, public employment programs, the alliance with Fidel Castro, and the negotiation of the 1977 Canal treaties that provided for the return of the Canal Zone to Panama.

For others, Torrijos was an inept leader who sold short the working class by adopting an externally oriented development strategy based on services, permitting the fortification of international capital with the establishment of the offshore banking center, allowing eviscerating amendments to the 1972 Labor Code, freezing wages and collective bargaining contracts in the late 1970s, reneging on the agrarian reform, retrenching eventually on his public programs, and conceding too much to the United States in the treaty negotiations. For still others, Torrijos was a misguided, perhaps corrupt, leader who followed ineffective economic policies that bloated the inefficient state sector, perpetuated the disincentives to export promotion, and saddled the government with a burdensome foreign debt.

More careful analysts recognized that Torrijos was all these things. Ricaurte Soler concluded that the Torrijos government was

"Bonapartist"; that is, it represented neither the working nor the capitalist class.[25] Nicolás Barletta, Torrijos's principal economic adviser and head of the newly formed Ministry of Planning and Economic Policy (MIPPE) from 1972 to 1978, argued that there were two groups of advisers in Torrijos's government, developmentalists (Barletta's group) and leftists, and that the two alternated in their influence. Barletta's interpretation of the sequence of events was: from 1968 to 1971, developmentalist ideas were ascendant; from 1972 to 1974, leftist ideas; 1975, stalemate; from 1976 to 1977, developmentalist, though programs were inconsistently implemented; after late 1977, leftist ideas.[26] Although there is much to dispute about Barletta's schema and it was undoubtedly influenced by his own decision to move to the World Bank in 1978, his view does provide a useful insight by suggesting an ongoing ideological/policy conflict within the Torrijos government. Whatever Torrijos's goals might have been, the concrete outcomes of his policies can be evaluated on their own merits.

Because Torrijos inherited a booming economy, initially there was little reason to change policy direction. The development strategy, drawn up by a team of economists around Barletta, called for a progressively outward orientation with major state investments in human capital and infrastructure. By 1968–1969 manufacturing growth had slowed to a standstill, whereas the export sector (goods and services) was expanding at a rate in excess of 10 percent per year. Barletta sought to build on the dynamic export sector by taking further advantage of Panama's geographical location, its highly educated and often bilingual labor force, its use of the U.S. dollar as its currency (since 1904), and its lenient 1927 incorporation laws. He perceived correctly an eventual slowdown in Canal traffic and sought to identify other international services to fuel Panamanian development. The 1960s growth of the eurodollar market as well as the Colon Free Zone made the formal establishment of an international banking center in Panama City an obvious choice. Barletta also promoted the expansion of the Colon Free Zone as well as other international services, including tourism, a reinsurance center (created in 1976), a transisthmian oil pipeline (completed in 1982), a centerport project, and a transnational corporation headquarters center, among others.[27]

In 1970, to promote the international banking center Panama passed a new banking law that provided for numbered bank accounts, secrecy, and tax exemption and disallowed reserve regulations and exchange restrictions for offshore accounts.[28] The center, which had already experienced some growth in the late 1960s, blossomed from 23 banks with $1 billion in deposits in 1970 to 120 banks with $50 billion in deposits in 1982. The center was deemed "strategic" by the Panamanian government, and, hence, no bank employee union has ever been recognized. In addition to increasing the available capital for domestic loans, the center spawned a major building boom—bank headquarters and residential structures for bank employees—in Panama City and stimulated improvements in Panama's communications infrastructure. Construction spending, with a fillip from Torrijos's public housing program, expanded from $51.4 million (current prices) in 1969 to $125.2 million in 1973, representing a real annual growth rate of 19.9 percent. Value added from financial services grew even more rapidly, from $59.3 million in 1969 to $191.6 in 1973, a real annual rate of 29 percent.

Torrijos, in search of a popular base for his new government, reacted to one other characteristic of the 1960s economy—sharp and growing inequality. He seized upon the 1962 agrarian reform legislation to initiate a land redistribution program. Between 1969 and 1972, 138 *asentamientos* (production cooperatives) were established, benefiting 5,340 rural families. A second and final round of redistribution between 1974 and 1977 created an additional 92 asentamientos, benefiting 4,065 additional families. Together these redistributions involved less than 5 percent of cultivable land and less than 5 percent of the rural labor force.[29]

Torrijos also sought support in the urban working class. One early measure, in December 1971, made payment of a thirteenth-month bonus mandatory. More significant, in 1972 Torrijos promulgated a new labor code. The code made collective bargaining obligatory for most private companies, payroll deduction of union dues automatic, wage reductions illegal, and worker dismissals extremely costly. An upsurge in unionization ensued, with an annual average of 5,083 new union members over the next four years.[30] In December 1972 Torrijos declared a general price freeze, and in 1974, with the freeze lifted, he decreed a catch-up, progressive wage increase for the private

sector. New labor benefits statutes also led to sharp increases in social security payments, which rose to approximately 14 percent of the
basic wage by 1970.[31]

Torrijos's populist programs required money, and he attempted to
accommodate this need with a major tax reform in 1970. The reform
raised the statutory rates of taxation on income, dividends, and property and increased the excise tax. It also increased audits and raised
the ad valorem import surcharge from 3.5 to 6.0 percent. Although
tax revenue in 1971 was 50 percent above its level in 1968,[32] with
widespread evasion and smuggling only one-third the expected additional revenue was forthcoming. As a result, a ballooning deficit
plagued Torrijos and the economy throughout the 1970s.

A major contributor to the fiscal deficit was the expansion of the
public sector of the economy. Originally, the plan was to limit new
state investment to infrastructure and utilities. Accordingly, the state
bought the U.S.-owned Power and Light Company in 1972 and na-
tionalized a short-wave company in 1973 and Western Union in
1974. One exception to the plan was the formation of the new state
sugar company, La Victoria; in 1972 that was intended to promote
the new asentamientos and provide employment for Panama's rural
poor. However, when the recession of 1973–1977 struck and private
investment (domestic and foreign) stagnated, Torrijos expanded the
productive state enterprise sector as part of his countercyclical policy.
In 1974, the state bought the bankrupt Chiriqui Citrus Company
and, in response to the short-term explosion of world sugar prices,
began a project to construct three new state sugar mills. In 1975,
Torrijos arranged to purchase the land of the United Fruit Company
and then to lease back to it more than 70 percent of that land. Also,
in 1975, the state cement company, Bayano Cement, was established,
and by the end of the decade there were also state enterprises in
wood, grains, and cattle production.

Even more so than elsewhere in Latin America, because of the international banking center, loan capital was readily available until
the late 1970s, and the Panamanian government took advantage of
this circumstance by borrowing heavily in dollars to finance its public
investments. Panama's public foreign debt rose from $145 million in
1970 to $2.2 billion in 1980. As either a share of GDP or in per cap-
ita terms, the latter figure represented the highest level of indebtedness in Latin America.

TABLE 2.4. *Private and Public Investment, 1972–1979*
(in millions of current balboas)

	Private Investment	Public Investment
1972	261.6	157.4
1973	325.1	104.7
1974	304.5	123.3
1975	253.8	261.4
1976	264.2	296.0
1977	171.2	238.0
1978	246.8	304.5
1979	418.6	231.0

Source. *Panamá en cifras*, various years.

On the whole, the public enterprises operated inefficiently, as alleged by conservative critics. Furthermore, particular ventures were glaringly inefficient such as the Felipillo, Alanje, and Azuero sugar mills,[33] and others were tainted by corruption.[34] The sugar mill expansion project followed the recommendation of a feasibility study by a Miami consulting firm. The government, however, clearly overreacted to the record high sugar prices of 1974–1975 by overexpanding productive capacity. Neither the domestic nor the U.S. market could absorb Panama's new production potential, and the new mills operated far below capacity. Moreover, a market-sharing arrangement was worked out with Panama's two private producers to the detriment of the government mills. Other public enterprises, though hardly paragons of efficiency, operated effectively and with surpluses, such as Bayano Cement, Intel, and the Colon Free Zone. Overall, the consolidated current accounts of Panama's public enterprises showed average annual surpluses of 9.6 million balboas during the 1970s[35] and 54.4 million balboas during 1980–1983.[36]

Nonetheless, clearly much of Torrijos's investment in public enterprise was planned to compensate countercyclically for the fall of private investment, both domestic and foreign, after 1973. There is little evidence that the investment in public enterprise per se crowded out private investment. In Table 2.4 we show a pattern of public investment growing the year after a drop in private investment, and vice versa. To the extent, then, that the state investments generated employment for the otherwise unemployed, the social efficiency of the investments exceeded the private efficiency (as would be indicated by the profit-and-loss statement of each individual enterprise).

The pattern of government spending in general was countercyclical. When the construction industry began to falter following the speculation-driven overconstruction period of 1972–1974, the government accelerated its infrastructural spending and prevented a collapse of the industry. The public construction program of low-cost housing in particular kept the industry afloat from 1975 to 1978. The problem with this program was not in its conception, according to Barletta, but in its management. He alleged that its growing deficits resulted from political payoffs and a general failure to write deeds and collect mortgages.[37]

As already mentioned, 1973–1974 marked the end of a long growth period for the Panamanian economy. Whereas real GDP grew at an annual rate of 6.3 percent between 1950 and 1973 (3.4 percent in per capita terms), between 1973 and 1977 real GDP expanded at only 1.7 percent per year; that is, in per capita terms, it fell at the annual rate of 1.0 percent. The vulnerability of Panama's transit economy was abundantly clear as growth nearly halted, given the high oil prices and world recession of those years. Most immediately affected were the Colon Free Zone and the Canal. Value added from the Free Zone fell drastically from $66.2 million in 1973 to $15.7 million in 1974 and $11.6 million in 1975. Canal value added in real terms fell by 15.7 percent between 1974 and 1976.

The 1973–1977 economic stagnation, however, was not entirely the product of world recession. Overexpansion of construction led to an initial pullback in this sector, the passage of the 1972 Labor Code, accelerating inflation, and subsequent price controls contributed to falling private investment. Furthermore, adverse weather in 1973–1974 reduced banana exports.

The budget deficit meanwhile exploded from 32.3 million balboas (2.5 percent of GDP) in 1972 to 195.2 million (11.8 percent of GDP) in 1974. Together with the concomitant reduction in private investment, Torrijos became convinced of the necessity for an accommodation between his government and private business as well as for more orthodox fiscal management. Discussions with CONEP (the National Private Enterprise Association) led to the well-known Declaración de Boquete on November 27, 1974. Many interpreted this declaration as the definitive turning point away from prolabor populism and toward private capital. Yet aside from setting up a special government office to deal directly with complaints from the private sector, the declaration offered no immediate, concrete policy measures.

Torrijos, however, did cut back on government expenditure and introduced a value-added tax during 1975–1976. This succeeded in cutting the fiscal deficit to 21 million balboas by 1976. Several pro-business measures accompanied this fiscal restraint. In January 1975, the government created a tax credit certificate (CAT) for nontraditional export products. The amount of the CAT, equal to 20 percent of local value added, is granted to products with a minimum of 20 percent local content.[38] Later in 1975, the state finance corporation, COFINA, was set up to provide financing for private-sector investment projects. In December 1976, Torrijos introduced three new fiscal incentives programs;[39] then, he took his biggest step, paradoxically with Communist party support, by promulgating the infamous Law 95, which amended the 1972 Labor Code.[40]

Law 95 attempted to loosen many perceived rigidities of the 1972 Labor Code and to reverse the trend in real wages, which had been increasing at 3.2 percent per year in the private sector from 1973 to 1976. Article 3 of Law 95 stipulated that collective bargaining contracts would be frozen during 1977 and 1978, preventing adjustments to the nominal wage for productivity increases or inflation.[41] Article 6 exempted new businesses from entering into a collective bargaining agreement before 1979. Article 13 weakened the provisions for job security in the labor code by permitting dismissal of "permanent" workers (those in regular jobs for over two years) for unjustified reasons in exchange for payment of a severance indemnity to the worker.[42]

Following the promulgation of Law 95, Torrijos's policy initiatives seemed to vacillate in their ideological orientation, pleasing neither working-class nor business organizations. After several years of falling per capita income and rising unemployment, in late 1977 Torrijos committed new funds for public housing and an emergency public employment program. Thus, after reducing government spending from 476.2 million balboas in 1976 to 433.4 million in 1977, Torrijos increased spending to 534 million in 1978 and 814.2 million in 1979. Fiscal deficits once again ballooned, rising from 98.2 million balboas in 1978 to 272.2 million in 1979. But courting both sides, in 1978 Torrijos attended the Annual Conference of Business Executives for the first time and called for an enhanced dialogue and closer cooperation between his government and business. Following the advice of the International Monetary Fund (IMF) and the World Bank, in January 1979, Torrijos put into effect a new export incentives law: it granted duty-free import of machinery, raw materials, and intermediate products; exemption from sales, export, and corporate income taxes; and a three-month exemption from restrictive provisions of the labor code.[43]

Torrijos's overtures to the private sector along with the removal of the uncertainty surrounding the negotiation of the Canal treaties (the new treaties were signed in September 1977) led to a healthy spurt of private investment. Private investment spending, which had decreased from 305 million balboas in 1974 to 171 million in 1977, grew to 247 million balboas in 1978 and 419 million in 1979. As noted above, supported by new U.S. loans resulting from the Canal agreements, government spending also increased, growing in nominal terms by 23.2 percent in 1978 and by 52.4 percent in 1979. These expansionary elements were joined by others: ongoing, strong growth in the international services (especially the banking center, Colon Free Zone, and the Canal); an economic reactivation in Costa Rica, Venezuela, Colombia, and the Caribbean in general; a reversal in the 1970–1978 downward trend in the terms of trade; a new boom in housing; new construction in the Zone and an additional $70 million-odd in government revenues provided for by the treaties; and new investment projects such as the transisthmian oil pipeline, La Fortuna hydroelectric, and the Marriott Hotel.

Together, these factors engendered a new economic expansion. Real GDP grew 6.4 percent per year between 1977 and 1982,[44] but the growth was not evenly distributed across the economy. In real terms, agricultural output stagnated, and the agricultural share in GDP fell from 12.7 percent in 1977 to 8.8 percent in 1982. Manufacturing output grew by 3.9 percent per year in real terms, but its GDP share fell from 11.3 percent to 9.3 percent. The principal stimulants of growth during the 1978–1982 boom were exogenous factors with ephemeral effect, and the hyperexpansionary fiscal policy left the government in 1982 with a record deficit (340.1 million balboas or 7.9 percent of GDP) and record foreign debt ($2.8 billion). IMF-styled austerity programs were implemented to confront this predicament; economic stagnation and political instability ensued. We discuss the post-1982 political economic crisis in chapters 6 through 8; for now, it remains to analyze the economic policies and performance of the Torrijos years.

Analyzing the 1970s

Did the outcome of Torrijos's policies represent a break from the oligarchical past? Did the underlying model of Panamanian development shift between 1968 and 1981?

Torrijos did denote a rupture in the political hegemony of the Liberal party, but insofar as this party represented economic interests they were those of a predominantly commercial class. A break with the interests of this class suggests a decreasing dependence on external sources of growth and/or a diminishing reliance on the trade and service component of the economy. As we have seen, the pattern of development in Panama became more international and service oriented after 1968. In a sense, this outcome merely followed Panama's geographical comparative advantage that had been reinforced by the development of the Canal-centered economy since 1914. If Torrijos's intentions were otherwise, the institutional context and the dynamic of economic change were too compelling for these intentions (absent a coherent political movement) to overcome.

In seeking to make sense of the Torrijos period, some have suggested that the oligarchy represented domestic commercial interests while the general catered to international capital. There is obviously a certain validity to this observation, but to some degree the interests of these two groups had already begun to merge prior to 1968. In any case, the overall pattern of an international service platform economy did not change.

The economic role of the government did expand during the Torrijos years. The share of government spending in GDP increased from 15 percent in 1968 to 27 percent in 1981. Public employment grew by 10 percent per year during the 1970s, and 75 percent of all new workers owed their jobs to the government. Yet much of this expansion responded to exigencies created by the slowdown in private spending and to the infrastructural needs of a modernizing economy. Similar growth in the public sector occurred in many Latin American countries during the 1960s and 1970s. Although during the mid-1970s the Panamanian state had tended to become involved directly in production, this had dissipated by the end of the decade. State enterprises accounted for less than 5 percent of manufacturing production in 1980.

What can be said about Torrijos's quest for a popular base in the peasantry and urban working class? Agrarian reform stopped well short of its goals: the redistribution program reached less than 5 percent of the rural population, and real agricultural output fell in per capita terms during the 1970s. Land tenure actually grew more concentrated over the decade: the number of holdings of less than one-half a hectare increased from 13,000 to 50,000, and the number of holdings between one-half and five hectares increased from 41,000 to 49,000 while the average size of the latter group's holdings decreased by 7.4 percent.[45] On balance, the agrarian reform was ineffective.[46]

Workers' gains in unionization, job stability, and real wages during the early 1970s were largely eroded by 1980. While real monthly wages in the public sector fell at an annual average of 1.3 percent per year between 1970 and 1980, real monthly wages in the private sector fell by 0.7 percent yearly. Only in the Canal Zone did average real monthly wages increase over the decade—at a rate of 2.3 percent annually. Throughout the economy, real monthly wages fell at an average annual rate of 0.8 percent during the 1970s.

Furthermore, unemployment rates increased, and labor force participation rates decreased during the decade. The official national unemployment rate went from 7.1 percent in 1970 to 8.8 percent in 1979, as the participation rate fell from 61.3 percent to 57.6 percent.[47] Despite an upturn in the business cycle in 1979,[48] had the average labor force participation rates of 1963–1971 been maintained, the unemployment rate in 1979 would have been 11.3 percent. As one would expect from the wage and unemployment trends, the share of employee compensation in GDP fell from 50.0 percent in 1970 to 45.7 percent in 1980.[49]

These trends contributed to growing poverty. According to an official study, in the early 1980s, 38 percent of Panamanian families lived in poverty. Of this group, nearly 60 percent could not purchase a minimal subsistence food basket using their entire incomes.[50]

By these indicators, Torrijos cannot be judged objectively to have been a worker's general. Furthermore, despite instability in economic policy and periodic extravagance of the government budget, the perception of the business climate in Panama by the mid-1970s was on the whole positive. *Barron's,* for instance, expressed such sentiments in July 1978:

The fact is that Panama's economy and management style are already dominated by U.S. attitudes and business methods at a level found nowhere else in Central America, which the unpredictable Torrijos, though often appearing to be far leftward leaning, has encouraged.[51]

Torrijos won over many sectors of international capital by providing a financially hospitable environment for the international banking center. Most politically astute bankers realized that the health and longevity of this center, as well as the entire business climate, would be in jeopardy if the negotiations around the Canal treaties were not successful. Through the banks, Torrijos gained some powerful allies to lobby in Washington for the eventual return of the Canal to Panama, the centerpiece of his program. Indeed, once the 1977 treaties were ratified by the U.S. Congress in 1978, foreign investment in Panama increased again: from a negative $365,000 in 1978 to a positive $50.7 million in 1979.

If Torrijos promoted both human capital and infrastructural development and, on balance, provided an auspicious business climate, then why did economic performance deteriorate during the 1970s? Economic growth, after all, slowed from a real annual rate of 7.7 percent in the 1960s to 5.5 percent in the 1970s, despite a substantial increase in the rate of investment (from 21.2 percent of GDP in the 1960s to 26.4 percent in the 1970s). Total employment expanded by only 18 percent over the ten years, and the nonservice sectors' (manufacturing, agriculture, mining, and construction) share in GDP fell from 33.9 percent to 26.5 percent. Total factor productivity, a measure of overall economic efficiency, actually declined during the decade.

One obvious factor behind Panama's deteriorating performance was the international economy. The post-1973 recession reduced world demand for the country's exports in goods and services and helped turn the terms of trade against Panama during the decade. The terms of trade deteriorated 26.6 percent between 1972 and 1978 before recuperating by 10.5 percent between 1978 and 1980.

Another factor was the stagnation of direct foreign investment in Panama's manufacturing sector. After briefly rising between 1970 and 1972, foreign investment fell off sharply until 1979. By 1980 the stock of foreign investment in Panama's manufacturing sector was the same as it had been in 1970. The uncertainty engendered by the pending Canal negotiations and the early unpredictability of Torrijos's policies were key deterrents to new direct foreign investment.

Also important was a general sense that the period of easy import substitution in Panama had come to an end,[52] that future manufacturing growth would depend on export expansion. Panama's price and incentive structure, however, discouraged investment in new agricultural and manufacturing exports. Import substitution manufacturing in Panama proceeded, as elsewhere, behind an appreciable wall of protectionism. Given Panama's small internal market, and its exclusion from the Central American Common Market,[53] domestic production could not take advantage of economies of scale; the result was less efficient production and higher prices. With low shares of domestic value added and general exoneration on import duties for imported inputs, these high prices were sustained by high effective rates of protection.[54] The small domestic market, along with social and political factors, also meant that the markets for most industrial products were dominated by a couple of large companies, at times in collusion, thus reinforcing the pattern of high prices. The high prices, in turn, meant a higher cost of living (pushing up wages) and more expensive domestically produced inputs (e.g., refined petroleum, electricity, sugar, cement, fertilizers, chemical pest controls, etc.). High prices were palatable to firms producing for the protected domestic market, but they made entrance into the competitive world market difficult.[55]

Also working against the development of labor-intensive manufactured exports, as called for in the IMF/World Bank strategy, was Panama's comparatively high wage structure for the region. The relatively high wages in part reflected the high cost of living, but more significantly they demonstrated the historical influence of the Canal Zone on the Panamanian wage structure.[56] Since the 1955 Remón-Eisenhower Treaty, with the exception of a short period after 1979, Panamanian workers in the Zone have been paid on the U.S. government wage scale.[57] Thus, in 1978 the average monthly salary of a Zone worker was $788, almost three times as high as the average monthly salaries in the public sector ($267) and the private sector ($288). The high salaries paid semiskilled and skilled employees in

TABLE 2.5. *Hourly Labor Costs in 1987*

	U.S. $/hr.	Panama = 100
Panama	1.77	100
Brazil	1.14	64
Mexico	0.84	47
Costa Rica	0.95	54
Guatemala	0.88	50
Honduras	0.53	30
Dominican Republic	0.79	45
Haiti	0.58	33
Jamaica	0.63	36
Hong Kong	1.98	112
Taiwan	1.84	104
South Korea	1.54	87
Thailand	0.35	20
Philippines	0.26	15

Source. Figures computed from International Labour Office, *Yearbook of Labour Statistics*, 1987.

Note. Includes estimated payroll taxes, fringe benefits, and bonuses.

the Canal Zone and the banking center naturally applied an upward pressure on the salaries for similar workers elsewhere in the Panamanian economy. In Table 2.5 we present data on the 1987 average hourly compensation costs for semiskilled production in export manufacturing industries for Panama and several other less developed countries. These figures, sensitive to fluctuations in exchange rate and differential accounting definitions, must be interpreted cautiously. Nevertheless, their magnitudes are sufficiently divergent to sustain the general pattern we describe.

On the basis of wage costs alone, Panama was not a very attractive country for foreign investors to take advantage of General System of Preferences (GSP) or Caribbean Basin Initiative (CBI) trade preferences with the United States. Downward wage rigidity resulted because the government could not devalue as long as the balboa was fixed at parity with the dollar (see the discussion of Panama's monetary system in chapter 4.) In other countries wage concessions could

TABLE 2.6.   *Average Output/Labor Ratios by Sector, 1985–1987*
(in thousands of balboas)

Sector	Value Added per Worker
Agriculture	1,122
Manufacturing	2,736
Construction	2,630
All services	3,844
Commerce	2,616
Finance	11,164
Transportation, storage, and communications	14,126

Source. Figures calculated from *Panamá en cifras* (1987).

be quickly eroded by currency depreciation, helping to maintain the competitiveness of their exports. Panama, without an autonomous currency, did not have this option.

Many distortions and problems of the Panamanian economy under Torrijos (and after) could be traced to its international service platform nature. The Canal distorted Panama's wage structure and created a disadvantage for labor-intensive export promotion. In fact, most of Panama's international services were more capital intensive, paid higher salaries, and generated less employment per unit of output than the remaining sectors of the economy, as illustrated in Table 2.6.

Herein lies another explanation for the slow employment growth during the 1970s; namely, most economic growth occurred in the service sectors. Despite the fact that real wages were stagnant during the decade and that unemployment grew, investment flowed to more capital-intensive sectors. This apparent misallocation of capital must be attributed in large measure to the distortion in relative prices created by the hegemonic role played by international services in the Panamanian economy.

The investment pattern toward capital-intensive services was underwritten by the international banking center. For example, in 1979 out of total domestic loans from the center of 2.7 billion balboas only 142 million (5.3 percent) went to agriculture, 239 million (9.0 percent) to construction, and 416 million (15.6 percent) to industry; that is, 70.1 percent of all loans went to services.[58]

As we shall see in chapter 4, the international banking center was a significant net contributor of funds to the Panamanian economy after 1970. Indeed, without the banking center it is unlikely that Panama could have shifted from its dependence on foreign equity capital in the 1960s to foreign debt capital in the 1970s. It is plausible to argue that the international banking center made capital too available to Panama, encouraging the country to live beyond its means. As Pou has pointed out in his study for the Panamanian government, real interest rates were actually negative for four consecutive years during the 1970s.[59] This is not an auspicious circumstance in an economy with a large budget deficit and exiguous private saving. The low real rates of interest contribute both to Panama's high investment ratio and preference for capital-intensive projects. That is, the international service branches of Panama's economy contributed to a double distortion: first, they engendered relatively high wages for the region; second, they provided unrealistically cheap capital, leading the economy away from an allocation of resources appropriate for its factor endowments and level of development.

From this perspective, one must also question whether the conclusion of the World Bank, the IMF, and others that Panama has exhausted its import substitution possibilities was not too hasty. On the basis of this alleged exhaustion, the World Bank argued that Panama had to orient its future development toward the foreign sector, but it may be that this "exhaustion" occurred precisely because Panama has followed an externally oriented model. Panama's international services rendered employment growth slow and wages relatively high. Demand for unskilled labor by these service sectors was minimal. High wages paid to fewer workers, given the powerful U.S. presence and cultural influence in Panama, have resulted in a high propensity to import. In this regard, it is worthwhile to quote the 1985 report on poverty published by the office of the archbishop of Panama:

The North American presence in Panama has brought to the country consumption norms and cultural patterns that are definitively foreign and that lead to higher levels of imports as a share of GDP than is common for countries at a similar level of development. . . . The operation of the canal in the middle of Panama has an opportunity cost that is the relatively small development of the country's other resources, especially agriculture, fishing and industry. [our translation][60]

Following Hirschman, it can also be argued that duty-free imports of intermediate and capital goods thwarted the potential development of secondary import substitution in Panama.[61] As late as 1986, only 3 percent of Panama's manufacturing value added was in capital goods.[62] Given the presence of the Canal, the natural potential to develop a ship repair and building industry went largely unexploited.

Certainly, one can question the thesis of exhausted import substitution on other grounds as well. The manufacturing sector, for instance, after stagnating between 1968 and 1977, grew at the healthy pace of 3.9 percent in real terms for the next five years. Over this period, manufacturing value added expanded by $163.2 million, and exports accounted for less than $20 million of this growth.[63] That is, once the uncertainty of the Canal negotiations was removed and the economy began to grow again, manufacturing output for the domestic market responded. This, of course, is hardly conclusive evidence against the exhaustion thesis, but absent compelling empirical evidence to buttress the exhaustion thesis this information is suggestive. We shall return to this point in our discussion of Panama's economic crisis in the 1980s in chapter 6 and its prospects for the 1990s in chapter 8.

In this chapter we have presented in broad strokes the evolution of Panama's economic policies and institutions. In the next two chapters we consider the institutions of the international service sector in more detail and assess their linkages to the domestic economy and their prospects for the future.

Chapter Three

Institutions of the Service Economy I: Canal, Pipeline, and Ship Registry

Unlike the famous entrepot economies of Asia, Panama's economy has been dominated by international services throughout its history. Whereas the economies of Hong Kong and Singapore began as centers of trade and transshipment, they developed a large, dynamic industrial sector as well as new international service institutions over time. With small domestic markets and populations of 2.5 million and 5.6 million, respectively, in 1986, Singapore's and Hong Kong's industrial sectors accounted for more than 30 percent of their GDPs. Panama, however, has never emerged from its overwhelming dependence on its entrepot functions. Indeed, as pointed out in chapter 2, the share of GDP contributed by the service sectors of Panama's economy, increasing over the last twenty years, surpassed 80 percent in 1988.

We now turn to a detailed consideration of the principal service institutions in Panama's economy. A central purpose in this discussion is assessing each institution's potential to contribute to future economic growth. It seems appropriate to begin with the Panama Canal; discussions of the transisthmian pipeline, flags of convenience, the Colon Free Zone, and the international banking center follow.

The Panama Canal

The Canal's checkered political history has already been discussed. Both Senator H. I. Hayakawa and commentator William F. Buckley, commenting respectively, seemed to find appropriate summary

47

phrases to describe this history in its relation to the United States: "We stole it [the Canal] fair and square"; and "What we have done to Panama is the equivalent of taking the falls away from Niagara."[1] The early economic history of the Canal and its key role in shaping the country's economic development have also been touched upon. Here we concentrate upon the economic effects of the 1977 Carter-Torrijos Treaties and the Canal's changing role in the world economy. Again, we begin with some background information.

The Canal is fifty miles long. Transiting ships, through a series of three locks, are lifted and lowered eighty-five feet. The maximum dimensions of transiting vessels are determined by the size of the locks (1,000 feet long and 110 feet wide). Canal restrictions limit transiting commercial vessels to a length of 965 feet, a beam of 106 feet, and a fresh water draft of 39.5 feet. Today, the largest ship the Canal can accommodate fully laden (the so-called PANAMAX ship) is approximately 65,000 deadweight tons (dwt). The Canal is able to accommodate roughly 93 percent of the world's fleet of some 27,000 oceangoing vessels of 1,000 gross registered tons or greater.

From the time the Canal first opened to world trade in 1914 through the early 1950s, the typical oceangoing vessel was a small tanker or general cargo vessel, displacing only 10 to 12 thousand dwt. Since the mid-1950s, however, huge increases in world trade have encouraged the building of larger and more specialized ships. Correspondingly, demand for Canal services has soared, and average ship size has risen dramatically. Likewise, in recent decades, many improvements have increased the Canal's transit capacity. The Gaillard Cut (or *Corte Culebra*) was gradually widened during the 1960s from its original 300 feet to its present 500 feet; modern lighting was installed to allow around-the-clock operations; the Canal channel has been deepened and curves straightened; and marine traffic control systems have been expanded and modernized. Several other Canal expansion projects are currently under study (we shall discuss these later in this chapter).

From August 15, 1914, when the first ship crossed the Canal until 1974, the Canal tolls were not changed. Following deficits of $1.3 million and $11.8 million in fiscal years 1973 and 1974, the Canal tolls were raised for the first time on July 8, 1974, by 19.7 percent. These toll rates, both before and after the increase, represented an enormous subsidy and saving to the user vessels that avoided an additional 7,872-mile trip around the southern tip of South America.[2] The U.N. Economic Commission for Latin America (ECLA) estimates that Canal users saved an annual average of $490 million during the 1960s.[3] By 1977, some savings estimates for steamship lines ran as high as $1 billion.[4] These savings resulted either in higher profits for the ocean carriers and/or lower cost, insurance, freight (c.i.f.) prices for the traded commodities.

Table 3.1 depicts the growth and stagnation in economic activity through the Canal since 1963. The number of yearly Canal transits peaked in 1968 at 15,511 following the earlier widening of the Gaillard Cut. Canal capacity today is probably closer to 14,500 transits as larger ships have reduced two-way traffic through narrow passages. As average ship size has grown (average vessel size in 1988 was more than three times what it was in 1955), alternative trade routes have become available, and patterns of world commerce have altered, the steady increase in Canal transits through 1968 has ended. Canal cargo tonnage peaked in 1982. The significant drop in tonnage since that date reflects the sharp decrease in Alaskan North Slope oil shipments through the Canal with the opening of the oil pipeline in western Panama, the increasing competition of alternative routes (particularly the land bridge) for container and vehicle cargo, and the decade-long recession in Central and South America.[5] Toll revenue, however, continued to climb in nominal terms due to rate hikes— 19.7 percent in July 1974, 19.5 percent in November 1976, 29.3 percent in October 1979, 9.8 percent in March 1983, and 9.8 percent in October 1989—but in real terms it declined by 19.7 percent between 1980 and 1988.[6]

In 1989 Canal business declined, resulting from slowing economic and trade activity in the United States and certain key Asian trading partners as well as selected developments affecting the important automobile, petroleum, and grain trades. A relatively flat pattern is now projected for 1990 (we discuss the long-run picture for Canal traffic later).

The tolls collected on the operation of the Canal, however, had no significant direct impact on the Panamanian economy prior to October 1, 1979, the day the Carter-Torrijos Treaties came into effect. That is, payments from the Canal Company to the government of Panama did not vary with toll revenues; rather, they were set in terms of a fixed annual annuity by the 1903 treaty: $250,000 per year, plus

TABLE 3.1.　*Canal Transits, Tolls, and Cargo, 1963–1988*

Fiscal Year	Number of Transits	Tolls (million $)	Long Tons of Cargo (million)
1963	12,005	57.9	63.9
1964	12,945	62.5	72.2
1965	12,918	67.1	78.9
1966	13,304	72.6	85.3
1967	14,070	82.3	93.0
1968	15,511	93.2	105.5
1969	15,327	95.9	108.8
1970	15,523	100.9	118.9
1971	15,348	100.6	121.0
1972	15,198	101.5	111.1
1973	15,109	113.4	127.6
1974	15,269	121.3	149.7
1975	14,735	143.3	140.6
1976	13,201	135.0	117.4
1977	13,087	164.7	123.2
1978	13,808	195.7	142.8
1979	14,362	209.5	154.5
1980	14,725	293.4	167.6
1981	15,050	303.1	171.5
1982	15,271	325.6	185.7
1983	12,954	287.8	145.9
1984	12,523	289.2	140.8
1985	12,766	300.8	138.9
1986	13,278	322.7	140.1
1987	13,444	329.9	148.9
1988	13,441	339.3	156.8
1989	13,389	329.7	151.9

Sources. Panama Canal Company, *Annual Report* (1973, 1979); Panama Canal Commission, *Annual Report* (1988). Various documents from the Canal Commission, Panama.

one lump-sum payment of $10 million. The 1936 treaty raised the yearly rental payment to $430,000, retroactive to 1934, and the 1955 treaty raised the annuity to $1.93 million. The latter was augmented gradually to approximately $2.5 million during 1975–1979 as the dollar devalued relative to special drawing rights (SDRs) in the 1970s.[7]

In addition to the rental payments, the Canal Company directly contributed to the Panamanian economy by employing more than 10,000 Panamanians in the late 1970s, purchasing goods and services from Panama, using refined oil from international companies operating in Panama to provide bunkering and chandlering services (oil sales and provisions) to the transiting ships, and stimulating auxiliary service activities. Overall, direct value added from the Canal rose from $44.1 million in 1950 to $63.9 million in 1960 to $152.0 million in 1970 to $343.8 million in 1979 (figures in current dollars); yet as a share of GDP, the direct contribution from the Canal fell from 16.5 percent in 1950 to 12.3 percent in 1979.

The Carter-Torrijos Treaties of 1977

At least from the time of the 1964 riots in Panama City following the U.S. flag-burning incident, the U.S. administrations recognized that political stability in Panama required a radical reworking of the basic terms of the 1903 treaty. That is, they understood that in one way or another the Canal would have to be unequivocally turned over to Panama. Omar Torrijos staked the honor of his government on achieving full sovereignty over the Canal and the Canal Zone.

Two treaties were finally signed by Carter and Torrijos on September 7, 1977. One treaty concerned the transitional comanagement of the Canal until the year 2000 when the Canal would be fully controlled by Panama; the other treaty concerned the operation of the Canal and its neutrality after December 31, 1999. The treaties contained several elements that many Panamanians saw as unacceptable: the majority control granted to the five U.S. commissioners on the nine-member board of commissioners for the new Canal Commission; the twenty-year-plus length of the transition period before Panama became the sole operator of the Canal; the provision giving the United States the right in perpetuity to safeguard the neutrality of the Canal; and the terms of the economic settlement that inter alia provided for far less revenue for Panama than Torrijos had been calling for.

Torrijos's concern for domestic opposition to the treaties prompted him to rush the required plebiscite and spend millions of dollars in a publicity campaign to garner support. Six weeks after the signing, on October 23, 1977, the Panamanian plebiscite was held and passed with 67 percent support. The U.S. Senate, facing both widespread ignorance about the Canal and well-organized opposition at home, proceeded with less dispatch.[8] After adding the so-called DeConcini Condition, which stipulated that if the Canal were closed for any reason after the year 2000 either the United States or Panama could take unilateral military action to reopen it, the Senate ratified the treaties on April 18, 1978. The Panamanian people never voted on the DeConcini Condition, but following the U.S. Senate vote at least some Panamanians expressed their opinions on it and the treaties during a vigorous protest in which two students were killed.[9] The initial treaties were further modified when the House passed implementing legislation on September 26, 1979—five days before the treaties went into effect—that granted the U.S. Congress control over the funds of the Canal Commission and gave the U.S. secretary of defense control over the five U.S. commissioners on the board.[10]

The treaties gave Panama immediate control over the railroad, the ports, the bowling alleys, barber shops, and other activities. The 2,700 U.S. citizens who worked in these facilities were given no job protection.[11] The United States was allowed to keep its fourteen military bases with its component of 10,000 plus troops in Panama, free of charge, until 2000. The Canal itself would be comanaged but U.S.-controlled (although the chief administrator became a Panamanian on January 1, 1990) until December 31, 1999. The jobs of the 2,000 U.S. citizens who worked on the Canal itself at the outset of the treaties would be protected until 2000, but many have left gradually as Panamanians have been trained to take their places. In late 1989, fewer than 1,000 U.S. employees remained.

The economic arrangements had several provisions: the annuity increased from $2.3 million to $10 million; an additional $10 million was paid for certain public services in commission-operating areas (police, sewerage, garbage collection, road maintenance); revenues were shared through a payment of $0.30 per net ton of transiting

TABLE 3.2. *Direct Revenues from the Canal*
(in millions of U. S. dollars)

	Fiscal Year(s)	Annuity	Public Services	Net Tonnage	Surplus	Total Revenues
1903 Treaty	1903					10
	1903–1934	0.24				5
1936 Treaty	1934–1955[a]	0.43				9
1955 Treaty	1955–1979[b]	1.93				50
1977 Treaty						
	1979[c]	2.5	2.5	13.0	0.0	18
	1980	10.0	10.0	55.0	2.7	78
	1981	10.0	10.0	57.0	0.0	77
	1982	10.0	10.0	61.2	0.4	82
	1983	10.0	10.0	51.2	0.0	71
	1984	10.0	10.0	45.0	0.0	65
	1985	10.0	10.0	52.8	2.7	76
	1986	10.0	10.0	57.0	1.1	78
	1987	10.0	10.0	58.0	2.0	80
	1988	10.0	10.0	59.9	0.0	80

Sources. Panama Canal Commission, *Annual Report* (various years); Elton et al., *Canal: desafío para los panameños,* 166–67; various documents from the Canal Commission.
[a]Payments made retroactive to 1934.
[b]Through September 30, 1979.
[c]For 1979, figures include only October through December.

cargo (to be adjusted for inflation first after five years and every two years thereafter); and surplus (profits), if generated, were shared up to $10 million annually. Table 3.2 above summarizes the Panamanian government's revenues from the Canal since 1903. Furthermore, President Carter pledged to provide Panama with $295 million in economic aid over five years and $50 million in military aid over ten years. The treaties also stipulated that Panamanian workers would be trained, on the Canal's budget, to take over the skilled jobs from the Americans. Whereas 69 percent of the Canal's labor force was Panamanian in 1979, by the beginning of 1989 this share had risen to 85 percent.[12]

Prima facie the 1977 treaties looked like a good economic deal for Panama. Indeed, to their U.S. opponents, the treaties looked like a wholesale giveaway, as if Carter and the Democrats had cowered before cries of imperialism. Yet in Panama some thought Torrijos had sold out, that more should be forthcoming to Panama to compensate for its exploitation over the years. Let us consider their economic arguments for a moment. First, the Panamanians cried foul when they learned that a deal had been struck to lower the wages of Panamanians working on the Canal by 17 to 25 percent. Economist Roberto Méndez, for instance, claimed that the new wage scale would cost Panamanians almost $4 billion in lost wages by the year 2000.[13] This claim loses its force when one realizes that the Panamanian government, fearing the tremendous costs implied after January 1, 2000, insisted on lowering domestic wages. Moreover, protests from the workers themselves led to retracting this wage decrease in January 1982.

Second, Torrijos had been speaking of $1 billion in financial compensation for past exploitation until only a few days before the final treaty was signed. The agreed-upon payments were expected to average $70 or $80 million a year, a far cry from Torrijos's projection. Critics argued that the historical rental payments (annuities) for the Canal were too low and that the operation of fourteen U.S. bases rent-free was worthy of indemnification.[14] After all, the United States at the time paid Spain $20 million annually for just three bases and made larger rental payments to both Greece and Turkey. Although the critics make a reasonable claim in this regard, it should also be pointed out that the alternative of no bases would severely dislocate the Panamanian economy. In 1990, the United States still pays no rent for its bases, but the bases generate a yearly demand for Panamanian goods and services on the order of $100 million.[15] The treaties provide for the termination of the present base leases by the year 2000, when the Panamanian government will either have to sign a new base agreement (presumably charging a fair rent) or face a sizeable drop in aggregate demand.

Third, the critics have argued that the $10 million in payments for public services is inadequate. No one questions that the state of the railroad and the ports connected to the Canal was in disrepair in 1979. The railroad, inadequately maintained from 1975 to 1979, suffered annual operating losses of $1 million during this period.[16]

By 1985, the Panamanian government's budget was allocating $5 million for railroad repairs and maintenance; actual work performed, however, appears to have been minimal. The condition of the railroad has gone from dubious to dangerous.

The treaties granted the United States preferential use of the railroads and ports and prohibited Panama from unilaterally suspending service. The situation at the Balboa (Pacific) and Cristobal (Atlantic) ports was yet more problematic. The Balboa port in 1979 was at least ten years behind other ports in the area and required $23 million minimally for modernization with problems ranging from inadequate containerization, storage, refrigeration, and repair facilities to faulty roads, docking pads, and structural maintenance.[17] With the shutting down of operations by U.S. lines in 1987, however, the Balboa port has lost significance and is now less active than Cristobal. With only two container cranes, Cristobal also suffers from poor maintenance; one or both cranes are frequently out of service. Other auxiliary maintenance costs such as managing the hydrographic basin, which required expenditures of $1.6 million in 1984, also fell upon the Panamanian government. Another maintenance cost is related to the ecology of the area: the badly deforested surrounding jungle requires urgent attention. When one considers as well the additional services that Panama provides the commission-operating areas, it is unclear whether $10 million is an adequate sum. But it does not seem appropriate for the critics to assume that Panama would be given the Canal area while the United States would continue to maintain its facilities. As long as the United States is just one of many users of these facilities, there is no reason the U.S. service payment should cover the entire costs of upkeep.

Fourth, the treaties provide for profit sharing with the Panamanian government up to $10 million a year.[18] The critics allege that the United States has used its majority control to deliberately undermine this provision by extending additional benefits to U.S. citizens employed by the Canal Commission; for example, the U.S. government has provided its employees with free lodging and electricity, free mail services, free trips to the United States, and two free trips per year for children who are students in the United States. Reportedly, there are plans both to install free-of-charge cable television systems in the homes of U.S. employees and to introduce an expensive employee relocation plan.[19] The intention behind the extension of these benefits is impossible for us to judge, but it might be pointed out that greater inducements to keep these skilled employees in Panama were probably necessary once the treaty was approved and the assumptions of their existence as "Zonians" were falsified.[20]

It is also important to remember that the Canal confers many indirect benefits on Panama's economy. For instance, in 1988, in addition to the $79.9 million of treaty payments to the Panamanian treasury, the Canal Commission spent $142 million in wages and salaries for Panamanian workers, $52 million in retirement and disability benefits, and $38 million in local purchases of goods and services[21] and U.S. employees of the Canal spent an estimated $7 million in the local economy in 1988.[22]

In the final analysis, whether the treaties prove a long-run boon to the Panamanian economy will have much more to do with the economic future of the Canal itself than with the particular payments for services specified by the treaties.

The Economic Future of the Canal

Apart from political problems, several recent developments in the patterns of world trade have weakened the competitive position of the Panama Canal. Since 1970, there has been a significant shift in world commerce away from bulk materials (e.g., oil, coal, grains, iron ore, lumber) toward processed and manufactured goods. The demand for some materials, such as iron ore and coal, is decreasing with the increasing use of plastics and high-tech materials; also, new processing methods, such as pelletizing iron ore, have resulted in less tonnage being shipped.[23] This shift in traded commodities, along with technological developments in shipping, has meant an increasing presence of containerships and auto/truck carriers in Canal waters. Since the 1970s, however, the development of intermodalism—coordination of water, rail, and truck transportation—has challenged the Canal for the business of container and auto carriers. Furthermore, the trend toward ever larger ships now means that some 7 percent of the world's commercial ships cannot pass through the Canal, while another 20 percent or more are restricted to one-way passage over the narrow eight-mile stretch of the Gaillard Cut.[24] The implications of these trends for future Canal traffic are extremely complicated to sort out and require a detailed analysis of trade routes, commodities and their prices, present and prospective suppliers, new technologies, projections of changes in Canal tolls and prices of alternative routes, and possible political events.[25] Below we merely sketch the complexity of such analyses and briefly summarize some relevant considerations and conclusions.

It is useful to keep the following facts in mind as we proceed. During the 1980s container traffic grew at a rate of approximately 10 percent per year, and by 1988 containerships carrying processed and manufactured goods accounted for 15 percent of Canal revenues.[26] Auto and truck carriers accounted for another 19 percent of revenue and grains an additional 12 percent. Roughly half of all Canal trade moves between the Far East and the U.S. Gulf and East coasts.

Grains are generally projected to provide the most secure source of Canal growth over the next twenty years. Yet coarse grain exports from the United States to the Far East are being challenged by substantial increases in local grain production in the developing nations of Asia: China has become a key corn supplier to Japan; South Korea is increasing production of corn and wheat; the green revolution has lifted India from a wheat importer to an exporter; and even Saudi Arabia is now exporting wheat. Brazil is increasing its competition with the United States for soybean exports. Plummeting grain sales provided a major cause of the Canal's record financial deficit in 1989. Hence, projections that grains will account for 30 percent of Canal traffic by 2010 may prove overly optimistic.[27]

Traffic growth of auto and truck carriers will be stunted by the saturation of the U.S. car market, slower population growth, Japanese investment in U.S. production facilities, and intermodalism. In 1989, it became cost effective to use the U.S. land bridge (rail shipment) rather than the Canal, and, according to some claims, political instability in Panama enhanced the attractiveness to shippers to make this shift.

Container traffic, however, is probably the most serious question in the Canal's future. The basis of this question is the development of intermodalism since the early 1970s and its explosive growth since 1984. Railroad deregulation, new port construction on the U.S. West Coast, and the introduction of double-stack trains in April 1984 have resulted in growth in land bridge traffic of more than 15 percent per year between 1983 and 1988.[28] Double-stack trains consist of twenty to twenty-eight articulated rail cars, carrying up to 280 forty-foot containers stacked two high. The typical double-stack train is one to one and a half miles long. These trains are estimated to reduce hauling costs by some 25 percent on average, and depending on the destination they save five to fifteen days over the all-water route through the Canal.[29] As a further complication, in 1988 American President Lines put into operation its first containership that was too large for the Canal, and the company was expected to introduce five more such ships by mid-1990. Most observers believe the trend toward larger containerships will continue. The Canal still retains a cost advantage over container shipment for many routes, and future land bridge growth is limited by installed capacity. Generally, rail shipment, viable only for containers and vehicle carriers, offers little competition for bulk cargo, which still forms the majority of the Canal's business.[30]

The prospective difficulties with container traffic, however, place a greater onus on bulk traffic. We have already mentioned that grains are the most promising bulk commodity group, but even they are problematic. The Canal has already lost most of its petroleum business to (post-PANAMAX) supertankers, to the pipelines across western Panama, and, since 1988, to the United States (see below). Coal and iron ore traffic has also been severely challenged by the modern, large bulk carriers and the practice of topping-off with coal on the route around South Africa. It is likely that coal and iron ore traffic will slow to a trickle or disappear entirely before the year 2000. Other bulk commodities face difficulties as well: banana shipments are threatened by the development of new groves in the Caribbean; lumber and sugar are threatened by source substitutes obviating the Canal route; phosphates and sulfur are similarly threatened by new production in Africa and the Middle East, and so on.

All this is not to say that the Canal "will become little more than a museum piece of 19th Century engineering prowess" by the year 2000.[31] The consensus projection from the mid-1980s seems to be that Canal traffic will grow between 0.5 and 2.0 percent per year over the next twenty years, although more recent estimates tend to predict slower growth.[32] A key variable in these projections is the assumption one makes regarding future toll rate increases. The 1986 study by Temple, Barker and Sloane Inc. (TBS), for instance, projected a 2.0 percent annual growth rate without transit cost increases, but the growth rate slows as transit costs increase: a 1.7 percent rate with a

25 percent increase, a 1.4 percent rate with a 50 percent increase, and a 0.8 percent rate with a doubling of transit costs.[33] Investments in modernization will be necessary if the Canal is to remain a contributor, however modest, to Panamanian economic growth.

Canal Modernization

The ongoing Canal modernization has accelerated since the 1960s. Richard Wainio, head of economic analysis for the Canal Commission, described some of these efforts:[34]

In the early 1960s, modern lighting was installed along the banks of the Canal and the waterway began operating 24 hours a day. The Gaillard Cut widening from 300 to 500 feet was completed in 1970; shortly thereafter, a multimillion dollar computerized Marine Traffic Control Center was constructed; more recently, the entire channel was deepened to assure sufficient water for lockages and deep draft vessels; all the original towing locomotives have been replaced with 80 more powerful models; the Canal tug fleet is being upgraded with the addition of modern tractor tugs, especially designed to handle large ships in confined spaces; high mast, high intensity lighting now allows PANAMAX ships—the largest vessels that use the Canal—to transit the locks at night; curves in the channel have been straightened and sections have been widened; state-of-the-art computer and communication systems have been installed; modern weather and water monitoring equipment acquired; and the list goes on and on.

Notwithstanding these past improvements, many believe that to remain competitive and avoid an absolute diminution in traffic the Canal must make significant investments in modernization. In 1982, representatives from Japan, the United States, and Panama formed a trilateral preparatory commission to establish the framework for an investigation to be conducted between June 1986 and June 1991 by a regular commission with a $20-million budget. Japan, the second largest user of the Canal and the largest user of the Colon Free Zone, had been pushing the idea of a new sea-level (i.e., without locks) canal. Investigating a sea-level canal has been the primary charge of the trilateral commission, although the commission has also been looking into creating a third set of locks for the present Canal as well as improvements in the transisthmian railroad and new pipelines. By early 1990, three-and-a-half years since the regular commission's formation, no evident progress has been made in its study of these

potential projects. Most observers attribute this unproductiveness to
political difficulties and the obvious lack of economic viability of a
new sea-level canal. Not only does the estimated cost of the project
exceed $20 billion, but a number of environmental concerns also re-
main unresolved.[35]

At present, the consensus is that the next important project necessary for making Canal transit more competitive is a second widening
of the Gaillard Cut. By implementing this project, ships with beams
longer than ninety-five feet—now nearly 30 percent of Canal traffic—could travel in two-way traffic throughout the Canal. This, in
turn, would reduce both average transit time to less than the present
eight to ten hours and the total Canal waters time, including waiting,
to less than the present twenty-four hours. Because the so-called
ships' value time ranges between $400 and $1,000 an hour, conserva-
tively estimated,[36] reducing Canal waters time effectively makes Canal transit more economically competitive. The widening would en-
tail the removal of some 35 million cubic yards of material at an
estimated cost of $400 million in 1987 dollars.[37] If undertaken, the
work could be accomplished in three stages, commencing in 1994
and ending in 2005. Before finally committing to the Canal's widening, however, the shipping companies would be systematically sur-
veyed to assess the perceived need for the cut. The decision to proceed, if taken before the year 2000, would also require the approval
of the U.S. Congress and the president.

If the Gaillard Cut is widened, then the next Canal bottleneck to
consider is the Pedro Miguel Locks. At such a time, the commission
could seriously consider adding another set of locks.

The former Noriega regime committed itself to one major project,
not involving the Canal directly: the development of a "centerport"
for storage and transshipment. The centerport concept first surfaced
from Barletta's planning group in the early 1970s. Its present incar-
nation entails several elements—some plausible, some not—but in
no case will the centerport offer the salvation its proponents predicted. It is plausible to set up a transshipment port at Telfers Island
in the Atlantic: (1) large shipping lines could then transfer cargo at
this central drop-off point for more efficient cargo routing; and (2)
large ships could unload containers at Telfers Island, which would be
loaded on smaller ships ("feeders") for local port delivery. Each inter-
lining method would permit ships to operate at fuller capacity. Basi-

cally, the idea expands and diversifies the already existing Colon Free Zone (to be discussed below).[38] Whether the plausibility of the transshipment port is converted into profitability will depend on the National Port Authority's ability to manage the project efficiently and flexibly. Unless the Endara regime can markedly improve the operation of the Port Authority, one cannot be optimistic.

The implausible part of the centerport project calls for upgrading the fifty-mile-long railroad across the isthmus and using the modernized rail as a land bridge to transport containers. The problem is that the loading and unloading of container cargo on long trains is a labor-intensive and time-consuming task that can be justified only if the cargo haul is over long distances.

A less glamorous project alternative would be a major improvement in Panama's dry dock (ship service) facilities. Bunkering (oil sales) has trended downward with larger, more fuel-efficient ships and less efficient refining and management in Panama. Chandlering (provisions to ships) has also suffered, and ship repair services remain a skeleton of its potential.

Overall, the Canal and its auxiliary operations offer little prospect of significant growth in the coming decades, even with major investments in maintenance and modernization. The Canal seems to be losing traffic to the aggressive land bridge operators more rapidly than anticipated. The Canal experienced a record deficit of $7.6 million in 1989.[39] Although some of this loss may be attributable to the country's political instability, it is not clear that the ocean carriers will reroute their cargo when the political situation is normalized. Even under the most optimistic political and economic assumptions, it is unlikely that the Canal will either resume its preeminent role in East-West trade or exert a dynamic influence on the Panamanian economy in the 1990s and after, as Panama gains full sovereignty over its own Canal.

The Transisthmian Pipeline

When oil began to flow from Alaska's North Slope in the late 1970s, the United States urgently needed a way to absorb the surplus production. From an output of 1.5 million barrels per day, the West Coast refineries could process only one million. Because the Alaskan reserves are considered strategic, shipment to the Far East is prohibited. Ecological considerations and constraints led to arrangements, beginning in 1979, for much of the oil to be shipped to the Gulf and East coasts via the Canal.

Because Alaskan oil was shipped typically in supertankers of up to 265,000 dwt—far too large to transit the Canal—it was necessary to set up a transshipment operation. The first solution was to construct an oil transshipment terminal in Charco Azul, south of Puerto Armuelles on the Pacific Coast of Panama near the border with Costa Rica, where the oil could be transferred from the supertankers to smaller ships that could pass through the Canal. The company Petroterminal de Panamá, S.A., was formed for this purpose as a joint venture between the government of Panama (holding 25 percent),[40] Chicago Bridge and Iron International (holding 25 percent), and Northville Industries Corporation of New York (holding 50 percent).[41] From 1979 to 1982 Canal traffic increased markedly due to this new operation: for instance, in 1980 and 1981, the 24.2 and 26.9 million tons, respectively, of Alaskan crude oil that passed through the Canal generated an additional $50 million annually in Canal revenues. The construction of the petroterminal port in Charco Azul created one thousand jobs with total labor payments of some $10 million. The actual operation of the transshipment port requires approximately 140 employees, of whom all but six are Panamanian.[42]

In July 1981, an agreement was reached among Northville, the Panamanian government, and Chicago Bridge and Iron to construct a pipeline from Charco Azul to the Atlantic Coast, through the rain forest and cordillera (up to 3,936 feet), at Chiriqui Grande. The holdings of the Panamanian government would be expanded to 40 percent at first and to 100 percent in July 1999. The construction of the pipeline employed 1,200 workers for more than eighteen months at a total cost of $363 million. The pipeline was estimated to cut transportation costs by 20 percent and reduce Canal transits by three boats per day. The investment on the pipeline paid for itself in three years.[43]

The pipeline has the capacity to pump up to 850,000 barrels per day; as recently as 1987, it handled close to this level. At capacity, the pipeline operation, albeit highly computerized, employs over 500 people, roughly an investment of $680,000 per job. In 1984, in addition to labor income of $8 million, the pipeline generated approximately $36 million in income tax, $11 million in user fees paid to the national government, $2 million in payments to the municipalities through which the pipeline passes, $9 million for electricity consumption, $15 million in purchases of goods and services, a $17-million contribution for constructing the David-Chiriqui Grande highway, $10 million in interest paid on Panamanian government tax notes, and $1 million for the employer's portion of social security.[44] By the end of the second year, the pipeline company estimated that it had put $220 million into the Panamanian economy in direct benefits. By another estimate, the pipeline contributed $154 million in value added to the economy in 1983, the first full year of its operation.[45] This made the pipeline the second largest enterprise in Panama, responsible for 3.5 percent of its GDP.

The pipeline's business remained buoyant until 1988 when two new pipelines, crossing from southern California to the Gulf Coast, were opened. Pumped oil through the Panamanian pipeline fell from 261.4 million barrels in 1987 to 213.6 million in 1988 (an 18.3 percent decrease).[46] Throughput fell off even more sharply during 1989; for the first six months of 1989 throughput was 41 percent below the level of the similar period of 1988.[47] By 1990, together the two U.S. pipelines, with their projected daily capacity of 1.2 million barrels, make the Panamanian pipeline redundant as a carrier of Alaskan oil, the output of which is dwindling anyway. From the investors' point of view the pipeline has already paid off handsomely; from Panama's point of view the future of the pipeline is questionable, perhaps limited to carrying mineral slurry.[48]

Flags of Convenience

In 1939, Standard Oil of New Jersey transferred a substantial share of its tanker fleet to Panamanian registry to circumvent technically provisions of the Neutrality Act while aiding Great Britain.[49] After World War II, shipping companies realized the economic benefits to foreign registration of their ships. Namely, many countries offered ship registry at lower costs, quicker processing, and fewer or less stringent regulations. Panama's ship registry laws, for instance, have fewer insurance requirements, looser health and safety regulations, and more lax employment standards than many industrialized countries. Because Panama has no income tax on offshore operations, shipping companies can shelter that part of their net income not returned to their home country.

In 1986, Panama held second place, behind Liberia, in the registry of the world's shipping fleet, with nearly 12,000 ships flying the Panamanian flag.[50] Aggressive marketing and pricing policies brought Panama from seventh in the mid-1970s to second place a decade later. The government's Shipping and Consular Department opened representative offices in dozens of new ports around the world, maintaining inspection procedures in more than 300 ports. Most new ships flying Panamanian flags are owned by Japanese, among the most active investors in the Colon Free Zone and the international banking center.

The ship registry business provides the Panamanian government with direct revenue in excess of $40 million a year.[51] In addition, an estimated $20 million plus is collected from the merchant marine of the Panamanian registered fleet who are obligated to purchase identity cards. It is, however, not clear how much of this latter sum finds its way into the government coffers. According to José Blandon, former Noriega consul in New York, the sale of identity cards was run as a monopoly by the company Marinac, owned by Noriega's brother-in-law, Ramón Sieiro.[52] Apparently many Panamanian ambassadors and consuls, agents for the identity card business, were paid generously.[53] Although the ship registry business prospered in the 1980s, ongoing stiff competition comes from Liberia, Honduras, and other countries.[54] Ship registry also produces several million dollars a year for Panama's law firms, which handle the registration and provide other maritime services.[55]

Chapter Four

Institutions of the Service Economy II: Free Zone and Banking Center

Colon Free Zone

Some three hundred years and twenty-five miles separate the Portobelo Fairs of Inca gold and the present Colon Free Zone (CFZ), a Latin American trade fair in its own right. The idea for the free trade zone at Colon (the Atlantic end of the Canal) was first proposed by the Colon Chamber of Commerce in 1929. It was not acted upon until 1948 when the Panamanian government set up an autonomous public entity with an endowment of thirty-eight hectares to operate a free trade zone. When the CFZ finally opened for business in 1952, it did so with ten companies on five hectares of land.

The chief proponent and planner for the CFZ was Thomas E. Lyons, a functionary of the U.S. Department of Commerce. Lyons argued that the Zone, where goods could enter and exit tariff-free and with little paperwork, would provide several advantages for international trade.

1. It would offer commercial agents a respite from rigid customs practices and government regulations.
2. It would establish a contact point for American and European manufacturers with their clients in Central and South America.
3. It would allow Latin American buyers, who formerly had to travel to Europe or the United States, to explore disparate merchandise in a compact area as well as make their purchases in nearby Panama.

4. It would provide companies cheaper and more convenient warehousing of inventory nearer their final markets and permit quicker and more competitive delivery.

Lyons also foresaw several CFZ benefits to the Panamanian economy.

1. It would stimulate construction employment connected to warehousing and infrastructure and generate ongoing employment related to the CFZ's management.
2. It would encourage the growth of commercial and financial expertise among the Panamanian managers.
3. It would generate rental income for the land.
4. It would stimulate business travel to Panama, which would enhance commercial contacts and promote the development of hotels, restaurants, services, and so on.
5. It would motivate some corporations, experiencing the tax, currency, and communications advantages of doing business in Panama, to locate manufacturing branches in the country from which they could supply the Latin American market.
6. It would increase both cargo and revenues for the Canal.
7. It would promote passenger traffic, especially by air.[1]

There is little question that much of Lyons's analysis was on the mark. International companies saw a host of advantages from participating in the CFZ: Panama's central location, excellent communications infrastructure, lax corporate laws and extensive tax benefits, use of the U.S. dollar as currency without restrictions, and, after 1970, proximity of easy credit from the international banking center induced hundreds of companies to set up business in the CFZ. In 1988, the CFZ, spread over 300 hectares,[2] involved more than 1,600 companies;[3] it was the largest free zone in the Western Hemisphere, second only to Hong Kong in the world. Although most companies used the CFZ for warehousing and sales, increasing numbers of employees were involved in light processing activities (repackaging, electronics, assembly, textiles, etc.). The processing activities were stimulated by both the tariff preferences made available by the U.S. Caribbean Basin Initiative Program after 1983 and the desire of Asian newly industrialized countries (NICs) to continue to benefit from the GSP preferences of a low-income country.

Most companies operating in the CFZ sign a contract with the government that specifies exemptions and tax benefits, including no income tax, over a period of up to twenty years. Smaller companies are sometimes taxed on their net export income from CFZ operations at a rate from 2.5 to 8.5 percent. The absence of income tax for most firms or its low level for other firms in the CFZ encourages many companies to employ the transfer pricing technique—overinvoicing exports or underinvoicing imports—to make their global profits appear in Panama, thus avoiding income taxes in other countries.[4] No firm pays either a capital gains tax on the sale of Free Zone assets held over two years or a municipal tax. No Panamanian import or export taxes, excise duties, or consular fees are levied on goods entering or leaving the CFZ, unless they are being sold to Panama. In the latter case, unless contraband, they are treated as normal imports.

Contraband trade, in and out of the Zone, was reportedly rampant in the 1980s.[5] The Panamanian Defense Forces controlled customs, managed the company that controls merchandise movement in and out of the CFZ, and monopolized the majority of overland trucking within Panama. Contraband trade, then, was rather straightforward as it was undertaken by the government itself.

In the CFZ value added—reexports minus imports—grew from $1.4 million in 1952 to $23.0 million in 1960 to $58.2 million in 1970 to a peak of $441.2 million in 1982 (i.e., 10.3 percent of GDP). In nominal terms, the yearly growth rate of the Zone was 18.3 percent between 1970 and 1982. From its 1982 peak, CFZ value added fell steadily to $122 million in 1987 (2.3 percent of GDP, with $1.501 billion in imports and $1.623 billion in reexports). Private employment in the CFZ followed a similar pattern: it rose steadily from 2,660 in 1972 to a peak of 6,974 in 1982, but then it fell to 5,822 by 1985. The most important factor behind this fall is the devastating effect of the debt crisis on normal trade with Latin America.[6] Both hard currency shortfalls and the greater difficulty in procuring short-term credits for trade financing have reduced trade levels and converted much ongoing trade to a direct, bilateral barter basis. Also hurting the CFZ has been increasing competition from the new free trade zones in Miami and elsewhere in the Caribbean.

Although this competition is likely to increase in the 1990s, it is a source of strength for the CFZ that it has become for many Japanese and Asian NIC companies the base for Latin American operations and reexports to the United States. In 1985, Japan, Hong Kong, Taiwan, and South Korea accounted for 54.5 percent of all imports into the CFZ.[7] Reexports from the CFZ fell by 8.5 percent during 1988, but this drop was reversed during 1989.[8] If the Latin American economies emerge from the debt crisis and if the Panamanian government can take advantage of the some 9,000 hectares of the reverted areas (from the 1977 treaties) around Colon, then the CFZ could resume its growth. There is little basis to believe, however, that the dynamic growth of its past can be replicated.

The International Banking Center
Panama's Monetary System

To understand Panama's banking system one must first consider its monetary history. Based on an agreement with the United States in 1904 and Law No. 84 of the same year, Panama has no paper currency of its own. Rather, the U.S. dollar circulates as legal tender, along with U.S. and Panamanian coins. The stated purpose of this agreement was to facilitate payment to workers engaged in building the Panama Canal. When the Canal was completed, however, the agreement remained. Panama calls its currency the balboa, but it has, according to the 1904 agreement, always run at parity with the U.S. dollar; the only exception was the brief period in 1941 when President Arnulfo Arias Madrid created the Banco Central de Emisión de la República. The new bank issued notes in denominations of one, five, ten, and twenty balboas, but when Arias was deposed in October 1941 the notes were invalidated and withdrawn from circulation.[9]

Law No. 84 also created the National Bank of Panama (NBP), which has served as a clearinghouse for checks and dollars. Until the creation of the National Banking Commission in 1970, the NBP also enforced the nation's sparse regulations and reserve requirements. Lacking both a central bank and its own currency, the monetary authorities have little control over the supply of money in Panama. Today, the banking commission has a minor degree of control through the reserve requirements imposed on domestic banking, but it would be only a slight exaggeration to compare Panama's control over its money supply with that of New Jersey. U.S. dollars enter the Panamanian economy from Panama's exports as well as from loans and transfers. When an excess of cash develops in the economy, private banks unload their excess dollars into their accounts at the NBP, which credits their accounts and sends the excess cash by plane to either a private bank in the U.S. (e.g., the Republic National Bank of New York) or the New York Federal Reserve Bank. When a cash shortage develops, the NBP draws on its accounts in the United States, and cash is flown back to Panama. These legal flows of currency have been complemented by often equally important flows of narcodollars in and out of the country.

This monetary system has had both advantages and disadvantages. The major disadvantages are Panama's inability to conduct its own monetary policy, its vulnerability to both the fate of the dollar and U.S. policy, and its inability to devalue the currency to promote current account balance in international payments. Panama's vulnerability to U.S. policy became painfully obvious with the imposition of stiff U.S. economic sanctions, including freezing the NBP's accounts in the United States, beginning in March 1988. One Panamanian analyst described the situation: "Panama is the only country that can be subjected to an economic blockade from its interior."[10] Certainly, one reason Panama's economy fell by some 20 percent during 1988 was its inability to follow an expansionary monetary policy in response to U.S. sanctions.

On the positive side, Panama has had no short-term shortage of foreign exchange as a result of difficulties in the balance of payments. Panama's access to foreign exchange and its international credit standing have been more directly a function of its public finances than its current account balance. The system has virtually guaranteed monetary and price stability, enabling Panama to avoid the crippling bouts of inflation that have afflicted the rest of Latin America. It has also facilitated international transactions, largely because the use of the dollar eliminates any exchange rate risk. Finally, the use of the dollar and the consequent absence of exchange controls greatly supported the growth of the international banking center.

The Birth of International Banking

Although the birth of Panama's international banking center is usually identified with Cabinet Decree No. 238 of July 2, 1970, prior corporate and banking legislation played a central role in promoting the center. For instance, the Commercial Code of 1927 provided easy and inexpensive incorporation procedures and established the principle of not taxing offshore operations. Law No. 101 of 1941 permitted the creation of dummy (or "paper" or "shell") companies. Law No. 18 of 1959 enhanced corporate secrecy and opened the way for numbered bank accounts. With these statutes in place, Panama's banking sector, in resonance with the rapid development of the eurodollar market, began to grow in the 1960s. The number of "real" banks grew from six in 1961 to twelve in 1965 to twenty-three in 1970, while employment in banking increased from 1,312 in 1964 to 2,518 in 1969 to 2,881 in 1970.[11]

The biggest impulse to the development of Panama's international banking center, however, was Cabinet Decree No. 238 on July 2, 1970. This decree reorganized Panama's banking system along more systematic lines, allowing both greater stability and efficiency. Several measures provided greater stability: abolishing paper banks, requiring a minimum paid-in capital of $250,000, establishing new regulations for reserves and capital structure in domestic banking, and creating the National Banking Commission with regulatory authority.[12] Although this structural stability itself attracted international banks, the decree also added flexibility in bank licensing and further defined secrecy provisions to lure offshore banking to Panama.

Three types of bank licenses were created: a general license allowed banks to conduct both domestic and offshore business; an international license permitted only offshore business; and representative banking authorized indirect banking through affiliation. Offshore banking was to be free of interest rate regulations and reserve requirements and exempt from income taxation. Enhanced secrecy was provided by Articles 63, 65, 74, 83, and 101. In summary, Articles 63 and 65 make several stipulations: the banking commission has the right to request specific information on accounts from the banks and the duty to conduct an inspection every two years, but the results of such inspections can only be published in the form of aggregate statistics; moreover, a bank refusing to submit to the biannual review will be subject to a fine of not more than $1,000. Article 74 forbids the commission "to conduct or order investigations concerning the private affairs of any bank's clients" and prohibits the release of any specific information unless judicially requested.[13] It further prohibits the publication of any information without the consent in writing of the bank or client concerned. Article 101 stipulates monetary sanctions to bank or commission employees who release any information in violation of the decree. These secrecy provisions are added to those that permit numbered bank accounts, which conceal the depositor's identity to all but one or two bank employees (usually the manager and/or a senior account manager). According to one expert, Panama's secrecy provisions are equal to those in any of the thirty-eight countries listed by the U.S. Internal Revenue Service commissioner as tax havens in 1981.[14]

In addition to the use of the dollar, easy and inexpensive incorporation, tax exemption, virtual regulation-free banking for offshore operations, and extensive banking secrecy, Panama offers many attractive attributes to offshore banking: geography; the business of the Colon Free Zone; an excellent, modern communications system; and bilingualism where English attracts U.S., European, and Japanese banks and Spanish attracts Latin banks (in the mid-1980s approximately one-third of the banking center's assets came from Latin America). Luis Moreno, former president of Panama's Banking Association and member of the banking commission, argues that a further attraction is the historical disposition of Panamanians "to serve with loyalty and efficiency international business."[15] Until the post-June 1987 political and economic crisis, advocates had claimed that Panama was attractive because of longstanding political stability and the sense of security provided by U.S. bases.

The Banking Center's Impact on the Economy

As is the case with Panama's other international service institutions, the banking center stimulated the country's economy in a number of ways.[16] As the banking center expanded from 23 banks and $854 million in assets in 1970 to 118 banks and $49.0 billion in assets in 1982, employment in the center more than tripled, from 2,881 in 1970 to 8,971 in 1982. After assets peaked in 1982, the number of banks peaked at 125 in 1983 and stabilized at around 120 thereafter; employment continued to grow through 1986 when it reached 9,197.[17] Roughly 97 percent of total employment in the center has been of Panamanians, with jobs ranging from skilled (managers, accountants) to semiskilled (bookkeepers, stenographers, secretaries,

tellers) to unskilled (janitors, drivers, security). Overall, average salaries in the banking center have been more than 50 percent above
those in the rest of the nonagricultural sectors of the Panamanian
economy.[18] The center has also stimulated substantial indirect employment via construction of bank headquarters, housing for
employees, hotels, and infrastructure and auxiliary activities (such
as professional services, reinsurance, Colon Free Zone, etc.). At its
peak in the early 1980s, Moreno estimated that for every person directly employed in the center at least four outside the center owed
their jobs to it; thus, the center's direct and indirect contribution to
GDP was between 3 and 4 percent.[19] The indirect effects were undoubtedly much stronger during the years of the center's rapid
growth (1970–1982) when massive construction projects were undertaken. They have fallen off sharply since 1982 as the center's
activity levels have declined.

Another significant contribution of the center has been to increase
the supply of loan capital available domestically. If one subtracts total
domestic deposits (bank deposits made by Panamanians) from total
domestic loans (loans from the banks of the center to Panamanian
government, business, and individuals), the difference is the net outstanding loan capital contributed to the Panamanian economy from
the international banking center. Table 4.1 depicts movements in net
loan capital from 1968 to 1988. During the years represented in this
table, the average outstanding net supply of capital to Panama was
$282 million, or 12.9 percent of the total loan capital issued by the
banking center. Of course, some net supply of capital to Panama from
the center would have been available in the form of foreign loans in
any event; hence, it cannot all be considered the center's contribution
to the economy.

Other benefits accruing to Panama from the banking center are the
tax revenues generated from personal income and corporate income
on domestic banking, capital gains to landowners, maturation of the
domestic financial system, and promotion of business tourism.

The economic gains provided by the center did not come without
their costs. First, the domestic loans supplied by the center were
skewed toward service-sector activities and consumption. In 1986,
for instance, 80.4 percent of loans went to nonproduction
activities.[20] In a related manner, it has been virtually impossible for
small industrial and agricultural businesses to receive loan capital

TABLE 4.1. *Supply of Capital to Panama from the International Banking Center*
(in millions of U. S. dollars)

Capital from IBC	1968	1970	1972	1974	1976	1978	1980	1982	1984	1986	1988
Domestic loans	262	420	766	1,367	1,628	1,843	2,531	3,351	3,764	4,189	3,996
Domestic deposits	217	341	602	796	995	1,553	2,406	3,527	3,371	4,275	2,937
Net loans[a]	45	79	164	571	633	290	125	−176	393	−86	1,059

Source. Luis Moreno, *Panamá: centro bancario internacional,* 102–3.
Note. Figures refer to amount outstanding on December 31 of each year except 1988, when they refer to June 30.
[a]Amount of net loans equals amount of domestic loans minus the sum of domestic deposits.

from the banks in the center.[21] Second, contrary to Moreno's claim that the center stimulated domestic saving,[22] the growth of the center has been accompanied by a decreasing domestic saving rate.[23] Naturally, we do not know that the center caused this fall in saving, but the decrease is consistent with our suggestion in chapter 3 that the center, by making foreign capital more easily available, engendered a lassitude about thrift as well as a dependence on foreign funds. In effect, as has been argued by Griffin,[24] the foreign capital substituted for domestic saving. Third, the existence of the center and the Panamanian government's control over the banking commission enabled the center to be used extensively for money laundering, which has contributed importantly to the economic and political instability of the late 1980s.[25]

General Noriega and Money Laundering

Of all the money-laundering centers in the world, Panama's international banking facility has been widely regarded as the most efficient and unique: the U.S. dollar circulates as legal tender, and foreign exchange regulations are completely absent. Therefore, it is understandable that in his April 5, 1988, testimony before Senator John Kerry's (D-Mass.) hearings on terrorism, narcotics, and international operations, popular financial author Martin Mayer argued that if the United States were serious about controlling money laundering it must force Panama to stop using the dollar and start printing its own currency.[26]

Martin Mayer might also have inquired into the U.S. government's many years of tolerating and even encouraging Manuel Noriega, long after his venality and involvement in drug trafficking was known by the State Department. In his testimony before the Kerry Subcommittee, Francis J. McNeil, former U.S. ambassador to Costa Rica and State Department intelligence officer, stated that in 1977 when he became deputy assistant secretary of state for Inter-American Affairs Noriega was already widely known as "the rent-a-colonel."[27] The deposition of one U.S. Drug Enforcement Agency (DEA) agent stated that the DEA "first received reports linking Noriega and narcotics before 1978."[28] And, on March 29, 1988, Norman Bailey, former senior staff member of the National Security Council under Ronald Reagan, stated before the Kerry Subcommittee that by 1981 there already existed "available to any authorized official of the U.S. government ... a plethora of human intelligence, electronic intercepts and satellite and overflight photography that taken together constituted not a 'smoking gun' but rather a twenty-one cannon barrage of evidence" of Noriega's involvement in crime and drugs.[29] By 1982, Noriega was working with the Medellin Cartel—smuggling drugs, protecting traffickers, guarding cocaine-processing plants in Panama, and laundering money.

But Noriega was also involved with supporting the contras in Nicaragua, and so the United States looked the other way. From the various witnesses before the Kerry Subcommittee, testimony corroborated that Noriega allowed three bases in Panama to be used for contra training, permitted contra leaders to enter and exit Panama freely, conducted an espionage operation on the Sandinistas from within Nicaragua, orchestrated the shipment of guns to the contras in Costa Rica and elsewhere (often on the same planes carrying narcotics to the United States), carried out a sabotage of a Sandinista arsenal in 1985, and agreed with Oliver North in September 1986 to sabotage production facilities in Nicaragua. During this time Noriega developed a close relationship with the DEA; through his gestures of cooperation he learned DEA intelligence that he shared with traffickers and launderers. The report of the Kerry Subcommittee sums up the U.S. policy vis-à-vis Noriega:

Noriega recognized that so long as he helped the United States with its highest diplomatic priorities, as Torrijos had done with the Panama Canal, the United States would have to overlook activities of his that affected lesser U.S. priorities. In the mid-1980s, this meant that our government did nothing regarding Noriega's drug business and substantial criminal involvement because the first priority was the Contra war. This decision resulted in at least some drugs entering the United States as a hidden cost of the war.[30]

Noriega's ubiquitous insertion into the Panamanian economy was part of the security package he proffered to his illicit business associates. General Gorman, former head of the U.S. Southern Command in Panama, stated: "[Noriega] behaved as though he was a businessman. He had holdings in all sorts of commercial enterprises: shipping firms; airlines; various kinds of importing and exporting activities. It was quite evident that very little was going on of a commercial nature in Panama from which he did not in some sense directly profit."[31] And José Blandon, former general consul for Noriega in New York, elaborated: "The course set by Torrijos was reversed by 180 degrees. Instead of returning to the barracks, the military forces expanded their involvement in government at all levels, including such normally civilian responsibilities as immigration and customs, the ports, railroads and airports."[32] Either Noriega or the Defense Forces controlled and/or owned numerous Panamanian activities, inter alia: shipping and shipbuilding; two duty-free airport companies selling liquor and general merchandise; Transit S.A., the company regulating traffic in and out of the CFZ;[33] gambling casinos; Arwell, the government advertising agency; Banco Cafetero; Banco Patria; extensive real estate; overland trucking; the newspaper chain Ersa; and Explonsa, an explosives producer. In addition, his brother-in-law, Ramón Sieiro, ran Marinac; this business grossing $20 million a year sold identity cards to crew members and officers of the 15,000-odd ships flying the Panamanian flag. Noriega also ran a multimillion-dollar operation of providing phony passports and visas to Asians and Cubans for entry into the United States. According to an estimate appearing in the *New York Times,* during the first eleven months of 1989 alone Noriega's visa sales to Hong Kong emigrants produced more than $130 million in revenue.[34] In this light, money-launderer Manuel Rodríguez's response to Senator Kerry becomes readily comprehensible.[35]

Senator Kerry: Did you have problems in the Bahamas?

Manuel Rodríguez: Yes, because Bahamas lacked a central power figure. You know, it's like having to deal with 50 different people. It was not anything like, say, Panama, where I could go to one source.

What, then, is money laundering, and how did it work in Panama? Money laundering describes a wide range of activities whose purpose it is to erase the source of (launder) ill-gotten monies or skim funds from cash-generating businesses to avoid taxes. U.S. law enforcement officials estimate that money-laundering activities "generate as much as $100 billion in illicit cash profits each year in the United States."[36]

For small-time drug traffickers money laundering is a relatively simple proposition; they can spend their profits. When larger sums are involved, however, it is necessary to save some of the profit. On the one hand, holding substantial amounts of cash is both insecure and costly because it entails forgoing interest earnings on the capital. On the other hand, to open large bank accounts with massive cash deposits provides an easy trail for a drug agent to follow. This is especially true in the United States since the passage of the 1974 Bank Secrecy Law, which obligated reporting all transactions over $10,000 to the Internal Revenue Service. The money-laundering gambit is to break cash earnings into small bills and pass the funds quickly through various bank accounts, to varying degrees anonymous or untraceable, in different countries until the source is obscured. The funds finally settle in an investment house that makes normal investments in stocks, bonds, real estate, and so on.

For reasons already indicated—without taxes on offshore deposits or exchange restrictions and with a venal *caudillo* controlling the necessary institutions—Panama has been an excellent haven for money launderers. Testimony of various launderers before the Kerry Subcommittee provided important insights into the details of their trade in Panama.

For example, Manuel Rodríguez described the cycle of his business. First, he took responsibility for counting, packaging, and shipping his clients' money to Panama. He paid Noriega approximately 1 percent to provide for the safe passage of the funds from the airport to a bank in the banking center. These monies, sent to Panama either air freight or in the suitcase of a passenger on a regular commercial flight, were collected in the runway by armoured cars. Rodríguez estimated that by the mid-1980s he was paying Noriega personally some $10 million each month for this service.[37] The funds were deposited in the account of a "shell" company or "dummy" corporation that Rodríguez set up by paying Panamanian lawyers several hundred dollars, often for the sole purpose of receiving a one-time deposit. The bank assigned a number to the account so that the teller and junior officers were unable to trace its origin.

The cash deposit was then moved through a cash withdrawal in the form of a teller's receipt, which left no paper trail to the receiving account, to several other numbered accounts in the same bank. From there, the monies were moved to a second bank, again in the form of teller's notes, and deposited in the accounts of another group of dummy corporations. Eventually, the funds were transferred to a legitimate investment corporation in the Dutch Antilles. When Senator

Kerry asked what banks Rodríguez used in Panama, he replied: "Well, we used just about every bank in Panama."[38]

Other witnesses described variations on this theme. One prominent variant, explained by the former manager of the Bank of Credit and Commerce International, entailed dollars being transferred to the National Bank of Panama (NBP) and then back into the United States. Reportedly, banks paid kickbacks to agents and security companies to acquire laundering business, and, further, the banks "tolerated cash skimming by officials of the NBP when the money was transferred for repatriation."[39] Another variant involved Colombian banks in the center (according to the Kerry Subcommittee Report more than 50 of 120-odd banks in the center were owned by Colombians[40]); after transferring funds back to the parent banks in Colombia, they were invested in newspapers, radio and TV stations, soccer teams, pharmaceutical companies, construction companies, and automobile agencies.

During the hearings Senator Kerry stated that from 1980 to 1984 approximately $3.5 billion was shipped through the NBP, mostly in small bills, to the United States; in contrast, the U.S. Federal Reserve shipped around $500 million to Panama in replacement currency over this period. Thus, a net of $3 billion was "washed" through the NBP during these years. Because drug traffic picked up in the mid-1980s, probably laundering via this route exceeded these figures after 1984. From the various testimonies, it appears that total laundering through Panama exceeded $10 billion a year in the mid-1980s. The cash surplus generated by money-laundering activities was probably an important liquidity cushion for Panama after the United States froze the accounts of the NBP in the United States (some $150 million) in March 1988.

The Future of the Banking Center

As mentioned, the level of assets in Panama's banking center peaked in 1982. In December 1981, the U.S. Congress passed a law permitting the establishment of offshore banking in the United States. Offshore deposits in the United States would be free from regulations and taxes as elsewhere, with the sole exception that deposits must stay in the account for at least forty-eight hours. When this law passed, there was little reason for U.S. banks to retain or introduce

TABLE 4.2. Comparison of Leading Bank Centers' Offshore Assets, 1980–1987 (in billions of U. S. dollars)

	Hong Kong	Singapore	Cayman	Bahamas	Bahrlin	Panama	Total
1980	38.0	44.6	84.5	na	31.4	34.2	375.4
1982	58.2	81.3	126.0	na	49.8	43.5	519.5
1984	78.7	101.3	143.1	147.0	55.0	32.3	563.6
1987	266.0	209.8	na	155.5	59.7	25.5	930.9

Source. Moreno, Panamá: centro bancario internacional, 58.

offshore books in Panama.[41] By early 1988, only two of the thirty-two international license banks were North American.[42]

The intensification of the international debt crisis in 1982, when Mexico declared that it could not meet its debt payments, affected all banks in Panama. This development, reinforced by the incipient stagnation in Latin America, restricted regional trading and severely curbed new multinational lending. Business at Panama's banking center was further curtailed. External assets in the banking center fell from their peak of $43.5 billion in 1982 to $31.9 billion in 1984.[43] Yet as the center in Panama contracted, the leading offshore centers elsewhere continued to grow.

At least a token effort to contain drug trafficking and money laundering was made in the Anti-Drug Law of December 1986. Some nominal regulations against laundering were imposed, and provisions to imprison or deport criminals were included. The basic institutions and practices of laundering, however, went unscathed. The law succeeded in bringing praise to Noriega from John Lawn, head of the U.S. DEA.

As a further gesture of his cooperation with the antidrug effort, in May 1987 Noriega orchestrated Operation Pisces, of which there are almost as many accounts as there are bankers in Panama. The basic thrust of the operation was to help the U.S. DEA receive information on the bank accounts of several suspected traffickers. Noriega sent the military into several dozen banks; at bayonet point, and according to most accounts without the proper judicial warrant, the military demanded to see the banks' records of more than one hundred accounts. Larry Rohter reported in the *New York Times* (August 10, 1987) that the operation resulted in freezing some $10 million in fifty-four accounts at eighteen banks and identifying another eighty-five suspect accounts.

The banking center reacted to Pisces with disbelief and apprehension. In one impulse Noriega had seemingly undone the years of trust and sense of stability in the center. Bankers objected not to identifying criminals but to violating the rules of the game when political ends were capriciously asserted over established business practices. Panama's banking center began to lose its glow.

Following on the heels of Operation Pisces Noriega dismissed second-in-command (and according to a 1983 accord, soon to become first-in-command) General Díaz Herrera. Díaz Herrera promptly retaliated by revealing to the public Noriega's illicit profiteering, his defrauding of the 1984 elections, his ordering of the assassination of Hugo Spadafora, and his alleged complicity in the Torrijos plane crash. Although most of these "revelations" had been made the previous year by *New York Times* reporter Seymour Hirsch or were already known, this time they came from a close associate of Noriega's within the Defense Forces. The anticipation of greater political instability engendered more nervousness in the banking center, and deposits began to plummet, falling from $32.9 billion in March 1987 to $25.9 billion by September 1987.[44]

In the succeeding months, matters only got worse as the United States gradually withdrew economic aid and, on February 4, 1988, brought grand jury indictments against Noriega for drug trafficking and money laundering. Twenty days later then President Eric Delvalle announced that he was relieving Noriega from active duty pending an investigation of the grand jury accusations.[45] The next day the Legislative Assembly met and dismissed Delvalle. Delvalle called for a general strike and went into hiding. After Noriega countered by closing the opposition press, the strike began on February 26, without the participation of the banking center. These events generated a new run on the banks, and several banks closed their doors.

On Tuesday, March 1, the Panamanian private banks met with the National Banking Commission to inform it that they would not be able to resist the withdrawals at the rate they were occurring and requested permission to close. In hiding, Delvalle called for freezing all Panamanian assets outside Panama. On March 2, the U.S. State Department advised U.S. banks not to disburse funds to the Noriega regime, and on March 3, U.S. federal district courts froze the accounts of the NBP in the United States. Major international banks in Panama announced their intention to close, and on the evening of March 3, the Panamanian government announced the indefinite closure of general license banks.

A profound banking crisis thus erupted: The NBP could no longer fulfill its clearinghouse role; confidence in the financial system was shattered. With banks closed, checking ceased, and transactions reverted to a cash or barter basis. Individuals hoarded cash, aggravating the already intense liquidity crisis. The economic consulting firm INDESA estimated that Panama's money supply fell by 50 percent. Deposits in the banking center, which had fallen to $24.4 billion in

December 1987, stood at $10.6 billion in June 1988. Total assets in the center had fallen from their peak of $49.0 billion in 1982 to $14.5 billion in June 1988.[46]

We discuss the economic repercussions as well as the political dimensions of this financial crisis in chapter 7. But for our present purposes, it is sufficient to note that Undersecretary of State for Latin America Elliot Abrams's prediction that Noriega would fall within a week was based on a severe miscalculation of both the resourcefulness of Panamanians and the resiliency of the monetary system. First, because surplus cash was regularly entering Panama from laundering activities, Noriega used this currency to establish large-dollar accounts in European banks, which the NBP then employed for clearing purposes. Second, the Panamanians began to develop new mediums of exchange. To pay public employees the government issued fractionated checks that, in turn, circulated as exchange instruments at a discount. Banks sold CEDIS *(certificados de depósito de inversión)* to depositors whose accounts were restricted by the banking commission. The CEDIS, negotiable instruments based on the restricted assets, were usable for any type of transaction. Issued in minimal amounts of $1,000, however, the CEDIS were used primarily for the purchase of major consumer durables.[47]

Abrams's notion that because Panama used dollars the United States could choke off its supply and bring down the economy along with Noriega proved fanciful. It was no more possible to eliminate the supply of dollars to Panama than it would be to do so to California. Instead, a crisis of confidence occurred, and, to avoid an unmanageably massive flight of capital, it was necessary first to close Panama's banks and then only gradually to reopen them by lifting the restrictions on banking activities step by step.

The first step was taken on April 18, when banks were allowed to engage in limited operations with their doors still closed. Checks began to clear again, but mostly on a bilateral basis between private banks. New demand and time deposits after this date were unrestricted. Restrictions on preexisting accounts were gradually relaxed. As of December 31, 1988, demand deposits became unrestricted, but withdrawals from savings accounts were limited to $100 per month, and time deposits of more than thirty days remained frozen.

After June 1988, withdrawals from unrestricted offshore accounts, which had dropped by 75 percent in the first six months of the year, stabilized through the remainder of the year. By early 1989, the initial bleeding of deposits was over, and the concern turned from the banks' balance sheets to their income statements. With the economy in depression domestic loans were not being repaid. Employment in the center had fallen by some 1,500, and seven banks had reportedly shut down operations.

The banking center's decline, begun back in 1982, seemed to have hit its nadir, but there was concern whether it could be rebuilt. There was consensus that any turnaround in the center's fortunes would not come before the political crisis was resolved and relations with the United States normalized. But there were doubts whether all the damage since Operations Pisces could be undone. Banks, after all, had begun to shift offshore operations to other existing or newly opened branches in the region, and new banking centers were planned in several countries. In any event, there was little expectation that Panama's center could return to its deposit and asset levels of the early 1980s.

Other International Services

As an outgrowth of the banking center, the idea of a reinsurance center was promoted in the late 1970s. According to the 1976 legislation, reinsurance companies do not pay income taxes and are required to pay only a registration fee. By 1987, some forty-six reinsurance/insurance companies had located in Panama City, in contrast to the 1978 projection that the reinsurance center would grow to more than two hundred companies "in the near future."[48]

There are discussions regarding the establishment of a data-processing teleport, where credit cards, airline tickets, and other receipts would be processed. Some entrepreneurs are optimistic that, given Panama's bilingualism and relatively low wage levels, an alluring fiscal benefits package could induce companies to move their billing operations to Panama. Other ideas—such as establishing Panama as a center for headquarters of multinational corporations or for a regional stock market—have surfaced, but they are in still early stages of planning.

All such concepts, congruent with the general perception of Panama's international (static) comparative advantage, are actively supported by the World Bank, IMF, and most of the political spectrum in Panama. As we argued at the end of chapter 2, serious questions about the price distortions, the trade vulnerability, the distributional consequences, and the dynamic implications for long-run development are raised by an economic strategy that relies on international service activities. Our discussion of these services in chapters 3 and 4 suggests that if these services promoted development, however distorted, in the past, there is little basis for optimism that they will do so in the future.

Chapter Five

Agriculture: Structure
and Performance

In chapter 1 we made the point that Panama had a powerful landed elite in neither the nineteenth century nor the early independence period. By the second half of the twentieth century, however, Panama was well on its way to acquiring one. In the language of neoclassical economics, land is "an abundant factor" in countries where the land/labor ratio is high and "a scarce factor" when that ratio is low. By this criterion, land would be scarce in El Salvador and abundant in Panama. This conclusion, however sensible on the surface, is an excellent example of the famous observation by Stuart Chase that common sense is that sense which tells us the world is flat; although true for some purposes, it is fundamentally false.

We show that the scarcity or abundance of land in Panama was a class question: for the wealthy, land was abundant and available for the taking; for the poor, it was desperately scarce. The land reform of the early Torrijos years changed this asymmetry, but not by much. The trend toward greater inequality of distribution, which can be documented from 1950, continued through the 1970s despite redistributing land and expanding the agricultural frontier. Inequality of distribution created a dichotomy between economic status and use of land. At one end of the distribution were the smallholders, who for the most part dedicated their resources to food production (much of it consumed by the household); at the other end vast estates produced for the market, usually bananas, sugar cane, and cattle. In consequence, an agricultural strategy oriented toward exports would be unlikely to significantly aid the smallholder.

Overall, agricultural output in Panama grew at a rather slow rate, particularly in the 1970s and 1980s when it was below the rate of population increase. During the 1970s, government policy shifted relative agricultural prices in favor of food crops, though not dramatically so. This policy seems to have both stimulated production and fostered increases in productivity. The World Bank, given its 1980s obsession with export promotion, took the Panamanian agricultural policy to task for allegedly fostering inefficiencies. In the bank's view, Panama's agricultural sector was well-suited to beef production. Given the probable social consequences of substituting grazing for food crops, and developed country protectionism, any Panamanian government would be wise to ignore this advice.[1] At the same time, Panama's crop exports—bananas, sugar, coffee—hold little promise of being growing suppliers of foreign exchange. If ideological considerations could be set aside, a pragmatic agricultural policy for Panama would be to continue and extend the self-sufficiency emphasis of the early Torrijos years.

Land and Inequality

In most of Latin America the unequal distribution of land that characterized the twentieth century was established in the colonial period and significantly modified during the nineteenth century when agricultural production became much more oriented to the world market. In Panama, however, the distribution of land at the end of the twentieth century was very much a product of developments during that century, even the second half of the century.

This point is demonstrated in Table 5.1, which covers farms of one hectare or more. The 1950 and 1960 agricultural surveys did not include farms smaller than one hectare, and our present purpose is to cover as long a time period as possible.[2] The first indicator of the recentness of the emergence of the landholding pattern is that in 1980 there was twice as much land in cultivation as in 1950. This is quite a large increase in comparison to other countries of Latin America, most of which show no measured expansion of cultivated land of note.[3] In the 1980s the agricultural frontier continued to expand, principally into the province of Darien, with most smallholder settlers migrating from the provinces of Los Santos, Herrera, and Chiriqui.[4] Second, and clearly related to the first, the proportion of

TABLE 5.1. *Farms without Legal Title, by Farm Size, 1950–1980*

Farm Size (hectares)	1950 (%)	1960 (%)	1970 (%)	1980 (%)
1 to 5	77	79	79	77
5 to 10	74	81	80	77
10 to 50	59	74	74	71
50 to 100	43	62	63	65
100+	14	26	31	43
Total	44	52	53	57
Total area in farms[a]	1,159	1,804	2,093	2,265

Source. República de Panamá, *Censos nacionales de 1980, Cuarto censo nacional agropecuario,* vol. 4, *Compendio general,* cuadro 8.

Note. Table excludes farms of less than one hectare in size.

[a]Total area in farms is presented in thousands of hectares.

untitled land, where producers operate without legal ownership, rose from 44 percent of the total in 1950 to 57 percent in 1980. This increase implies that 71 percent of the land brought into cultivation during the thirty-year period still lacked documentation of legal ownership at the end of the period. It is safe to assume that the actual percentage of land brought into use without legal ownership must have been substantially higher because some owners would have successfully gained official title during the three decades.

Land-hungry peasants seeking plots to cultivate did not foster this extralegal of land; quite the contrary process was involved: medium and large farms expanded onto unused public lands. Between 1950 and 1980 the number of farms in the one-to-five-hectare range increased, almost exclusively through subdivision, for their area actually declined from 96,000 to 80,000 (see Table 5.2). The proportion of these farms without title remained virtually unchanged at 77 percent. At the other end of the distribution, farms over 100 hectares in size increased by 692,000 hectares from 1950 to 1980 (Table 5.2). The proportion of all untitled land in this the largest size range rose from a mere 14 percent to 43 percent. Virtually all the untitled land was property of the state (96 percent in 1980),[5] so that the large estates expanded through the de facto privatization of public land.

TABLE 5.2. *The Distribution of Land in Panama by Farm Sizes,*
1950–1980

	Distribution, Absolute[a]			
Farm Size[b]	1950	1960	1970	1980
1 to 5	96	93	72	80
5 to 10	106	118	90	89
10 to 50	390	547	598	592
50 to 100	156	284	363	402
100+	411	762	970	1,103
Total	1,159	1,804	2,093	2,266

	Percentage Distribution			
Farm Size[b]	1950	1960	1970	1980
1 to 5	8.3	5.1	3.4	3.5
5 to 10	9.2	6.5	4.3	3.9
10 to 50	33.6	30.3	28.6	26.1
50 to 100	13.5	15.8	17.4	17.8
100+	35.5	42.2	46.4	48.7
Total	100.0	100.0	100.0	100.0

	Changes in Distribution, Absolute[a]			
Farm Size[b]	1950–1960	1960–1970	1970–1980	1950–1980
1 to 5	−3	−21	8	−16
5 to 10	11	−28	−1	−18
10 to 50	157	51	−6	202
50 to 100	128	79	39	246
100+	351	208	133	692
Total	644	289	173	1,106

TABLE 5.2. *(continued)*

Percentage Point Changes

Farm Size[b]	1950– 1960	1960– 1970	1970– 1980	1950– 1980
1 to 5	−3.1	−1.7	0.1	−4.8
5 to 10	−2.6	−2.2	−0.4	−5.3
10 to 50	−3.3	−1.8	−0.4	−7.5
50 to 100	2.3	1.6	0.4	4.3
100+	6.8	4.1	2.3	13.2
Total	0.0	0.0	0.0	0.0

Source. República de Panamá, *Censos nacionales de 1980, Cuarto censo nacional agropec-uario,* vol. 4, *Compendio general,* cuadro 8.

[a]Absolute distribution and absolute changes in distribution are presented in thousands of hectares.

[b]Size of farms is measured in hectares.

The expansion of farming onto the extensive margin involved a growing concentration of control over land, rather than increased access to land by smallholders and the landless. This pattern is shown in Table 5.2. In 1950, agricultural units of greater than 100 hectares held nearly 36 percent of the land in farms, and this proportion rose steadily: 42.2 percent in 1960, 46.4 percent in 1970, and 48.7 percent in 1980. At the same time, the proportion of land in farms less than 50 hectares declined continuously, from 51 percent in 1950 to 34 percent in 1980; the land held in farms of less than five hectares declined absolutely, from 202,000 hectares in 1950 to 169,000 in 1980 (a fall of 17 percent).

Table 5.3 provides the distribution of farms by size for 1970 and 1980, along with the land distribution, this time including holdings in the smallest size range.[6] Using Tables 5.1 through 5.3, one can assess the process of land concentration in Panama and the impact of agrarian reform on that process. The first land reform measures were begun in the early 1960s, when the Agrarian Reform Commission was created. The stated goal of the reform was to aid rural families having incomes less than 200 balboas per year; in the mid-1970s they were estimated at 70,000.[7] The vehicles to achieve this goal were land entitlement and land distribution. According to

TABLE 5.3. *Distribution of All Farms and Land, 1970 and 1980*

Number of Farms and Area

Farm Size[c]	Farm Distribution[a]			Land Distribution[b]		
	1970	1980	Change 1970–1980	1970	1980	Change 1970–1980
0.5 to 1	6.8	11.8	5.0	4	7	3
1 to 5	34.3	39.0	4.7	72	80	8
5 to 10	14.0	13.8	-0.2	90	89	-1
10 to 50	28.3	27.7	-0.6	598	592	-6
50 to 100	5.5	6.2	0.7	363	402	39
100+	3.1	4.1	1.0	970	1,103	133
Total	92.1	102.6	10.5	2,097	2,273	176

Number of Farms and Area
(in percentages)

Farm Size[c]	Farm Distribution[a]		Percentage Point Change	Land Distribution[b]		Percentage Point Change
	1970	1980	1970–1980	1970	1980	1970–1980
0.5 to 1	7.4	11.5	4.1	0.2	0.3	0.1
1 to 5	37.3	38.0	0.7	3.4	3.5	0.1
5 to 10	15.2	13.5	-1.7	4.3	3.9	-0.4
10 to 50	30.8	27.0	-3.8	28.5	26.0	-2.5
50 to 100	6.0	6.1	0.1	17.3	17.7	0.4
100+	3.4	4.0	0.6	46.3	48.6	0.3
Total	100.0	100.0	0.0	100.0	100.0	0.0

Source. República de Panamá, Censos nacionales de 1980, Cuarto censo nacional agropecuario, vol. 4, Compendio general, cuadro 8.
[a]Farm distribution measured in thousands of farms.
[b]Land distribution measured in thousands of hectares.
[c]Farm size measured in hectares.

official reports, by the mid-1980s the commission had granted land titles to 23,098 people for ownership of 347,945 hectares. It had also acquired 536,513 hectares, 105,597 through expropriation, which it distributed to 21,027 families.[8] The expropriated land area represented only 5.0 percent of total agricultural land in 1970 or 4.4 percent of the total in 1980. Virtually all this activity, particularly the land distribution, occurred during the Torrijos period.

The first aspect of the agrarian reform, land titling, in itself had no direct impact on poverty reduction or access to land by the landless. In the context of Panama the titling of land probably helped the large farmers more than the small. As shown in Table 5.2, from 1950 to 1980, the area in large farms expanded dramatically. Although the figures suggest that a large number of smallholders received title to their land, it is also the case that the titling of medium and large estates endorsed the increasing concentration of property that occurred through expansion onto public lands from 1950 to 1980. The entitlement program not only endorsed the concentration of land but also actively fostered it. To secure title, the user of a plot of land was required to purchase it, invariably from the state. The purchase prices on a sliding scale favored the smallholder, but large units also sold at bargain prices.[9]

The second major aspect of the agrarian reform, land acquisition and redistribution, apparently had little impact on the concentration of landed property. Table 5.2 shows that 77 percent of the increase in land in agriculture went to farms of 100 hectares or more between 1970 and 1980, the years when the land distribution program was most active. A more disaggregated analysis reveals that the largest farms did not account for the increase, but those between 100 and 500 hectares. Still, it remains the case that in the 1970s, hardly a period of curtailing the economic power of large landowners, large-scale farming extended and tightened its grip on the agricultural sector. Furthermore, because large-scale farming was expanding onto state land, it was easily within the administrative power of the Torrijos government to arrest and even reverse the process had there been the will to do so.

Notwithstanding the clear evidence on the concentration of landholding during the 1970s, one finds in the 1985 World Bank report the perpetuation of the myth of a radical Torrijos land reform. Assessing the land reform, the report states:

The principal objective of this massive effort was initially social: the transfer of resources to the rural poor, especially the beneficiaries of the ambitious land reform which the Government undertook during 1969–73. Over 16 percent of Panama's farm land changed hands in five years.[10]

Altering the ownership of 16 percent of the country's farmland would not seem "massive"; even so, it is unclear to what this 16 percent refers. If the reference is to the amount of land expropriated, as pointed out above the correct share is between 4.4 and 5 percent; if it refers to the total amount of land distributed (however acquired), the share is well above 16 percent. In any event, the bank fails to tell the reader at any point in its review of the agricultural sector that the major benefactors from titling and new land acquisition were the rich, not the poor.

Assessing the Panamanian Land Reform

Although the Torrijos government's agrarian policy unquestionably favored the larger landholders, smallholders and the poor did benefit: the populist rhetoric was not empty. Inspection of Table 5.2 shows that a rapid increase in the concentration of land took place from 1950 to 1970, when farms larger than one hundred hectares augmented their share from 35.5 percent to 46.4, accounting for 63 percent of the new land brought into use over the twenty-year period. At the same time, farms of one to ten hectares actually lost land, though the number of such farms increased. When one disaggregates the largest size category, the process of land concentration is revealed to be even greater.[11]

Compared to this rapid pace of land concentration up to 1970, the rate for the next decade was quite moderate. As Table 5.3 shows, the land in very small farms (0.5 to 5.0 hectares) actually increased, a growth that kept pace with the rise in the number of farms. As a consequence, average farm size in the smallest category did not fall during the 1970s, as it must have done during the two previous decades. Furthermore, the number of very small farms (0.5 to 5.0 hectares) increased faster than the rate of growth of the rural population—5.7 percent per year compared to 2.4 percent. This increase in the number of very small farms seems to partly explain the relative reduction in landlessness during the 1970s. It must be stressed, however, that, with a few exceptions, the gains of the very smallholders did little or nothing to eliminate their poverty.[12]

In most circumstances in Panama five hectares or less is poverty farming, particularly given the simple slash-and-burn techniques at this scale of production that require use of fallow to rejuvenate the fertility of the soil. The 1970 agricultural census indicates the poverty of the smallholder: 47 percent of all farms reported no cash sales, a proportion almost exactly equal to the percent of farms of one to five hectares in the total.[13] The increase in very small farms did not alleviate poverty, which was merely manifested in subsistence and below-subsistence agricultural production. The alternative to this form of poverty would have been for peasants to abandon agriculture. Thus, for smallholders agrarian reform generally maintained rural poverty—where at least food supply and shelter were more reliable—rather than urban poverty. Although this result was not insignificant, it did little to improve the overall income distribution.

To some extent the small gains of the smallholders might have been at the expense of the farms in the 5-to-50-hectare range, which slightly declined in number. But it would be misleading to interpret the Torrijos reform as principally redistributing land from medium to small producers, for more significant change came at the top of the distribution. In 1970, there were 326 farms of 500 hectares or more, and this number remained the same in 1980.[14] The increase in large farms occurred at the next step down, in the 100-to-500-hectare range, where the number rose by 35 percent and the amount of land by 33 percent. This pattern of change at the top of the distribution probably represented the modernizing and rationalizing of large-scale agriculture in Panama. As we pointed out in chapter 1, the Panamanian hinterland was settled late, so that arable land was relatively abundant throughout this century. As a result, large-scale producers adopted a land-extensive method of production. To insure against plant blights, the banana estates left land idle, a practice common throughout Central America and the isthmus. Cattle ranches also employed land-extensive grazing, which partly accounted for the low quality of Panamanian beef. Prior to land reform the Panamanian government's policy of allowing free access to public land resulted in considerable inefficient use.[15] This inefficient land use was quite consistent with modernizing and rationalizing large farms. The inefficiency arose from what in practice was a cheap land policy for large farms, but not for small. The private cost of land to large farms was below the social cost; that is, had land not been made available to larger holders so cheaply, its more efficient use would have resulted from the perspective of society as a whole. Cheap land for large estates meant land was either underutilized (left idle) or used extensively in relation to the labor working on the estates. The land acquisitions under the agrarian reform program, rather than discouraging large-scale production, encouraged more efficient use of land on large estates by limiting, at least to a degree, the extent of idle land (a point demonstrated in our discussion of land use). In this way the agrarian reform served the interests of both the capitalist farmer and the very smallholder, though the former benefited considerably more than the latter.

The agricultural frontier in Panama, continuing its expansion into the 1990s, will probably do so into the next century. Therefore, the task of effecting a more equal distribution of land in the country would be considerably easier than in the rest of Latin America. Estimates suggest that the amount of land cultivated in 1980 might be doubled,[16] which, if true, could provide an opportunity for the state to pursue a social and economic policy in the countryside that would bring the benefits of growth to the vast majority of rural Panamanians. Because the policy would not necessarily require substantial land redistribution as such, it would hardly be a radical policy course. Furthermore, few, if any, economies of scale in agricultural production exist in Panama, so the policy would not involve any significant trade-off between equity and growth. However, a clear commitment by the state to equitable access to new land would be required, along with major infrastructural investments. The data from 1950 to 1980 clearly show that when left to private initiative with little state direction, the settling of new land tended to increase, not decrease, the concentration of land. Without purposeful state action, land is abundant for the rich in Panama, but scarce for the poor.[17]

Determinants of Land Allocation

In the paradigm of neoclassical economics, relative prices determine the allocation of resources. This approach to allocation is limited for at least two reasons. First, it implicitly assumes that resources are fully employed, for if they are not, the prevailing price vector of the

economy is derivative from not only the composition of aggregate demand but also its level.[18] Second, even when prices perform their allocative function, the social relations in which producers find themselves affect their response to market signals. A case in point is how
large and small agricultural producers behave when offered monetary
incentives by markets. A wealth of theoretical and empirical research
demonstrates that rational behavior on the part of smallholders
would be risk averse by assigning priority to production for household consumption over production for monetary gain. This frequently results in a dramatic difference in the pattern of land use by
size of farm, differences well summarized for Panama in the Merrill
report:

A strong tendency exists for small farmers to use more of their land for crops
than large farmers. A much greater proportion of land in large farms is used
for pastures, a pattern which is not unexpected. Very small farmers use their
land intensively in order to survive. Farmers that have more land, but are
still small, continue to emphasize crop production. . . . Large farms frequently are held for capital appreciation and use only a small proportion of
their land for crop production, devoting most of their land to extensive livestock production.[19]

This same point can be put another way: small farmers farm to
survive, and large farmers farm to make money. For the latter in particular, the allocation of land may derive from relative prices.[20] But
the allocation of land by small farmers in contrast to large farmers is
primarily a consequence of the social relations of production of each
group. This point emerges clearly from the Panamanian data.

Land Use and Distribution

As noted above, from 1950 to 1980, 1.1 million hectares of new land
were brought into agricultural use. Of this total, producers applied
only 116,000 hectares (10 percent) to crops of any type—grains,
beans, sugar, bananas, and so on.[21] These figures imply an annual increase in crop area of 1.3 percent per year over the thirty years, compared to the 3 percent rate of growth of total population and 2 percent for the farm population. No doubt orthodox economists,
particularly those from the World Bank, IMF, and other multilaterals, would argue that this pattern of land use at the extensive margin
reflected the market signals received by producers.

This argument suffers because it presumes the domestic demand for agricultural products to be independent of the supply, but such is not the case in Panama or elsewhere. The distribution of arable land inter alia determines the rural distribution of income, which in turn determines the effective demand for agricultural products by the lower classes, directly for the peasants and indirectly for urban workers. Were the distribution of land more equal in Panama, more rice, corn, and other basic foods would be planted for on-farm consumption. The statistics on rural poverty analyzed in chapter 6 suggest that supplying adequate food to the rural population at prevailing levels of productivity among smallholders in 1980 would have required an increase of 50,000 hectares in the area for crop production. The demand for basic food products was also depressed by the effect of unequal land distribution on wages. The urban wage (at least in the lowest wage sectors) is determined in large part by rural incomes because the latter sets the opportunity cost of migration. A very unequal distribution of land keeps this opportunity cost down and urban wages correspondingly low. The intervention of trade unions and the state into wage determination does not amend this conclusion, for the wage levels set by such interventions are not arbitrary but derivative from the baseline set by market forces.[22]

Several factors—the operation of the postulated process, a land-poor peasantry, low effective demand for food, and a small proportion of land in crops—show themselves in the data on land use. In Table 5.4, the proportion of land applied to crops and pasture is given by size of farm. The residual remaining from the sum of these two categories is nonagricultural land, largely forests and fallow. By reading down any year in Table 5.4, one sees the rapid decline in the proportion of land applied to crops; the reverse is the case for grazing land. By reading across the last row of each part of the table one sees that the share of land assigned to crops has declined over time, while application of land to pastures has risen. Although a variety of livestock was commercially raised during the period, the pasture land refers almost exclusively to cattle. Inspection of land in crops in Table 5.4 produces an apparent contradiction: for all farms taken together, the area in crops declined from 20.4 to 15.6 percent over the thirty years, but in no single size range was the decline nearly this great; indeed, the share of land to crops rose in three of the five categories.

TABLE 5.4. *Agricultural Land Use in Panama, 1950–1980*
(in percentages)

Farm Size (hectares)	Land in Crops			
	1950	1960	1970	1980
0.5 to 1	nd	nd	nd	73.4
1 to 5	71.7	74.6	69.6	70.8
5 to 10	43.1	50.8	40.6	43.5
10 to 50	19.8	22.9	18.6	18.4
50 to 100	8.2	9.9	10.2	9.3
100+	7.9	6.0	8.8	10.1
Total	20.4	18.2	15.3	15.6

Farm Size (hectares)	Land in Pasture			
	1950	1960	1970	1980
0.5 to 1	nd	nd	nd	4.6
1 to 5	14.0	8.1	10.8	12.5
5 to 10	26.4	18.2	25.6	30.2
10 to 50	42.1	35.9	45.5	53.9
50 to 100	54.4	49.2	60.2	63.8
100+	63.6	65.1	71.7	69.8
Total	47.4	45.4	54.5	57.3

Source. *Censos nacionales de 1980*, vol. 4, *Cuarto censo nacional agropecuario.*

The concentration of landholding explains this apparent anomaly, as demonstrated in Table 5.5. Table 5.5 gives both the actual area of farms, by size range assigned to crops for each census year, and the crop areas, simulated on the assumption that the 1950 distribution of land prevailed in 1960, 1970, and 1980. This allows the allocation of land within a size range to change in the observed pattern, but it does not allow shifts of land among size categories. The result of this

TABLE 5.5. *Actual and Simulated Land in Crops, 1950–1980*
(in thousands of hectares)

	Actual Land in Crops			
Farm Size[a]	*1950*	*1960*	*1970*	*1980*
1 to 5	69	69	50	56
5 to 10	46	60	37	39
10 to 50	77	125	111	109
50 to 100	13	28	37	37
100+	32	46	86	111
Total	237	328	321	353
	Simulated Land in Crops[b]			
Farm Size[a]	*1950*[c]	*1960*	*1970*	*1980*
1 to 5	69	112	121	133
5 to 10	46	84	78	91
10 to 50	77	139	131	140
50 to 100	13	24	29	28
100+	32	38	66	81
Total	237	397	424	474
Simulated − actual total	—	69	103	121

Source. *Censos nacionales de 1980, Cuarto censo nacional agropecuario,* vol. 4.
[a]Farm size measured in hectares.
[b]The table assumes that the 1950 distribution of land held for each decade.
[c]Actual figures.

hypothetical exercise is striking: *ceteris paribus,* had the distribution of land remained the same, in 1980 an additional 120,000 hectares of crops would have been planted, for an increase of 34 percent over the actual figure.

A number of reasons leads one to think that this result indicates what actually would have happened absent increasing land concentration. First, had there been more small farmers (or had small farmers had more land), more basic foodstuffs would have been produced

TABLE 5.6. *Land in Basic Food and Export Crops
(as a percentage of total crop area)*

Crop	1970	1980	1983
Basic foodstuffs	81.9	65.4	62.6
Export products	18.1	34.6	37.4
Total	100.0	100.0	100.0

Source. Maria Eugenia Gallardo and José Roberto López, *Centroamérica en cifras: la crisis,* 66.

for both on-farm consumption and sale to low-income urban dwellers, a particularly important development for rice and corn production. Second, the resource base of the smallholder is not conducive to grazing livestock as a primary commercial activity. Given the rather simple techniques of animal husbandry practiced by smallholders in Panama, more income can be gained from crops than from grazing on a small plot of land. Smallholders cannot afford the land-extensive character of cattle raising. Furthermore, cattle raising uses relatively little labor, and a characteristically small farm takes advantage of the available family labor at a low opportunity cost (frequently zero). In terms of cost calculations, it may be quite irrational for the smallholder to specialize in cattle raising even if by a strict accounting measure it yields a higher return than crop cultivation.

The increasing concentration of land affected not only the distribution of land between crops and grazing but also the composition of crop production itself. Evidence is abundant that in Panama large estates produce crops for export—bananas and sugar are most important—and small farms rarely grow these. This is implied by the finding that a large proportion of farms generated no cash sales at all (47 percent in 1970 and 37 percent in 1980),[23] and it is also indicated directly by studies of land use on smallholdings.[24] Therefore, one expects that the data would reveal a decline in the area in food crops over time, as shown in Table 5.6. From 1970 to 1983 the proportion of crop land devoted to the basic staples of the Panamanian lower-class diet—rice, corn, and beans—declined by almost twenty percentage points, from more than 80 percent to near 60 percent. This decline is all the more striking because during the 1970s and early 1980s the government used a policy of producer price supports to encourage the production of these crops, particularly corn. Although there are no data on area planted in crops by size of farm, the statistics in Tables 5.4 through 5.6 provide circumstantial evidence for a strong distributional impact on the allocation of land and labor in Panamanian agriculture.

In summary, the evidence in the tables suggests that the area in crops would probably have increased substantially had the Panamanian state not endorsed a process of land concentration from 1950 onward. The consequences of this increase could only have been favorable for the economy. First, because crops use more labor than cattle raising, employment would certainly have risen. Second, rural poverty would have been reduced because smallholders would have had more land. Third, more rural employment and higher peasant incomes might have created labor shortages and pushed up urban wages at the bottom of the pay scale, thus reducing urban poverty. Fourth, the reduction of rural and urban poverty would have contributed to expanding the domestic market and provided an impulse to more dynamic development. Furthermore, all this could have been achieved by merely blocking the increased concentration of land ownership. No redistribution would have been necessary, though redistribution would have made the gains greater.

Overall Agricultural Performance

Agriculture has never been the leading sector of the Panamanian economy. Even in terms of foreign exchange earnings, the major agricultural export, bananas, took second place to the service sector. Before formal independence, agriculture to a great extent served as a catchment area for those who could not find wealth and fortune in the urban service sector. The arrival of the banana companies and subsequent development of more commercialized ranches and large estates changed the character of rural areas. In a reversal of the usual pattern in Latin America, the development of powerful rural landed interests was subsequent to and partly fostered by the prior rise of urban wealth and formal independence.

Table 5.7 presents the growth performance of agriculture spanning five decades, from 1946 to 1988. The record is not impressive because growth in output above the rate of population expansion was sustained for only four of the nine time periods in the table, with three

TABLE 5.7. *Growth of Agricultural Value Added in Panama,*
1946–1988
(in constant prices)

| | Average Annual Growth Rates[a] | |
Period	5-year	Decade
1946–1949	3.6	
1950–1954	1.5	
1955–1959	4.3	
1950–1959		2.9
1960–1964	3.7	
1965–1969	6.3	
1960–1969		5.0
1970–1974	1.5	
1975–1979	1.8	
1970–1979		1.7
1980–1984	1.4	
1985–1988	0.3	
1980–1988		0.9

Sources. For 1946 to 1964, CEPAL, *Statistical Bulletin for Latin America,* 9,
nos. 1–2; for 1965 to 1978, SIECA (1981), 476–77; for 1979–1987, *Panamá en*
cifras (1988); and for 1988, IDB (1989).
[a]Simple average of annual growth rates.

of those four strung together from 1955 to 1969. Particularly poor
was the growth performance during the 1970s and 1980s, and for the
forty-three years as a whole, agricultural production per capita fell
slightly.

By comparison to the countries of Central America and the rest of
Latin America, however, the performance was not so much poor as
mediocre. As Table 5.8 shows, in the 1960s Panamanian agricultural
output grew faster than for Latin America as a whole; then it was
half the Latin American rate for the 1970s. For the 1980s, Panama's
performance was a bit above the average (and above the rate for the
three Central American countries not racked by war), but hardly impressive at 2.2 percent.

Table 5.9 crudely decomposes the growth performance by calcu-
lating the increase in the land and labor inputs, (through 1980 only

TABLE 5.8. *Average Annual Growth Rates of Agricultural Output in Constant Prices, Panama and Latin America, 1960–1988*

Value Added by Country	1960–1970	1970–1980	1980–1988	1970–1988
Costa Rica	5.2	2.6	1.7	2.4
Guatemala	4.4	4.7	0.1	2.6
Honduras	5.5	3.0	1.6	2.6
South America	3.2	3.5	1.9	3.0
Panama	5.4	1.6	2.2	2.0
Food value added[a]	1.7	2.8	1.0	2.1

Source. For value added, see Inter-American Development Bank (1989), 467; for food production, see FAO, *Production Yearbook, 1975, 1979, and 1987.*
[a]Production of cereals only, through 1987.

because no later data are available on land in agricultural use). The table again makes the point we stressed earlier: the growth of Panamanian agriculture since 1950 and probably before was landextensive. From 1950 to 1980, output increased by less than 150 percent, while the amount of land in use roughly doubled. As a result, real value added per unit of land (the "productivity of land") rose very little, by only 26 percent over thirty years for an annual rate of less than 1 percent. The period of the greatest land-extensive growth was the 1950s, when output per hectare actually fell. From 1960 to 1980, land productivity rose at just over 2 percent per year. In contrast, the labor input increased by much less,[25] and around 1970 it began to decline. As a consequence, the land-labor ratio rose dramatically, by two-thirds over thirty years, and labor productivity doubled. This somewhat unusual pattern of scale change in agriculture has important implications. The thirty-year period was characterized by land being the relatively abundant factor and labor being relatively scarce.[26] A successful long-term development strategy for Panamanian agriculture must incorporate mechanization and other laborsaving techniques, particularly if significant expansion of the agricultural frontier were to occur. The relative scarcity of labor reinforces the point made earlier that in Panama land is abundant and labor scarce for medium and large holdings engaged in production for the market, while quite the opposite is the case for the smallholder. Smallholders in Panama lack sufficient land to supply their own

TABLE 5.9.   *Indices of Agricultural Value Added and Factor Productivity in Panama, 1950–1980*

Value Added (V.A.) and Level of Inputs[a]

Year	V.A.	Land	Labor
1950	100.0	100.0	100.0
1960	128.1	155.7	109.6
1970	215.8	180.6	120.2
1980	246.7	195.5	117.4

Factor Productivity and Land-Labor Ratio[b]

Year	Land	Labor	Land/Labor
1950	100.0	100.0	100
1960	82.3	116.9	142
1970	119.5	179.5	150
1980	126.2	205.2	167

Sources. For value added, see Table 5.8. For land, see Table 5.2. For labor, FAO, *World-wide Estimates and Projections of the Agricultural and Non-agricultural Population Segments, 1950–2025,* 137.

[a]Index of value added in constant prices, land in hectares, and agricultural labor force.

[b]Index of value added divided by indices for land and labor, followed by land index divided by labor index.

consumption, much less generate a surplus. The able-bodied from small farms must seek outside wage employment during part of the year, for they are land-constrained on their small plots. However, this institutional land constraint arises from a lack of access to additional land, often due to an inability to obtain loans to purchase land. In Panama, as elsewhere, land shortage for the poor farmer is perfectly consistent with land abundance in the aggregate.

Agricultural Policy and Food Production

Panama's pattern of agricultural growth is open to various interpretations: rapid in the 1960s, it was followed by slower growth, (except for food) in the 1970s and still slower growth in the 1980s. In the view of the World Bank, the growth reflects that during the 1960s the agricultural sector was largely left to market forces and then subjected to increasing government regulation during the following decade.[27] In its 1985 report the bank's judgment on government intervention was consistently negative, a reflection of that organization's bias against the public sector.

Before assigning cause to the slowdown in agricultural growth, it should be noted that the record is more complex than it might first appear. Although overall agricultural growth declined from the 1960s to the 1970s, looking back at Table 5.8 we see that the rate of expansion of food production increased from 1.7 to 2.8 percent before dropping sharply in the 1980s. Panama presumably should receive relatively better marks for improving its capacity to feed itself during the 1970s.[28] Part of the explanation for this relative improvement lies in government policy; namely, there is a consensus that its producer price support program effectively raised the return on the production of the two major staples, rice and corn. The price support program, like all such policies, benefited producers proportional to their sales. Because small and medium producers accounted for a substantial proportion of marketed food output, price supports must therefore have had a substantial impact on the incomes of poor farmers.[29]

Somewhat surprisingly for an organization that formerly and frequently advocated higher producer prices for small farmers all over the world, the World Bank judged the Panamanian price support program ill-advised and recommended its wholesale elimination in favor of "market incentives."[30] In question is considerably more than the optimal strategy for agriculture; at issue in the debate over price supports is Panama's development strategy itself. As argued in previous chapters, the basis upon which Panama grew in the 1960s and 1970s was no longer possible during the 1980s and beyond; a new development strategy was required. The World Bank's vision for Panama essentially sought to increase the role of foreign trade in an economy already relatively open by any quantitative measure. An alternative strategy, perhaps the only viable one for Panama at the end of the twentieth century, would place greater emphasis upon production for the domestic market. In this strategy the development of agriculture would be crucial to increase self-sufficiency in food supply, reduce poverty, and raise commodity exports. Achieving these goals would necessarily require purposeful government intervention; the goals could not be attained by leaving the allocation of resources to the signals of domestic oligopoly and unstable world markets. Therefore, the question about whether the government interventions in the agricultural sector during the 1970s and 1980s were functional or dysfunctional goes to the heart of broad issues of development policy.

Whatever the distribution of income in a country, political stability requires that governments implement policies to ensure an adequate supply of basic foodstuffs. The political consequences of shortages, and in the extreme famines, make food policy important even if governments do not stress problems of distribution and poverty. Broadly speaking, two strategies are available to small countries such as Panama; the strategies are not mutually exclusive, especially in the context of abundant land. On the one hand, policy interventions can raise the return on the production of food for the domestic market; in effect, this becomes an import substitution strategy for the agricultural sector. The instruments for such a policy would be tariffs and quotas to regulate imports and support prices, subsidized credit, and technical assistance to foster domestic production. If the support prices translate directly into retail prices, then an income transfer from net food buyers to net food producers results. If subsidies lower retail prices below support prices (or not so far above as they would otherwise be), then the income transfer occurs via the fiscal system, from taxpayers in general to food producers and consumers. Some form of market intervention in food characterizes all the developed market economies. Protectionism and domestic subsidies are particularly high in Western Europe and Japan.

On the other hand, access to food can be sought as an indirect outcome of an export-oriented trade policy, in which the agricultural sector is oriented to external demand and domestic food deficits are covered by imports, which are financed, of course, by agricultural or nonagricultural exports. This approach, frequently described as "free trade," engenders many misconceptions, as if it were achieved in the absence of policy intervention. Furthermore, advocates usually allege that this strategy allows greater efficiency in allocations because tariffs, quotas, and so on involve "market distortions." This view implies that conforming a country's domestic price structure to the international price structure—often called "border prices"—is more desirable than not doing so. As such the World Bank justifies jettisoning the Panamanian price support system: "Efficiency of resource use implies that costs of Panamanian products, regardless of whether primarily for export or for domestic consumption, should approach internationally competitive prices."[31]

One could argue whether this proposition is true in the abstract, but it has little practical importance for agricultural policy: first, international prices for agricultural products are rarely competitive, free market prices; instead, they reflect regulations and myriad interventions. This is the case for rice and corn, whose price supports in Panama the bank found particularly offensive. The international trade in corn is dominated by the United States and Canada, and these countries have both price supports and export subsidies. Nor are these minor programs. In 1986, the United States government spent $11.9 billion on corn price supports (acreage reduction)—a sum 2.3 times the entire GDP of Panama in that year.[32] The major countries exporting rice also practice market interventions. Perhaps it would be the optimal policy for all governments to eliminate their interventions into agricultural markets, but until they do, it is not the case that a particular country will necessarily gain by doing so.

There is a second compelling reason to be cautious about embracing the World Bank food strategy for Panama even if international agricultural markets were not "distorted" by protectionism. In a perfect world where a country's international payments were in balance, relying on commercial imports of food would not be problematic, assuming marketing and distribution were not issues. But, as a practical matter, countries, and particularly small countries, suffer from periodic external shocks beyond their control. At such moments, a heavy burden of adjustment is placed upon the exchange rate. If exchange rate adjustment does not quickly correct a current account or financial deficit, governments are usually forced to restrict imports or borrow in the short run. Thus, heavy reliance upon food imports implies that the balance of payments dictates access to food. Due to the instability of world commodity and financial markets and the heavy burden of external debt, for more than a decade Panama has been under great balance of payments pressure. In this context to shift to a food policy that relies on imports would be ill-advised. Finally, the implications of income distribution are important for each approach. A policy of greater national self-sufficiency tends to raise the incomes of poor farmers more than a trade-oriented policy because promoting cash crops for export tends to lead to land concentration, separating small producers from their food source.

With these considerations in mind, the success of the program to foster greater self-sufficiency in food can be assessed. Table 5.10 provides statistics on the two main staples of the low-income diet, rice and corn. The former is considerably more important than the latter, for an estimated 87 percent of corn production was used as animal feed in the 1980s.[33] Both benefited from price supports under the program begun in the early 1970s. But for the support prices to effectively stimulate increased production for the domestic market, they need either to raise the prices of internally traded foodstuffs relative to export prices or to prevent the internal prices from declining as much as they would absent price supports. This relative price shift increases the return to domestic production and, with a positive supply response, increases the output of internally marketed food.

Unfortunately, available information about actual relative prices, input use and prices, credit supply, and technical support is not sufficient to isolate the effect of government price policy on resource allocation and production levels in agriculture. There is, however, enough evidence to call into question the World Bank's contentions that government price supports: *(a)* had a negative impact on agricultural growth and *(b)* caused a significant shift in resource allocation engendering inefficiency.

Table 5.10 provides an index of increases in domestic wholesale food and export prices from 1975 to 1987. The column headed "all" is the official index of producer prices for the agricultural sector, followed by indexes for rice, corn, and commodity exports. A glance at the table suggests that the support system shifted relative prices toward production for the domestic market. The export price index was lower than the rice, corn, and composite indexes in every year except 1979.[34] When one compares the trend in producer prices for rice and corn to world market prices, the effect of incentives would be more striking.[35] Had the Panamanian government not introduced a price support system, world market prices would have discouraged domestic production of rice and corn. Hence, the available evidence is consistent with the proposition that price policy successfully shifted relative profitability in favor of food production.

The purpose of this relative price shift was to increase production and raise the incomes of poor farmers. Table 5.11 provides the basic

TABLE 5.10. *Indices of Producer and Export Prices, 1975–1987*

Year	Producer Prices			Export Prices
	All	Rice	Corn	
1975	100	100	100	100
1976	103	105	101	99
1977	110	105	101	99
1978	123	100	102	99
1979	127	103	105	114
1980	140	140	116	111
1981	158	140	124	119
1982	162	140	136	114
1983	169	130	142	116
1984	173	135	145	118
1985	173	135	143	117
1986	175	135	142	115
1987	173	135	145	116

Sources. World Bank, *Panama: Structural Change and Growth Prospects,* 266; *Panamá en cifras,* (1979–1983), 14–15, and *Panamá en cifras,* (1983–1989), 16–17.

information to assess the success in achieving the first goal; here five-year averages smooth out the effects of variation due to natural factors such as weather. One sees that the results were rather contradictory. In the case of rice production, the growth rate from the midpoint of 1960–1964 to 1985–1987 was 2.2 percent, below the rate of population growth for those years. However, the rate of increase was substantially greater between the early 1960s and early 1970s, when there were no price supports, than it was between the early 1970s to the mid-1980s, when there were price supports. Furthermore, if one focuses on the early 1970s to the early 1980s, when support prices rose relative to export prices, then the rate of increase for rice is still less than that from the 1960s, 2.5 percent per year compared to 2.8. The production performance for corn is even more at odds with expectations: output averaged 80 thousand metric tons in the 1960s but only 61 thousand in the 1970s. Also inconsistent with the trend in producer prices was the tremendous increase in

corn production for 1985–1987, when the price supports were ineffective. Clearly, variables other than output price were having a significant impact on production outcomes.

Even more indicative of the impact or lack thereof of the price support incentives was area planted. Presumably the relevant decision
variable in response to prices is not output as such, but the level of
input use. In the case of rice, for 1965–1969 land use was more than
20 percent higher than subsequent use. The area in corn also declined
substantially in the 1970s, though in this case it increased a bit in the
mid-1980s. As argued in the section on land use, these declines in
part reflect the long-term concentration of landholding. In Table 5.2,
we saw that the amount of land in farms of less than 10 hectares declined by 42,000 hectares from 1960 to 1980, a period during which
the land in corn and rice fell by about 50,000 hectares (Table 5.11).
From Table 5.4 we know that these smallest farms applied about 85
percent of their land to crops, mostly corn and rice. Assuming that
half was corn and rice, we can account for 21,000 hectares of the decline in area planted in corn and rice, but we would still be left with
29,000 hectares, almost 60 percent of the decline.[36] Changes in production costs for different products, making the producer price a
poor indicator of relative profitability, probably explain the
decline.[37]

We can conclude that, with respect to rice and corn, the price support system produced modest results. Because relative prices favorable to the two basic grains changed, probably the land applied to
their use would have declined even more than the observed magnitudes in the absence of price supports, and output would have increased by less. That is, agricultural pricing policy did not shift net
resources into basic grain production but slowed the shift of resources out of their production. We have direct evidence of this for
land, and it is highly unlikely that production, even on small farms,
became more labor-using (recall that the agricultural labor force in
1980 was less than in 1970). The exception to this pattern is an
apparently modest shift of capital into grain production, at least
in the case of corn. The evidence for this shift is presented in Table
5.12, which shows that the share of mechanized corn production increased from 12.7 percent during 1976–1979 to 31.8 percent during
1985–1987.

In Table 5.12, production is divided between "traditional" and "mechanized";[38] the latter farms are virtually all over 100 hectares. From Table 5.11 we see that the land in corn increased by 8,000 hectares from 1975–1979 to 1985–1987 (though to a level well below that prevailing in the mid-1960s). Of this increase 75 percent went to mechanized farms, more than doubling their amount to 11,000 hectares: their share increased to 15 percent of total corn land, and their production share rose to more than 30 percent. At the same time, yield per hectare on mechanized farms increased both absolutely and relatively to traditional farms. Table 5.12 shows the variation in yields by demonstrating that output per hectare rises with farm size. The two parts of Table 5.12 indicate that the increase in corn production resulted from expanding modern, mechanized production relative to both small-scale traditional production and the more rapid growth of yields on the modern farms. Unfortunately, no similar data are available for rice, but the increase in rice yields suggests a similar pattern applies to that crop as well.[39]

The foregoing discussion leads us to the overall conclusion that the price policy expanded food production more than would otherwise have been the case, but not as a consequence of shifting resources to these crops. This conclusion contrasts to that of the World Bank. One of the Bank's three major criticisms of the price support program was that it resulted in a misallocation of resources. The Bank concluded that the progress made toward self-sufficiency was achieved only at "a considerable cost." If this was meant as an empirical assessment for basic grains, then it appears not to be true. If the Bank's conclusion is meant as a theoretical generalization about the consequences of market interventions, then it refers to the consequences of deviations from Pareto optimality,[40] and it only holds under assumptions so restrictive as to render it of little policy significance (i.e., perfect competition, "properly behaved" long-run cost curves, etc.). As a variation on the allocation argument, the Bank took the price support program to task for its "inconsistency" and alleged that the degree of price incentive varied across commodities.[41] This criticism assumes what it seeks to prove. Only if one accepts that markets unregulated by governments would produce an ideal result, does it then follow that a uniform rate of incentive across products is a sound policy. If one lacks faith in the perfection of markets, then differential incentives may be not only appropriate but also desirable. When markets fail, the purpose of interventions is to create a more socially efficient set of relative prices than that which the market would generate.

The Bank's second argument against the price supports is that they had the effect of worsening the distribution of income. This conclusion is based upon a subjective judgment about what would happen absent price supports, but the Bank attempts to present it as empirical fact: "Neither have pricing policies acted efficiently as means of redistributing income to poorer groups. . . . Far from redistributing income to the rural poor, current pricing policy effectively subsidizes relatively efficient farmers."[42]

In the case of corn, Table 5.12 shows that small producers generate a lower output per hectare than large producers. If this reflects overall efficiency of production, then support prices bring greater absolute gains to larger producers, but without support prices the small producers might not exist at all. Furthermore, because small producers devote a larger share of their land to corn, their relative income gains from the subsidies would surpass those to larger producers, thereby leveling the distribution of rural income.

The Bank's final argument against price supports for food products for the domestic market was that Panama lacks a comparative advantage in these commodities. Here again, the argument is unconvincing. The evidence presented for Panama's comparative disadvantage is a table showing output per hectare for seven products; Panama is compared to the average for South America, North America, and the world.[43] The table shows that yields in Panama in 1981 were lowest for five of the seven, including rice, corn, dry beans, sugar cane, and cocoa, and next to lowest for potatoes and sorghum. From this information, the Bank concludes that Panama's comparative advantage was not in grains.

This is a rather startling conclusion because the average productivity of a single input (or "factor") tells one nothing about a country's comparative advantage. The message of Hecksher-Olin trade theory is precisely that the average productivity of each factor should vary across countries, according to relative factor scarcities.[44] As we argued earlier in this chapter, twentieth-century Panama has been a land-abundant country, which implies that output per unit of land should be lower in Panama than for countries that are "labor-

TABLE 5.11. *Annual Averages for Production, Yield, and Foreign Trade in Basic Foodstuffs, 1960–1987*

	Rice[a]			
	Area[b]	*Production[c]*	*Yield[d]*	*Imports[c]*
1960–1964	103	111	1.08	5.4
1965–1969	130	154	1.19	—
1970–1974	102	147	1.43	—
1975–1979	109	167	1.55	—
1980–1984	103	188	1.82	—
1985–1987	96	189	1.98	—

	Corn[a]			
	Area[b]	*Production[c]*	*Yield[d]*	*Imports[c]*
1960–1964	89	73	0.81	4.3
1965–1969	106	86	0.81	1.2
1970–1974	67	54	0.80	—
1975–1979	76	67	0.89	8.7
1980–1984	68	64	0.94	28.4
1985–1987	84	96	1.20	30.9

	Land and Production, Rice and Corn	
	Area[b]	*Production[c]*
1960–1964	192	184
1965–1969	236	240
1970–1974	169	201
1975–1979	185	234
1980–1984	171	252
1985–1987	180	285

Sources. SIECA, *Compendio estadístico centroamericano,* 200–201; *Panamá en cifras* (1979–1983, 1983–1987); FAO, *Production Yearbook 1987,* 49–50, 77–78, 118, 125; and MIDA, *Resumen anual de la situación agropecuaria,* 11.

Note. —indicates that the measure is less than 0.1.

[a]All units measured in thousands.

[b]Area measured in hectares.

[c]Production and imports measured in metric tons.

[d]Yield figure is the simple annual average; therefore, it may not exactly equal production divided by area. It is also measured in metric tons.

TABLE 5.12. *Corn Production and Yields by Type of Farm, 1981*

	Production			
Years	Mechanized Production Share (%)	Yields per Hectare[a]		
		Traditional	Mechanized	Ratio
1976–1979	12.7	0.84	1.60	1.9
1980–1984	21.7	0.82	2.14	2.6
1985–1987	31.8	0.95	2.72	2.9

	Size of Farm (in hectares)	
Size Range	Production Share (%)	Yields[a]
Below 5[b]	20.6	0.83
5 to 10	12.9	0.94
10 to 50	37.3	0.94
50 to 100	15.1	1.09
Over 100	14.1	1.19
All farms	100.0	0.96

Source. MIDA, *El plan alimentario de emergencia*, cuadros 9, 16, and 17.
[a]Yields measured in metric tons.
[b]Lower limit not specified in source, but presumably it refers to 0.5 hectares.

abundant" or "capital-abundant." From its table on yields the Bank's conclusion would follow only in a world where land was the single factor of production. But even if one accepts the Bank's implicit vision of a land theory of value, its table is still quite arbitrary. The conclusion about corn and rice being at a comparative disadvantage derives from ranking these commodities with respect to some external average relevant for international trade. But where the products stand in the ranking depends upon how many commodities are in the table, which even includes products that Panama does not produce. Absent from the table are coffee, bananas, onions, and tomatoes, only a few of the more important products. Finally, constructing the table from other years does not change the general conclusion that yields are low in Panama, but it does alter the ranking of the seven commodities in the table. The ranking is key because comparative advantage refers to what a country does relatively, not absolutely, well. The whole point of this version of trade theory is that a country can produce and export a product even if it uses more of some resources to do so than all other countries because it will necessarily use relatively less of other inputs.

On the basis of this distressingly imprecise work, the World Bank's report concludes that Panama's comparative advantage lies in beef. Given the relative land abundance of the country, this conclusion was not outlandish and could have been reached in a more rigorous manner. However, emphasizing beef does not preclude a simultaneous emphasis on grains, particularly because almost 90 percent of corn was fed to animals in the 1980s.

Invoking the comparative advantage argument indicates the narrowness of the Bank's approach to the concept of efficiency, for it lacks any reference to dynamic comparative advantage. If the evolution of international trade patterns in the 1970s and 1980s taught us no other lesson, then it was that what countries can successfully trade and/or produce for the domestic market is dynamic and continuously changing. New exports and domestic competition for imports do not emerge suddenly, but they result from a process of reducing cost through technical change, developing human capital, and taking advantage of returns to scale. Certainly with respect to rice, production in Panama showed promise of achieving international competitiveness. Output per hectare—the World Bank's measure of efficiency—increased at a compound rate of 2.6 percent annually from 1965–1969 to 1985–1987 (see Table 5.11). This rate of increase, sustained for almost three decades, suggests that the policy of protecting rice production was feasible and over time may have yielded internationally efficient production.

On balance, the policies of protecting agriculture with tariffs and encouraging food production through price supports seem to have met with moderate success. It was probably ill-advised for the Panamanian government to yield to World Bank pressure after 1985 and abandon this policy package.

Export Performance of Agriculture

Compared to other countries in the Central American region, Panamanian agricultural exports are undiversified, and the other countries could hardly be described as enjoying diversified export structures. Of the five major agricultural exports from the region—coffee, cotton, beef, sugar, and bananas—only the last two earn substantial foreign exchange for Panama. Since the beginning of the twentieth century, bananas represented the largest share of Panama's agricultural exports. In the 1980s bananas still earned more foreign exchange than any other single commodity, an average of 25 percent of total commodity exports from 1980 to 1987. After bananas, the most important primary product was shellfish, at just below 20 percent of commodity exports in the 1980s. Much further down the list come other agricultural products; sugar and coffee are the only exports surpassing $10 million for any year in the 1980s. The policy question naturally arises: will fostering new agricultural exports be a viable and rational strategy for a Panamanian government?

Writing in the early 1970s, the Merrill report predicted that foreign exchange earnings from bananas would grow slowly if at all for the rest of that decade. Table 5.12 shows that this accurate prediction also applies to the 1980s. The problem with banana exports during these two decades was the slow growth of world demand, and demand is unlikely to improve in the 1990s. Partly in anticipation of this problem, agricultural policy sought to foster sugar production. In its 1985 report the World Bank took the Panamanian government to task for fostering an inefficient sugar industry and particularly criticized the state's participation in the sector. But the Bank's critique neglected to point out that Panama had been encouraged to produce sugar by outside agencies, including the Bank itself. The most important form of encouragement was the grant of a U.S. sugar quota, even though it was generally recognized that Panamanian sugar was not competitive at spot market prices.[45] The hope that subsidized sugar exports to the United States would compensate for declines in the world market price of bananas was partly realized, with foreign exchange earnings exceeding $40 million in the early 1980s (see Table 5.13). However, the Reagan administration's progressive reduction of quotas for Central American and Caribbean countries resulted in a sharp and probably permanent fall in sugar exports.

TABLE 5.13. *Production, Yield, and Foreign Trade in Export Crops,*
1965–1987

Bananas[a]

	Area[b]	Production[c]	Yield[c]	Exports Quantity[c]	Value[d]
1965–1969	na	828	na	500	44
1970–1974	14.2	1007	71	616	60
1975–1979	13.6	1028	76	622	65
1980–1984	na	1140	na	663	69
1985–1987	na	960	na	731	78

Sugar Cane[a]

	Area[b]	Production[c]	Yield[c]	Exports Quantity[c,e]	Value[d]
1965–1969	22	889	40.9	22	3
1970–1974	29	1404	49.2	41	20
1975–1979	42	2432	59.4	106	29
1980–1984	45	2359	48.9	107	43
1985–1987	32	1673	52.8	66	21

Coffee[a]

	Area[b]	Production[c]	Yield[c,e]	Exports Quantity[a]	Value[d]
1965–1969	26	4.8	0.19	1.0	1
1970–1974	23	4.7	0.21	2.0	2
1975–1979	25	5.4	0.22	2.0	6
1980–1984	23	8.4	0.37	4.4	13
1985–1987	33	11.7	0.35	6.9	21

Sources. SIECA, *Compendio estadístico centroamerica,* 200–201; *Panamá en cifras* (1979–1983, 1983–1987); FAO, *Production Yearbooks,* 1979, 179, and 1987, 207, 220, 225.
[a]All units measured in thousands.
[b]Area measured in hectares.
[c]Production, yield, and quantity measured in metric tons.
[d]Value is presented in millions of U.S. dollars.
[e]Raw sugar, i.e., milled but not refined, is presented.

TABLE 5.14.   *Head of Cattle and Land in Pasture, 1965–1985*

Year	Number of Cattle (in thousands)	Area (in hectares)	Head/Hct. (index)
1965[a]	967	980	100
1970	1,188	1,141	104
1980	1,405	1,300	108
1985[b]	1,447	1,330	109

Source. SIECA, *Compendio estadístico centroamericano; Panamá en cifras* (1981, 1986).
[a]Area extrapolated as half the difference between 1960 and 1970 figures.
[b]From FAO, *Country Tables* (1989), 216, assuming the percentage increase in pasture land to be equal to the percentage increase for all farmland.

The third crop export, coffee, has shown little promise for Panama. Over twenty years, export earnings rose spectacularly in percentage terms, but this was from a tiny base. By the end of the 1980s, however, coffee had probably reached its commercial limit because climatic and soil conditions in Panama appear unfavorable. In the early 1970s, the Merrill report passed a negative judgment on coffee due to a host of difficulties unlikely to be overcome.[46] Even the World Bank, which in the 1980s tended to see bright export prospects everywhere, rejected coffee as an export earner.[47]

The World Bank's report of 1985 recommended that Panama diversify into beef exports as a major foreign exchange earner. As we have seen, Panama had a large ranching sector: almost 60 percent of agricultural land was in pasture in 1980. As Table 5.14 shows, the number of cattle increased from about 1 million to nearly 1.5 million from 1965 to 1985. This increase, entirely directed to beef for the domestic market, was achieved through an expansion of grazing land, and in 1985 the ratio of cattle to land was only 9 percent above the ratio in 1965.

According to the World Bank, the absence of beef exports resulted from bad policy.[48] The Panamanian government accepted this view, and by the late 1980s the Bank's objections were no longer relevant. Whether the policy change will result in developing substantial beef exports remains to be demonstrated. There is, however, the prior question of whether fostering beef exports is a wise economic and social policy for a Panamanian government. On the demand side, beef has the advantage for the exporting country that both the income and the price elasticities of demand are greater than unity: that is, when the world price of beef declines, total sales revenue rises; and when incomes in the importing countries increase, beef sales increase more than proportionally to the income increase.

The negative aspects of fostering beef exports in Panama, however, may well outweigh this advantage. The income distribution consequences would be serious. Panamanian beef production is land-extensive, so it would occur on large estates and thus worsen the distribution of farm income and land. Moreover, of all agricultural activities, it probably generates the least employment. And for beef to be exported in quantity in the medium term, market interventions would be necessary to depress domestic demand.[49]

The market for Panamanian beef would almost certainly be the developed countries. Few Latin American or Caribbean countries are likely to liberalize their import regulations, for most must protect their own cattle sectors. The experience of beef exporters to the Western developed countries was unhappy in the 1980s. By using regulations on contamination levels in meat as a protectionist instrument, the Reagan administration virtually eliminated beef imports from Central America; there is no guarantee that Panama would not suffer the same fate. The European Community was, if anything, more protectionist; given its unwillingness to liberalize with respect to U.S. beef, it seems much less likely to welcome production from underdeveloped countries. A decision to undertake the investments to make beef a major export seems ill-advised when considering the domestic social and economic consequences and the high likelihood of protectionist barriers abroad.

Overall, Panama appears to have little prospect for substantially expanding foreign exchange earnings from the agricultural sector.[50] However, there is scope for significant foreign exchange saving through further import substitution. The policies of the 1970s, aimed at greater self-sufficiency in rice, corn, and market vegetables such as onions and tomatoes, were essentially sound, albeit partial.

Protection and Efficiency

The argument against government action to foster greater agricultural self-sufficiency is that it results in allocative inefficiencies. However, the absence of regulations produces more efficient allocation only if markets are competitive. Yet, as argued in the Merrill report, in Panama pervasive oligopolistic marketing structures require government intervention:

The oligopolistic nature of food marketing channels should make it easier for the government to control prices and to regulate food quality. . . . It seems unlikely that there will be any less need for government price controls in the future than there has been in the past.[51]

Furthermore, that same report judged that the unequal distribution of income in Panama in no small part resulted from "the market power position enjoyed by domestic producers in many industries."[52] The report argued that these oligopolies, particularly in food marketing, were quite efficient; therefore, regulating prices rather than attempting to enforce competition would be the correct policy.[53] On balance, it seems implausible to argue that markets in Panama would produce efficient outcomes if left free of price and other direct government interventions. Not only are domestic markets dominated by a few firms, but also substituting tariffs for import quotas and then lowering tariffs would do little to make domestic agricultural markets competitive because imports have been controlled by a few trading companies throughout the history of Panama, a condition underwritten by government policy. Even after implementing the IMF/World Bank liberalization measures in early 1986, food imports were controlled by government-licensing policy. Generally, the government granted an import license for a particular good to only one firm. Under Noriega at least, this monopoly privilege was exchanged for a handsome payoff or profit-sharing arrangement.

The lack of competitive markets does not argue for across-the-board state intervention. But it does lend support to a more interventionist agricultural policy aimed at increasing food self-sufficiency and reducing rural poverty.

Chapter Six

Prelude to Crisis

In the preceding chapters we have established an institutional and analytical framework for understanding Panama in the 1980s. For reasons internal and external to Panama, it was a decade of great turmoil, accompanied by shrinking incomes, escalating unemployment, and growing political corruption and instability. On the surface, however, the 1980s in Panama began innocently enough. In the political sphere, Torrijos's program of gradual democratization seemed to be proceeding on schedule. The first step in returning the military to the barracks was the indirect election by the National Assembly of Municipal Representatives in 1978 of a civilian president and vice-president—Aristedes Royo, a former minister of education, became president, and Ricardo de la Espriella, a banker, became vice-president. Law No. 81 of October 1978 legalized political parties, and Torrijos wasted no time in forming his own coalition, the Democratic Revolutionary party (PRD). On September 28, 1980, nineteen representatives were elected to a fifty-seven-member National Council of Legislation, with restricted legislative powers.[1] In 1984 Torrijos planned to proceed to direct, open elections for a new, fully endowed legislative assembly, a president, and two vice-presidents.

In the economic sphere, by 1980 Panama was in the midst of a moderate recovery that had begun in 1978. As discussed in chapters 3 and 4, Panama's service sector was flourishing. The Canal treaties brought an additional $75 million in revenue to government coffers along with various indirect benefits, and Canal traffic was booming with the growth in world trade and the new transshipments of Alaskan North Slope oil. Between 1977 and 1982 Canal tolls almost doubled, from $163.8 million to $324 million. The Colon Free Zone was also growing rapidly, with value added practically quadrupling from $118 million (5.7 percent of GDP) in 1977 to $441 million (10.3 percent of GDP) in 1982. Assets in the international banking center more than doubled, and employment grew by 50 percent between 1977 and 1982.[2] Even the manufacturing sector, which had stagnated between 1968 and 1977, expanded at a real annual rate of 3.9 percent from 1978 to 1982. Indeed, a March 1981 publication of the IMF, overlooking the fleeting factors underlying Panama's recovery, declared Panama to be a success story of applying IMF policy: "The results have been impressive; Panama is one of the few countries where fiscal adjustment and a progressive revival of domestic economic activity have recently blended successfully."[3]

Beneath the surface, however, problems were brewing. Under the influence of Panama's twelfth standby loan from the IMF, signed March 23, 1979, real wages throughout the economy fell by 1.6 percent in 1979, 2.3 percent in 1980, and 3.0 percent in 1981.[4] Official unemployment rates hovered around 9 percent while labor force participation rates had fallen some five percentage points from the early 1970s.[5] Labor unrest surfaced time and again in the form of national work stoppages and demonstrations. To better understand this social restiveness and consequent political instability it is instructive to look more closely at the prevailing inequality in Panama at the outset of the 1980s.

An Overview of Inequality in 1980

Whether measured absolutely or relatively to other countries, Panama in 1980 exhibited a high degree of inequality. Panama's neighbors in Central America were justifiably infamous in the 1970s and 1980s for being among the Latin American countries with the most unequal distributions of income. Yet as Table 6.1 shows, by a number of measures, distribution in Panama in 1980 was even more unequal, with the exception of El Salvador. Furthermore, when one uses the Gini coefficient to summarize the degree of inequality, Panama stands with El Salvador, well apart from the other four countries.

Particularly indicative of the degree of inequality is the last part of Table 6.1, which gives the average incomes per head for each group. In 1980, Panama's per capita income more than doubled that of Gua-

TABLE 6.1. *The Distribution of Income in Central America and Panama, 1980*

Country	20 pct. poorest	30 pct. <median	30 pct. >median	20 pct. richest	Gini coef.[a]
Guatemala	5.3	14.5	36.1	54.1	0.46
El Salvador	2.0	10.0	22.0	66.0	0.60
Honduras	4.3	12.7	23.7	59.3	0.51
Nicaragua	3.0	13.0	26.0	58.0	0.51
Costa Rica	4.0	17.0	30.0	49.0	0.42
Central America	3.7	13.4	25.6	57.3	0.50
Panama	2.7	10.0	27.0	60.3	0.58

Implied Income per Capita by Range[b]

	20 pct. poorest	30 pct. <median	30 pct. >median	20 pct. richest	Average income
Guatemala	111	203	364	1,134	419
El Salvador	47	155	341	1,536	465
Honduras	52	102	168	616	215
Nicaragua	62	178	356	1,200	413
Costa Rica	177	501	884	2,165	884
Central America	90	228	423	1,330	479
Panama	120	304	823	2,710	904

Sources. Gallardo and López, *Centroamérica en cifras: la crisis,* 153–57; originally from CEPAL, *Notas sobre la evolución social del istmo centroamericano hasta 1980,* 15.
[a]Gini coefficient, where zero indicates perfect equality and one indicates maximum inequality.
[b]Implied per capita income is given in U. S. dollars (in 1970 prices).

temala (in 1970 prices), yet the poorest 20 percent in Panama earned an average income just nine dollars greater than in Guatemala. Perhaps most striking of all, average income for the richest 20 percent in Panama was almost twenty-three times the average for the poorest 20 percent, roughly twice the size of the same ratio for Guatemala (ten times), Honduras (twelve times), and Costa Rica (twelve times). The low income levels for the population below the median income in Panama imply a high incidence of poverty, given in Table 6.2, which again compares the Central American countries.

When one recalls that per capita income in Panama in 1980 was 2 percent above that of Costa Rica, the measured poverty incidence for the country indicates a poor performance indeed. It is striking that in terms of unweighted averages Panamanian income per head was 140 percent higher than the average for the four low-income Central American countries; but its degree of rural poverty compared to these countries was only 20 percent less, and the incidence of urban poverty was only 13 percent lower. The contrast in poverty incidence between urban areas for Panama and Costa Rica is particularly telling: 43 percent compared to a mere 14 percent, for countries with similar per capita incomes. In Panama's defense we should point out that its degree of "extreme" urban poverty was substantially lower than for the average of the four poor countries of Central America. But even here the difference between Panama and Guatemala appears quite small in relation to the per capita incomes of the two countries.[6]

A study by Cordero indicates that the number of families in poverty increased by 45,300 between 1975 and 1980,[7] with a reduction in rural poverty, relative to urban poverty, due to migration. After rendering the 1980 estimates consistent with an earlier 1975 study, he concludes that rural poverty—defined in terms of nonsatisfaction of basic needs—declined from 83 percent of families in 1975 to 72 percent in 1980. Simultaneously, however, the incidence of urban poverty rose from 33 percent to 47 percent.

The unexpectedly high incidence of poverty in Panama derives in great part from the country's pattern of development. In urban areas, the emphasis upon financial and commercial services during the postwar period generated large inequalities between the elite and the lower classes and skewed distribution of wage and salary incomes. At the top of the wage and salary scale are the several thousand employees of the Canal and the international banking center whose average remuneration is well above what can be earned in the rest of the urban economy, not even considering rural wage earners.

A further indication of the high degree of inequality in Panama can be found in the trend in basic food consumption indicators from the early 1960s through the mid-1980s. The first three columns of Table 6.3 give per capita indices of caloric consumption, protein con-

TABLE 6.2. *Rural and Urban Poverty in Central America and
Panama, 1980
(in percentages)*

Country	Degree of Nonsatisfaction of Basic Needs		
	Extreme[a]	Nonsatisfaction[b]	Total
Rural			
Guatemala	51.5	32.2	83.7
El Salvador	55.4	21.0	76.4
Honduras	69.7	10.5	80.2
Nicaragua	50.0	30.0	80.0
Costa Rica	18.7	15.5	34.2
Central America	54.7	24.7	79.4
Panama	38.3	29.0	67.3
Urban			
Guatemala	16.8	30.2	47.0
El Salvador	44.5	13.1	57.6
Honduras	30.6	13.3	43.9
Nicaragua	21.6	24.0	45.6
Costa Rica	7.4	6.2	13.6
Central America	27.8	18.9	46.8
Panama	11.8	31.1	42.9

Source. Gallardo and López, *Centroamérica en cifras: la crisis,* 158–61, based on country studies by the Economic Commission for Latin America and the Caribbean, 1981.

[a]Food insufficiency means household income is insufficient to purchase minimum caloric and protein requirements.

[b]Basic needs insufficiency means household income is sufficient to purchase minimum diet, but insufficient to cover minimum housing, transport, health, and education costs.

sumption, and national income. Both caloric and protein consumption increased by 5 percent from the first half to the second half of the 1960s, while per capita income rose 25 percent. During the 1970s the nutritional indicators changed hardly at all, while per capita income increased substantially. An improvement in the nutritional indicators occurred in the 1980s, but over a period of more than twenty

TABLE 6.3.   *Indices of Calorie and Protein Consumption Compared with Per Capita Income, Panama, 1960–1986*

Years	Per Capita			Ratios	
	Calories	Proteins	Income	Calories/Y	Proteins/Y
1960–1965	100	100	100	100	100
1965–1970	105	105	125	84	84
1970–1975	105	102	151	70	68
1975–1980	103	105	172	60	62
1980–1986	107	110	187	57	59
1980–1986[a]	2,618	67	$2,550		

Sources. Organización de las Naciones Unidas para la Agricultura y la Alimentación, *Informe sobre el Instituto de Investigación Agropecuaria (IDIAP) de Panamá*, 143; República de Panamá, Dirección de Estadística y Censo, *Estadística Panameña, situación económica, hoja de balance de alimentos: años 1984–85; Panamá en cifras* (1988), 251.

[a]Average level of per capita income in 1987 U.S. dollars; calories in units per capita per day; and proteins in grams per capita per day.

years the increase in both caloric intake and protein consumption was slight, at an annual compound rate of 0.3 percent and 0.4 percent, respectively. The last two columns of the table present the contrast between the creditable rise in per capita income (3 percent per year) and the miniscule improvement in nutritional indicators, by dividing the latter by the former. These ratios show that the increase in per capita income did not translate into a substantial improvement in food consumption in Panama even on average, much less for the poor.

Of course, Engel's Law tells one that the expenditure on food tends to fall as a proportion of income as income rises.[8] However, one would expect food expenditure to rise absolutely in real terms, particularly for a country in which 40 percent of the rural population and 12 percent of the urban population suffered from food insufficiency in 1980 (see Table 6.2). The contrary result, that per capita income could rise rapidly with little or no increase in basic food consumption, can only be explained by a pattern of growth in which few if any benefits reached the lower classes. Again the contrast with Costa Rica is striking. Over the same period covered in Table 6.3, Costa Rica's per capita income increased by less than Panama's, but

TABLE 6.4. *Foreign Debt and GDP, 1980–1987*
(in billions of dollars)

	1980	1981	1982	1983	1984	1985	1986	1987
Public foreign debt	2.52	2.68	3.17	3.41	3.64	3.64	3.84	3.73
Total foreign debt	na	na	3.93	4.39	4.42	4.73	4.79	4.76
Current price GDP	3.56	3.88	4.27	4.37	4.56	4.90	5.12	5.20
GDP (1980 prices)	3.56	3.71	3.91	3.92	3.91	4.04	4.15	4.27
Index, real GDP per capita	100	102	105	103	101	103	104	104

Sources. World Bank, *Structural Change and Growth Prospects;* CEPAL, *Panamá: La situación económica a principios de 1989; Panamá en cifras,* various years.

the per capita consumptions of calories and proteins each rose by 27 percent in Costa Rica, compared to 7 and 10 percent in Panama. It is little wonder, then, that, with expectations raised under Torrijos but few real gains for the great majority of Panamanians, politicians had little room to maneuver as the decade of the 1980s began.

Political Change and Austerity Policies

Panama's post-1969 period of political stability definitively ended with the sudden death of Torrijos on July 30, 1981, in a mysterious plane crash. The political leadership vacuum was filled by a three-man struggle within the National Guard. After some skillful maneuvering, deceit, and possible support from the United States, Manuel Antonio Noriega emerged as the maximum leader of the National Guard in August 1983, which he promptly expanded and upgraded into the Panamanian Defense Forces.

The political uncertainty engendered by Torrijos's demise contributed to falling investment expenditures, which began in 1982. Scandal-ridden mismanagement of public housing, substantial cost overruns in public works, lower world petroleum and sugar prices, a sudden reversal in the fortunes of Panama's international services,[9] and the onset of the Latin American debt crisis in 1982 ended Panama's short-lived recovery and exploded its fiscal deficit.[10] By the end of 1982, Panama had the highest per capita foreign debt and highest debt share of GDP in Latin America.[11]

At the time of Panama's twelfth standby agreement with the IMF in March 1979, the fiscal deficit reached 12 percent of GDP. Panama successfully implemented the conservative budgetary measures of this agreement, including a pledge not to create new state enterprises, and by 1981 the fiscal deficit fell to 5 percent of GDP. For the reasons already outlined, however, the budget deficit's share jumped to 11 percent of GDP in 1982. The IMF standby loans signed in 1982 and 1983 and the World Bank structural adjustment (SAL) and technical adjustment (TAL) loans of 1983, in the context of the newly proclaimed Latin American debt crisis, ushered in Panama's most severe programs of fiscal austerity to date.

As expected, these programs exacerbated an already unstable political environment. Rapid turnover among the generals was reproduced among the figurehead presidents. Alleging nothing more than an earache, President Aristedes Royo resigned in July 1982 and was succeeded by his vice-president, Ricardo de la Espriella, who, in turn, resigned in February 1984. The vice-president under de la Espriella then assumed the presidency until the fraudulently elected Nicolás Ardito Barletta assumed office in October 1984.

Barletta, a former vice-president of the World Bank, was Noriega's (and apparently the U.S.) candidate in the 1984 elections, the first direct elections in Panama since 1968 when a military coup overthrew the elected Arnulfo Arias. The same Arnulfo Arias was Barletta's opponent in the 1984 elections. By all accounts, the election was close; several weeks after the election, Barletta was proclaimed the victor by 1,713 of 600,000 votes cast.

Despite widespread and universally accepted claims of fraud, the United States quickly recognized the Barletta government.[12] A 1987 staff report for the U.S. Senate Foreign Relations Committee concluded: "U.S. standing in Panama suffered a sharp blow in 1984 when American policy-makers appeared to play an important role in selecting, nominating and electing a candidate (Nicolás Barletta) acceptable to the U.S."[13] In part because of a yet more austere fiscal program and in part because he intimated investigating the killing of Hugo Spadafora, Barletta's tenure too was short-lived; he was forced out by Noriega in September 1985.[14] Barletta was followed by his vice-president, Eric Arturo Delvalle, owner of the Azucarero Nacional, S.A., one of the two privately owned sugar mills in Panama (Delvalle's fate will be discussed in the next chapter).[15]

The Economic Consequences of Debt and Austerity

The principal difference between IMF/World Bank austerity programs in Panama and those elsewhere in the region is that Panama's monetary system did not offer the possibility of a currency devaluation. That is, there was no "automatic" mechanism to redress imbalances in the balance of payments' current account, and there was no indirect way to force real wages down. This represented bad news for policy makers: attacks on real wages were now necessarily explicit, and the policy makers were thereby held directly accountable. But the circumstance also provided good news: Panama avoided the cycle of devaluation-inflation-devaluation-hyperinflation so common throughout Latin America.

Panama's first stringent IMF standby agreements of the decade, signed in 1982 and 1983, were complemented by two World Bank structural and technical investment loans in 1983. Together these loans amounted to $307 million and facilitated Panama's 1982–1983 debt rescheduling with its foreign creditors. Panama's austerity program contained the following elements:

1. a commitment to lower the fiscal deficit from 11 percent of GDP in 1982 to 5.5 percent in 1983 and 1984 by obligating the government to reduce spending on housing, transfer payments, social services, and physical infrastructure and to increase rates on public services, taxes, and debt-service payments;

2. a reorientation of public investment with the understanding that subsidies to public enterprises would be cut back and unprofitable companies would be eliminated or sold to the private sector;

3. a customs reform, including the replacement of import quotas and associated price controls with tariffs, the gradual reduction of tariffs, and the introduction of uniform tariffs;

4. a restructuring of incentives to promote investment in nontraditional exports; and

TABLE 6.5.   *Government Deficits, 1982–1986*
(in millions of U.S. dollars)

	1982	1983	1984	1985	1986
Government spending	1,625	1,370	1,493	1,365	1,757
Budget deficit	471	248	399	359	241
Deficit share in GDP	11.0%	5.6%	8.7%	7.3%	4.7%
Government debt service	477	479	541	509	838
Debt service share in government spending	29.4%	35.0%	36.2%	37.3%	47.7%

Source. *Panamá en cifras*, (1982–1986), 188–210.

5. a reform of housing, public health, and social security programs and better management of the lands reverted to Panama in the 1977 treaties.

Without always attaining the desired results, government policy faithfully pursued most of these policies. Government spending other than that on debt service fell by 20 percent in nominal and 30.9 percent in real terms between 1982 and 1986. During these years, in nominal terms spending for government investment and transfer payments decreased by 63.1 and 23.7 percent, respectively, while government debt-service payments increased by 75.7 percent (from $477 million in 1982 to $838 million in 1986).[16] Initially, the fiscal deficit fell to its target level in 1983 (5.6 percent of GDP), but in 1984 and 1985—as debt service grew, net capital flows turned negative,[17] the domestic economy stagnated, and public protest erupted— government deficits increased both absolutely and as a share of GDP. As presented in Table 6.5, only a severe SAL II and new IMF standby signed in 1985 and implemented in late 1985 and 1986 reduced the budget deficit below the 1983 level.[18]

The drastic reduction in public investment created serious infrastructural problems and helped undermine the IMF/World Bank project of increasing nontraditional exports. Inadequate maintenance and modernization of Panama's ports, railroad system, and road network resulted in excessively high transportation costs for current and prospective exporters. For instance, shipping costs per container from Panama to Miami were often two to three times higher than those from Venezuela to Miami.[19] Furthermore, the absence of container and refrigeration facilities, port delays, periodic ship damage due to improper docking cushions, inter alia, led some shipping companies to reduce or terminate service to Panama's main ports of Balboa and Cristobal.[20]

To reduce the public enterprise sector, several companies were, in fact, sold off to the private sector at bargain prices. It should be noted, however, that the World Bank *(a)* employed a skewed measure of public enterprise inefficiency (as discussed in chapter 2), *(b)* discounted the financial improvements in many enterprises, *(c)* overlooked the special circumstances causing losses in others (e.g., the special deal between the state sugar corporation and the private sugar companies owned by Delvalle and Chiari, to the latter's benefit), and *(d)* ignored the fact that most public enterprises in deficit in the early 1980s had been rescued from a previous deficitary situation as private enterprises (e.g., Air Panamá, Aeroperlas, Cítricos de Chiriquí, Ingenio Las Cabras, Hotel Contadora, Hotel Panamá).

To liberalize trade the World Bank's recommendations were followed assiduously. Tariffs replaced nearly half of Panama's quantitative import restrictions between March and October 1983 and most of the rest by March 1985. New tariffs were established at levels the Bank considered reasonable, with a schedule for their further reduction. These measures were accompanied by some easing of price controls. To further offset the incentive bias against export investments, the government established the Investment Promotion Council in 1982 to advertise the sweeping tax benefits of the 1979 export promotion law and to facilitate export licensing requirements.

In part as a result of these efforts, nontraditional exports experienced a modest growth between 1980 and 1985 from $90.3 to $101.0 million. Although the Bank attributes the failure of nontraditional exports to grow more rapidly to Panama's presumed pro-import substitution incentive structure, it seems that the problem runs deeper. First, the Bank sees nontraditionals as the salvation of Panama's debt problem and the hope for its long-term development; yet the absolute level of nontraditional exports is diminutive relative to Panama's foreign debt, and in 1987 their value represented only 10 percent of debt-service payments. Furthermore, the Bank is urging the same model of developing nontraditional exports upon all of

Latin America. To the extent that the model successfully increases the production and export of new products, markets are likely to become glutted, and prices for exports are likely to decrease, at least in relative terms. Second, as discussed in chapter 2, distortions in Panama's price structure from its international service orientation make applying this model even more problematic for Panama than for other countries in the region. Third, before nontraditional export production can "take off," large public investments in infrastructure will be necessary and easier access to loan capital for domestic investors will have to be achieved. These conditions are not easy to establish in the context of IMF/World Bank austerity programs.

Fourth, the U.S. tariff preferences granted to Panama and other countries in the region under the General System of Preferences (GSP) and the Caribbean Basin Initiative (CBI) are neither as extensive nor as reliable as they need be to stimulate substantial sums of new investment. During the first five years of the CBI program (1983–1987, prior to the imposition of U.S. trade sanctions), U.S. imports from Panama scarcely increased at all, rising from $377.4 million in 1983 to $388.5 million in 1987. A significant part of the problem for Panama and other nations in the Caribbean Basin was that at the same time the United States was exhorting these countries to rapidly augment their exports it was drastically curtailing its importation of sugar. U.S. sugar imports from the Caribbean Basin decreased by more than 84 percent between 1981 and 1987.

Equally troublesome is the unpredictability of U.S. trade preferences. Two examples make this point. In November 1986 the U.S. International Trade Commission (ITC) decided to impose a 46.5 percent duty on Costa Rican flowers. Not only were the ITC's methods dubious in determining Costa Rica's domestic costs of production, but the finding that export-related tax credits were countervailable also threw a monkey wrench into the whole concept of policy measures for export promotion. Although the duty was placed on Costa Rican flowers, Panamanian exporters saw it as a direct threat to themselves. Because any damaged U.S. producer can bring a suit before the ITC without regard to U.S. government intentions or the CBI preferences, Panamanian exporters tended to treat the case of Costa Rican flowers as symbolic of what happens whenever the CBI effort bears fruit and initial export success is achieved. In its 1985 report the World Bank relates the other telling incident:

Within months of the start of production of one of the Hong Kong owned maquila industries, the US Department of Commerce made the first of three calls for a reduction of imports from Panama to the USA of the sole products of the plant (women's woolen sweaters). According to Asian investors interested in the exploitation of Panama's commercial policy status with the USA, production levels will never reach proportions that will trigger protective measures. However, given the experience of the first producer of a sensitive product, this forecast appears unlikely to materialize. The future of such activities is therefore most uncertain and will depend on the dynamics of commercial diplomacy between the USA and Panama. (p. 96)

Fifth, the issues of relative profitability and investment options between production for the domestic and international markets must be examined more carefully. The Bank's argument of incentive bias in favor of production for the domestic market leads to the expectation of more dynamic investment for internal production. Yet industrial and agricultural investment and per capita production have been stagnant since the late 1960s, as their joint share in GDP has fallen from 38.6 percent in 1968 to 17.8 percent in 1988. If protection for final outputs and free trade for necessary inputs have raised the return on import substitution so far above that for export production, why is there not additional investment in the former until the rates of return equalize between the two sectors? Part of the answer lies in the fact, usually suppressed in the Bank's call for wholesale liberalization, that Panama does not have competitive financial and product markets. The option for the investor is not between production for the internal or foreign market, but more typically investment in real estate, domestic finance, or in capital flight. Perhaps the Bank would respond that only completely open markets and competitive wage levels prevent capital flight, but this vision provides little positive hope for either increasing living standards for the majority of Panamanians or promoting the country's long-term economic development.

The next round of policy reforms came in 1985–1986 with a new IMF standby loan and SAL II from the World Bank. The reforms continued and extended the 1982–1983 reforms. Again, they brought Panama not only fresh monies from the multilaterals ($98.8 million) but also new loans ($60 million) and debt rescheduling with its foreign creditors.[21] The program also renewed popular protest and political instability.

The government announced the new austerity/"readjustment" program in July 1985. The fiscal plan called for reducing the public deficit to 3.5 percent of GDP in 1985 and to 2.6 percent in 1986, to be accomplished by reduced spending, increased taxes, and higher fees for public services. According to the plan, projected debt-service payments would increase to 40 percent of exports of goods and nonfactor services in 1985 and to 57 percent in 1986 (in large measure due to the concentration of scheduled amortization payments in these years).

Yet with negative real GDP growth in 1984 for the first time since 1951, with official unemployment rates trending upward to the record levels of 10.1 percent in 1984 and 12.3 percent in 1985, with a sizeable current account surplus developing in both 1984 and 1985, and with the manufacturing sector operating only at some 30 percent of capacity,[22] the contractionary medicine prescribed by the IMF/ World Bank did not sit well with either the Panamanian people or their newly elected legislature. The program was rejected by the National Legislature in September 1985, but the Delvalle government imposed the bulk of it anyway the following month.

The structural readjustment program was enacted by the infamous "three-in-one" laws of March 1986. Law One sought to weaken the labor code and thereby promote employment and productivity. One provision reduced maximum overtime pay to 25 percent above the base wage for small enterprises and enterprises producing for export. The effects of this provision on employment generation were at best contradictory since it encouraged overtime work relative to new hiring. Another provision increased the trial period before a worker achieved "job stability" from two weeks to three months. It also enabled an employer to pay workers with more than ten years of work experience a severance bonus and then rehire them without offering job stability. Another exempted all enterprises with fewer than ten employees from the provisions of the Labor Code.

Law Two primarily concerned itself with deregulating agriculture: eliminating price controls, reducing tariffs, abolishing quotas on imported foods, and closing the Instituto de Mercadeo Agropecuario, the principal regulatory body in agriculture. Law Two also introduced a 3 percent c.i.f. tariff on imported machinery for enterprises producing primarily for the domestic market. Law Three, addressing trade liberalization, called for tariff reduction over five years in equal steps to a maximum of 60 percent ad valorem on c.i.f., with the exception of a few strategic products whose protection rates could settle as high as 90 percent.

The thrust of Law Two as it pertained to agriculture was critically analyzed in chapter 5. By imposing an import tariff on imported machinery the government intended to discourage capital-intensive technologies and provide an incentive for import substitution to move from consumer to capital goods production. The idea is commendable, but the low 3 percent level is clearly inadequate for either goal. The direction of Law Three—that is, the gradual reduction of protection to motivate more efficient, competitive production—is also commendable. More competitive production, which would enhance export opportunities, is desirable in any economy. The problem in Panama and elsewhere has been that price deregulation and fiscal incentives alone are insufficient to motivate efficiency. Domestic and international market distortions along with stagnant domestic demand under IMF austerity policies, inter alia, have thwarted the push toward competitiveness.

The 1985–1986 IMF/World Bank program had the predictable effect of improving Panama's financial indicators without improving the real economy or the citizens' living standards. During 1986–1987 real output per capita grew at 0.7 percent annually, real wages and salaries decreased by 0.4 percent per year, the official unemployment rate averaged 11.2 percent, the current account balance remained positive at levels similar to the preceding three years, and the public-sector deficit fell to less than 1 percent of GDP.

The structural components of the program, in fact, were not given a fair test. The gross mismanagement of the Noriega government, the general political instability, and the imposition of severe economic sanctions by the United States brought Panama into a deep depression during 1988–1989. It is to an analysis of the 1988–1989 crisis that we turn our attention in the next chapter.

Chapter Seven

Crisis, Instability,
and Intervention

The immediate cause of the U.S. invasion of Panama in December 1989 was the desire of the Bush administration to remove Manuel Noriega from power and install a pro-U.S. regime. As we made clear in previous chapters, the cause of this extraordinary violation of international law had much deeper roots in which Noriega's role was either incidental or accidental. In this chapter we analyze the last five years of the 1980s. We approach these crisis years on two levels: first, we consider the underlying structural causes; and second, we discuss the conjuntural events that eventually produced the violence, destruction, and transformation of December 1989.

The dictatorship of Manuel Noriega was the result of three characteristics, which both individually and collectively resulted in a fundamental destabilization of Panamanian society. The first characteristic is historical: Panama, beyond reasonable doubt, was created by the United States. As recounted in the opening chapter, during the nineteenth century there waxed and waned a Panamanian separatist movement of some substance. Possibly had the government of the United States not intervened in 1903 to create Panama, the Panamanians themselves may eventually have gained their independence. The point is moot, for it is the curse of the Panamanian nation that it can take no pride in its formal creation and that its founding fathers could be justifiably branded as agents of a foreign power. Indeed, in perhaps an even more bitter turn of history, the first time more than a handful of Panamanians would die defending their land would be in December 1989, under the direction of Manuel Noriega. Panama's political and economic dependence on the United States produced an entrenched, yet somewhat schizophrenic and cynical, nationalism.

The first characteristic is closely related to a second: the severe distortion of political life resulted in chronic instability. As we argue in chapter 1, political instability in Panama resulted from both the absence of a ruling class in the usual sense at the time of independence and the overwhelming hegemony of the U.S. presence that made a mockery of the term "domestic Panamanian politics." From Washington's point of view, no such category of Panamanian internal affairs existed. The entire country and its political arena were treated as areas of legitimate U.S. intervention. Under the treaty of 1903, the U.S. government had the right to control and regulate the waterways that fed the Canal, no matter how deeply they reached into the countryside. Similarly, the U.S. government always considered the most domestic of Panamanian political matters to be tributaries that eventually emptied into the Canal Zone. The distortion of Panamanian politics by the U.S. presence took many forms, and one of the important ones in the long term was the debilitation of the upper classes. In Panama as in few other Latin American countries (perhaps pre-1959 Cuba would also qualify), the elites depended upon the support of the U.S. government to rule (again, never as obviously as in December 1989).

The third characteristic was economic: the emergence of a profoundly denationalized economy. This economy was characterized by fundamental distortions that shifted profitability away from the commodity-producing sectors. The strategy based upon internationally oriented services never provided a pattern of growth that could spread benefits to the majority of the population. By the 1980s it could no longer successfully serve the nonmilitary elite, either.

Together these three interrelated characteristics produced a deep and irreversible crisis. The form of the crisis was the Torrijos coalition's inability to produce a legitimate successor to the general, but its essence was the denationalization of Panamanian society. In every country of Latin America, nationalism, in part, is a reaction to U.S. influence. However, in the case of Panama, the essence of nationalism was opposition to U.S. influence, for eighty years symbolized by the Canal. Since 1903 the U.S. government, through various agents and agencies, has actively participated in the political life of Panama. To a degree the same is true for all Latin American countries, but the frequency and reach of U.S. intervention in Panamanian politics has been singular. The U.S. government treated Panama as a client state, unwilling to tolerate independent political developments or politicians.

Why the Political Crisis Occurred

Of the many imponderables associated with the crisis in relations between the governments of Panama and the United States during the second half of the 1980s, the most perplexing is why it occurred at all. Answering this question is key to understanding the unfolding of events that eventually led to the U.S. invasion and installation of the Endara government. It is established fact that Manuel Noriega enjoyed close relations with agencies of the United States government, not only the Central Intelligence Agency but also the U.S. military. His role as a U.S. intelligence informant began in 1960 while he was still a cadet at an elite military academy in Peru. His relationship to U.S. intelligence agencies became contractual in either 1966 or 1967 when then head of the Chiriqui province garrison, Major Omar Torrijos, asked Noriega to set up the province's first intelligence organization. In this capacity, Noriega could keep close tabs on the growing communist influence in the unions at United Fruit Company's banana plantations in the area. After helping Torrijos squelch a coup attempt in late 1969, Noriega was promoted to national chief of intelligence and, thus, became an even more valuable informant for the United States. Noriega's espionage role continued until the mid-1980s,[1] despite extensive evidence of his involvement in illegal activities associated with the drug trade, arms sales, and counterintelligence.[2]

Noriega seems to have served the interests of the U.S. government in a satisfactory manner for a long time. Why then did the Reagan administration provoke a political conflict that would eventually leave Panama in economic ruin and political chaos? Most commentators beg this question, going directly to an analysis of the destabilization campaign of 1987–1989.[3] The explanations offered are not very satisfactory. First, some argue that U.S. policy toward Noriega changed with the discovery of his alleged criminal activities: trafficking in drugs, murder, commerce in prohibited technology goods with Cuba,[4] supplying arms to leftist guerilla groups, and election rigging. This explanation is unsatisfactory on two counts. Because other heads of governments in Latin America and elsewhere have engaged in these activities, it would be necessary to explain why Noriega was singled out for punishment. Furthermore, observers generally agree that the U.S. government was aware of these accusations long before it chose to rid Panama of Noriega: the drug charge apparently was known in the early 1970s; the election rigging, of which the U.S. embassy in Panama was well aware, occurred in 1984;[5] and the most celebrated murder (of Hugo Spadafora) happened in 1985, when there were immediate accusations of military involvement.[6] Knowledge of Noriega's crimes at best provides a prima facie motive as to why the United States might have initiated a confrontation anytime after Barletta's removal from the presidency (considered in chapter 6).

Complementary to the explanation of criminal activity was the argument that Noriega's drug dealings motivated intervention. If the drug allegations are true in 1988, then they were also true when he took control of the military in 1983, at which point he would have been considerably easier to remove than at the end of the decade. However, as Senator Paul Simon pointed out on April 28, 1988, "We tolerated [Noriega's] drug dealings because he was helping the contras."[7] And, according to the February 1988 congressional testimony of José Blandon, Noriega's erstwhile consul in New York, Noriega allowed the training of contra soldiers in Panama at the request of Oliver North. The general also allowed North and North's associate Secord to establish three dummy corporations in Panama as fronts for contra funding. And, according to the congressional testimony of Francis J. McNeil (April 1988), Noriega offered to run sabotage missions in Nicaragua. Moreover, according to *Wall Street Journal* reporter Frederick Kempe, Noriega actually ran an ongoing espionage mission against the Sandinistas from Managua and conducted at least one sabotage mission—exploding several forceful bombs at Managua's military headquarters—in March 1985. Kempe adds that Noriega directly contributed to the contras, allowed Howard Air Force Base to be used as a counter-Sandinista spy base in direct contravention of the Canal treaties, and even offered to assassinate Nicaraguan leaders in 1985.[8] Little wonder, then, that when Senator Jesse Helms introduced legislation in 1985 to cut off economic aid to Panama, CIA director William Casey urged the senator

to withdraw it. According to a Senate source, "Casey was very ada-
mant about it. He said Noriega was doing things for the U.S. that
Helms didn't know about."[9] Clearly, Noriega's drug dealings did not
present an insurmountable obstacle to cooperation with him in the
view of U.S. officials. Indeed, the Reagan administration appeared to
actively conceal the general's drug role. In 1986, after briefing Attorney General Edwin Meese III about his investigation into drug trafficking in Central America, U.S. Attorney (in Miami) Jeffrey Kellner
was told by Meese to suspend his inquiry.[10]

Other actions of the U.S. government suggest that it was not in-
tensely concerned about the general's drug-related activities until after it decided he had to go. As surprising as it may seem in retrospect,
in May 1986 John Lawn, director of the U.S. Drug Enforcement
Agency, sent a letter to Noriega expressing "deep appreciation for
[your] vigorous anti-drug policy."[11] Sent only a month before the revelations of Noriega's crimes in the U.S. press, the letter reflected either
extraordinary ignorance and naivete or a purposeful public endorse-
ment of the general. And in May 1987—a year after the newspaper
revelations about Noriega's drug involvement—Attorney General
Meese, the highest ranking law-enforcement official in the United
States, congratulated the Panamanian government on its cooperation
in a joint U.S.-Panamanian antidrug action. One can presume that
no such cooperation would have been possible without Noriega's
agreement. Furthermore, the U.S. Justice Department was not the
only law-enforcement agency complimenting Panama: only the previous month, the International Police Organization (INTERPOL)
presented Noriega with its medal of honor for his contribution to
the struggle against terrorism and drug trafficking.[12] But by journalistic reports, in June or July 1987 the Reagan administration
apparently decided to force Noriega out.[13] It seems unusual to
commend a government for aiding in drug enforcement one month
and then decide to overthrow it for drug trafficking the next. Thus,
the drug trafficking explanation of Noriega's overthrow is not
convincing.

Some Latin American nationalists argue that the decision to move
against Noriega was part of a larger campaign to prevent the Canal
from passing out of U.S. control and timed to preempt the Panamanian presidential election scheduled for 1989. By this argument, the
U.S. government feared the victory of a president antagonistic to its

interests in a Noriega-managed election. To avoid this outcome, the United States acted to remove the general and clear the way for a Panamanian government that would permit revision of the Torrijos-Carter Treaties to allow U.S. bases to remain in the country and authorize U.S. control over the Canal after 2000. The extension of this argument was that the timing of the December 1989 invasion was set by the treaty requirement that the Panama Canal Commission be headed by a Panamanian as of January 1, 1990. According to this argument, the Bush administration needed a client government to appoint a client administrator.

Although this explanation was ridiculed in the U.S. press, it is not groundless. The 1977 treaties passed the Canal to Panama unconditionally on January 1, 2000. Notwithstanding this legal obligation, in Panama on October 23, 1986, U.S. ambassador Arthur Davis delivered a speech in which he tied the transfer of the Canal to domestic political changes: "Fully functioning democratic institutions in Panama are the best guarantee to Americans and Panamanians alike for success in the turnover of the Canal to Panama." Without precisely saying that the U.S. government would not transfer the Canal to a Panamanian regime of which it disapproved, Panamanians so interpreted the statement, explicitly so by the head of the mainstream Christian Democratic party.[14] A nationalist did not have to be paranoid to conclude that contingency plans to block transfer of the Canal were being prepared.[15]

Despite Davis's statement, it is difficult to believe that the campaign to overthrow Noriega and the subsequent invasion was primarily motivated by U.S. hopes of a major revision of the Canal treaties. Certainly some U.S. politicians would cancel the treaties and maintain U.S. control of the Canal indefinitely, if such were possible. Ronald Reagan fervently attacked the Carter-Torrijos Treaties during the presidential campaign of 1980, and politicians of similar views could be found in the White House and Congress.[16]

However, given the decline in the relative importance of the Canal (see chapter 3), it is difficult to believe that treaty revision would have been the primary motivation of the campaign against Noriega. That such could be a by-product of an extended U.S. military occupation of Panama could not be ruled out. But this would be the consequence of invasion, occupation, and puppet governments, not the cause of the interventions of the 1980s.

Still others argued that the real motivation for overthrowing Noriega was to guarantee access to military bases after 2000, when the treaties required their removal. This argument has some prima facie credibility because in the 1980s the military bases represented the most important U.S. asset in Panama. Until the 1980s when Honduras permitted "temporary" use of its territory for U.S. military installations, only two countries in the hemisphere had U.S. bases: Cuba and Panama, both countries that the United States held in a semicolonial relationship. Compared to the bases in the former Canal Zone, the Guantanamo Naval Base in Cuba had been of minor strategic importance even before the Cuban revolution limited its use. On a tactical level, the Panamanian bases served important functions for all the major direct or surrogate U.S. military interventions in the region—Guatemala (1954), Cuba (1961), the Dominican Republic (1964), Chile (1973), Grenada (1983), and El Salvador and Nicaragua throughout the 1980s. On the ideological level, until 1983 the United States operated in the Zone the famous School of the Americas for the indoctrination and acculturation of Latin American military officers, many of whom became some of the more infamous dictators in the hemisphere, which prompted the nickname "School of the Tyrants."[17]

After the 1960s the military significance of the interoceanic waterway declined,[18] while the importance of the military bases in the Zone increased.[19] The significance of the Canal has declined for two main reasons. First, technical change in the transport industry has drastically reduced costs of transcontinental movement of freight over land; thus, a smaller proportion of tonnage would go through the Canal even if it were to be expanded and modernized (see chapter 3). Second, for military purposes the Canal declined in significance because the major U.S. warships were too large to use it.

However, if the end were to secure use of the bases, it is not clear that antagonizing Noriega would be the means. Until the breakdown of relations, Noriega had moved the Panamanian government and the Defense Forces away from the progressive foreign policy of Torrijos. He had also cooperated with U.S. ventures in the region and had risked popular indignation by permitting major U.S. military exercises in the country for three consecutive years.[20] Nevertheless, maintaining U.S. bases in Panama, hardly a trivial interest for the U.S.

government, may have eventually contributed to the decision to invade as U.S. relations with Noriega grew increasingly hostile. To be sure, according to the Independent Commission of Inquiry into the U.S. Invasion of Panama headed by former Attorney General Ramsey Clark, during the first five months of 1989 the Bush administration had offered to drop U.S. drug trafficking charges against Noriega in exchange for an agreement to extend the leases of U.S. military bases beyond the year 2000.[21]

Our interpretation of the U.S. motivation for the post-1987 campaign against Noriega contains several aspects. First, our explanation involves the key issue of succession within the Panamanian Defense Forces. By the mid-1980s, General Noriega was a serious embarrassment to the Reagan administration: he had overthrown a president whose election while fraudulent had been endorsed by the United States; revelations about his allegedly criminal activities had provoked an outcry in Congress, which became an election issue in 1988; and he began to balk at actively supporting U.S. policy in Central America (a topic we discuss at greater length). From this point of view, the question becomes, why did the Reagan administration not move against Noriega sooner? The answer remains: The U.S. government feared that if Noriega were removed, he might be replaced by Roberto Díaz Herrera, second-in-command of the Defense Forces until June 1987 and Torrijos's first cousin, who was perceived by the White House to be a "leftist."[22]

During 1986 and the first half of 1987, U.S. policy toward Noriega was ambivalent, indicating a strategy of seeking to pressure and influence rather than remove him. Although there were strong criticisms, there were also episodes of close cooperation (e.g., the military exercises). With the dismissal of Díaz Herrera from the Defense Forces in June 1987,[23] U.S. policy dramatically changed.[24] In a 1988 article, Millet argued that Noriega "made a major mistake" in removing Díaz Herrera.[25] Indeed he did, but not primarily for the reason Millet suggests—the inflammatory accusations issued by the ousted colonel. The removal of Díaz Herrera represented a miscalculation on Noriega's part because it removed the threat that he might be replaced by a "leftist" and thereby freed the Reagan/Bush administrations to follow their interventionist instincts.

Presented with the apparent opportunity to rid itself of Noriega, the Reagan administration seemed motivated to do so because of its obsession with pursuing its contra strategy against Nicaragua.[26] The general had been cooperative to a degree, but the increasing failure of that strategy required a more active involvement, which a post-Noriega regime might supply. Some evidence suggests that the White House saw in Eric Arturo Delvalle, Noriega's puppet president, a more receptive audience for its policy toward Nicaragua. The White House had for some time been pressuring Noriega to more actively support the contras. The most publicized episode was a December 1985 visit to Panama and meeting with Noriega by Admiral John Poindexter, who would later be indicted for his part in the Iran-contra arms scandal. Reports at the time suggested that Poindexter, among other things, had sought Noriega's agreement to train contras in Panama. Reportedly, Noriega's growing commitment to the Contadora peace process led him to resist many of Poindexter's initiatives. Subsequently, Poindexter was reported as one of the unnamed sources revealing Noriega's crimes to U.S. journalists in mid-1986, leaks designed to pressure the general into a more procontra policy.

By mid-1987 events had come together to prompt the Reagan administration to act against Noriega. The dreaded Díaz Herrera was out of the succession to the command of the Defense Forces, and matters were going badly for the contras in both Nicaragua and Washington. Opposition in Congress to contra aid had solidified; Daniel Ortega, president of Nicaragua, made a dramatic trip to Washington that proved a diplomatic coup (he met with Speaker of the House of Representatives Jim Wright); and the Central American presidents were moving toward a regional peace solution, which would result in their signing a joint accord in August 1987 (the "Arias Plan"). Pressure mounted for a peaceful solution to the Nicaraguan conflict that would result in the worst-case outcome from the point of view of the Reagan administration: disintegration of the contras and formal acceptance of the Sandinista government by its neighbors. Something very close to this occurred in 1989.

Finally, a consistent theme in U.S. policy toward Panama has been concern for political stability (albeit by the U.S. definition). While Díaz Herrera's June 1987 denunciations did not reveal any new information about Noriega, they were startling because they came from within the power structure.[27] The inferred breaking of the ranks precipitated an outburst of popular protest, perhaps perceived detrimental to U.S. interests by policy makers in Washington.

In a sentence, we argue that the U.S. government moved against Noriega as part of its plan to rid Central America of a leftist regime in Nicaragua and moved no sooner largely because it feared creating such a regime in Panama if it did. Although we cannot conclusively establish this hypothesis, it is consistent with other circumstantial evidence. During the propaganda campaign against Noriega in 1988 and 1989, U.S. officials made it clear that their goal was neither to dismantle nor even reform the Defense Forces. Indeed, on March 3, 1988, with the economic warfare raging, Marlin Fitzwater, U.S. presidential spokesman, said that the Reagan administration envisioned the military "playing an important and constructive role under a civilian regime."[28] For his part, Secretary of State George Shultz almost waxed eloquently on the virtues of the Defense Forces, referring to the need to "maintain its integrity" (perhaps an unfortunate choice of words); he described the Panamanian military as "a strong and honorable force that has a significant and proper role to play and we want to see it play that role. . . . We're for the Panamanian people, and for that matter for the Panama Defense Force."[29] This was a strange position to take if Washington sought to eliminate the drug trade because there is general agreement that the Panamanian military was riddled with corruption, particularly among its leadership.[30] On this issue the Reagan administration came into conflict with the Panamanian opposition that it allegedly supported and rejected the opposition's demand that a list of officers be retired along with Noriega.[31] This tolerance for a military command, described by a member of the U.S. Southern Command as "a band of thugs and thieves,"[32] is inexplicable if the Reagan administration were primarily concerned with ending drug trafficking or protecting the security of the Canal. It is, however, perfectly consistent with a policy of fostering a more reliable and conservative commander of the Defense Forces who would form a government more pliant with regard to U.S. regional strategy. The Reagan administration justified its blind eye to the activities of the other high officers by claiming it as part of a policy to provoke a split in the ranks of the Defense Forces. Of course, when the invasion came, the Defense Forces were dismantled, but this proved a necessary result of the initial military action and subsequent survival of the Endara government.

Destabilization and the U.S. Economic Sanctions, 1987–1989

The policy of economic sanctions began with the decision to suspend U.S. economic aid to Panama in July 1987. The World Bank followed suit in November by cancelling a planned loan of $50 million. Then, in December the U.S. government suspended Panama's sugar quota and instructed all U.S. directors of multilateral agencies to vote against proposed loans and aid to Panama. These measures were little more than short-term annoyances. The United States planned to accelerate matters by destroying Panama's monetary system, a plan initiated after Noriega's indictment in Miami for drug trafficking, on February 4, 1988.[33] The principal instrument of the campaign of economic sanctions was a March 3, 1988, document issued by the U.S. State Department freezing $50 million of deposits of the Banco Nacional de Panamá (BNP) in New York banks.[34] The BNP promptly notified commercial banks in Panama that it would be unable to carry out its internal check-clearing function and required the commercial banks to limit withdrawals. The next day, March 4, Panama's National Banking Commission, concerned with escalating capital flight as well as liquidity pressure, closed Panama's banks.

From press reports and statements by U.S. officials, apparently the new set of economic sanctions was designed to provoke a cash-flow crisis in Panama ("starve the economy of cash," as the press frequently put it). This was to be achieved by freezing the BNP's deposits in the United States and blocking the payments of various revenues to the Panamanian government. Given the rationale that the sitting government was illegitimate and that Delvalle was the legal president, payments were diverted to an escrow account at the New York Federal Reserve Bank for the Delvalle government in exile. This diversion of funds proved embarrassing in subsequent months when the U.S. National Security Council had to block an investigation of Delvalle for allegedly embezzling the funds directed to his imaginary Panamanian government.[35] The inspiration for this strategy came from the special characteristic of the Panamanian monetary system— its use of U.S. dollars. The strategy was simple: Panama used dollars; if the Reagan administration could cut off Panama's overseas supply of dollars, then the economy would grind to a halt for lack of liquidity ("cash" as some crudely put it). In other countries governments can always meet their obligations by "printing" money (at the risk of inflation, of course), but this was impossible in Panama because it lacked a national currency.

With the banks closed, businesses in Panama accepted neither checks nor credit cards for payment. Cash, increasingly the only medium of exchange, grew shorter in supply as the psychology of crisis led to money hoarding. On March 11, Reagan announced that the United States would withhold the $6.5 million monthly payment for the Canal and would suspend Panama's trade preferences that affected approximately 30 percent of Panama's exports to the United States.[36] On the same day, Delvalle's lawyers made public an agreement with the New York–based majority shareholder of the transisthmian pipeline company to direct payments due the Panamanian government to Delvalle's escrow account at the Federal Reserve Bank in New York (instead of to Noriega). And in an action more symbolic than significant, the U.S. government grounded Air Panama's two planes and cancelled its daily flights between Miami and Panama City (though flights by U.S. carriers continued).

Matters came to a head on March 14, when Noriega's government missed its first payroll of about $30 million to 145,000 public employees (20 percent of the labor force). Among these employees were 800 dock workers, who reacted with a strike; they were soon joined by 80,000 other organized workers throughout the country.[37] This national strike made it appear that Noriega's grip on the country was weakening, but we must stress that the strikers' primary demand was that they be paid, not that the government change. Evidence neither suggests that Noriega enjoyed any popularity among the strikers nor implies that the strikers were committed to the cause of the National Civic Crusade, the major domestic opposition group.[38]

Faced with these pressures from organized labor, Noriega's government announced a plan for partial wage payments with commemorative coins, but the offer was rejected. Emboldened, the National Civic Crusade, which had suspended its first strike for the trade fair, called for a second on March 21. At this point Under Secretary of State for Latin American Affairs Elliot Abrams, in a flush of anticipated victory, began uttering his daily predictions that Noriega was "hanging onto power by his fingertips" and that his days were numbered.[39] Yet, on March 26, with the dock workers on strike for their twelfth day, the Panamanian government took over the Balboa docks and two large flour mills. This decisive action marked the turning point of the crisis. The government quickly began to devise alternative means of payment for employees and simultaneously received taxes and fees from multinational companies operating in Panama. With the liquidity shortage apparently waning, workers gradually returned to their jobs, and by the end of March the National Civic Crusade strike was disintegrating.

Among the payments Noriega received was $2.5 million (U.S.) at the end of March from Eastern Airlines, Texaco, and United Brands. This source of revenue for the Panamanian government represented a major loophole in the Reagan administration's tactic of "cash strangulation," and one can only wonder why it was not anticipated. When corporate payments began to flow, White House officials obtained from the U.S. Internal Revenue Service a ruling that the U.S. foreign tax credit would apply only to profit taxes paid into Delvalle's escrow account, not to Noriega. Relatively speaking, small sums of money were involved. Only in the short term could these U.S. measures exert serious pressure, for many tactics were possible to circumvent the U.S. liquidity war if Noriega lasted long enough, which he did. Freezing the Panamanian government's assets and diverting payments did not in practice have the full powerful effect anticipated by the United States. As of mid-July 1989, after the campaign had been in progress fifteen months, barely $300 million in blocked property and assets were held in the United States, about half of which was immediately liquid ("cash").[40]

Perhaps recognizing the urgency of the moment, the Reagan administration dispatched 1,300 new troops to the Canal area to join the 10,000 already there. It is possible that White House strategists looked back (fondly no doubt) to the days when the mere appearance of force could bring Panamanian governments to heel. Noriega, however, countered with the formation of armed "dignity brigades" in urban working-class areas; these would prove more effective than U.S. planners expected when the invasion came.

The situation was quickly slipping out of Washington's control (if, indeed, it had ever been within it), and subsequent measures came forth with an air of desperation. On April 8, 1988, the U.S. Treasury Department announced the next punitive measure in the liquidity war: payments of all taxes and fees to the Panamanian government were prohibited. The consequence of this bold move quickly proved farcical. For failure to pay its electricity bill, the U.S. embassy found itself without power, prompting the White House to modify its latest move to exempt payments of utility bills, departure fees, and taxes on airplane tickets.

As the sanctions began to prove themselves ineffective in removing Noriega, the U.S. government found itself increasingly isolated and under diplomatic attack. At a meeting of SELA (Latin American Economic System) on March 29, 1988, twenty-two Latin governments (including Pinochet's Chile) called for an end to U.S. sanctions and pledged to consider economic aid to Panama. Eventually aid did come from Mexico (concessionary oil sales), Western Europe, and Taiwan, among other sources. In addition, Latin governments offered their central banks to aid Panama in financial intermediation to end the liquidity crisis. By early May the financial pressure had dissipated sufficiently for Noriega's government to permit the reopening of banks in the country, albeit preserving extensive restrictions on withdrawals.[41] Diplomatically, the United States suffered repeated defeats as countries accepted Noriega's new president, Solis Palma, as the de facto head of state. The most blatant embarrassment for the Reagan administration came when the new West German ambassador presented his credentials to Solis Palma on June 14, 1988.[42] The general had weathered the storm, and the Reagan administration's policy to remove him had unambiguously failed.

If there were to be an overthrow of Noriega, the time was ripe in mid to late March. Indeed, a palace coup was assayed, but uncertain support from a divided U.S. administration and poor communication among the putschists doomed it to failure.[43] At another level, it was a problem that the requisite political organization, which could take advantage of Noriega's difficulties, did not exist. In consequence, the U.S. sanctions generated enormous economic damage without seriously threatening the rule of the man they sought to remove from power. The legacy of the U.S. campaign proved to be a scarcely weakened Noriega, a decimation of the Panamanian banking system,[44] a shattered private sector,[45] and untold misery for the country's poor. In brief, the U.S. campaign brought the economy to its knees and an indicted drug dealer to his feet. By various estimates, as of early June 1988, open unemployment had at least doubled to more than 20 percent,[46] and all economic indicators were down sharply.[47]

Estimates of the fall in economic activity during 1988 range from the official figure of 17.2 percent up to 25.6 (according to the economic consulting firm Indesa).[48] The U.S. State Department estimated that as much as 40 percent of this decline could be attributed to the sanctions,[49] implying that absent sanctions real GDP would have fallen by 10 percent. This estimate of the impact was certainly too low. From 1980 to 1987, Panamanian GDP increased by 22 percent, compared to only 10 percent for all other Latin American countries (except Cuba); moreover, the Panamanian economy had grown at a real rate of 4.7 percent in 1985, 3.4 percent in 1986, and 2.4 percent in 1987. In 1988 Latin American economies as a whole (including Panama) grew at 0.6 percent, and Canal cargo increased by 5.4 percent; thus, it appears unreasonable to assume that Panama's economic growth in 1988 would have been negative without U.S. sanctions. Without a formal modeling of the economy, one could reasonably estimate that virtually the entire decline in GDP resulted from the impact of the sanctions.

The political change generated by these heavy economic costs was not the fall of Noriega, but initially quite the contrary: increased international sympathy and perhaps even some incremental domestic support for Noriega, who was seen by many as a victim of and bulwark against U.S. aggression in Panama and Latin America. The "forces of democracy and reform" from the private sector had been weakened, the environment for the international banking center had been spoiled (perhaps irreparably), and the U.S. government had been isolated and ostracized by the community of nations. Eventually, however, it is likely that the prolonged economic suffering engendered by the U.S. sanctions made the Panamanians more open to a change of government, to one offering the prospect of better relations with the United States. In this respect, the economic sanctions in Panama had a parallel effect to the contra war (combined with economic sanctions) in Nicaragua, and the ultimate electoral victory of Violeta Chamorro.

Election, Coup, and Invasion

Having successfully defied the attempt (admittedly clumsy) to depose him, in mid-1988 Noriega began to reconsolidate his rule over Panama. In this venture he proved less successful than in his short-term survival. The situation in Panama from July 1988, by which time the immediate threat of overthrow had passed, until the U.S. invasion of December 1989 was increasingly unstable: the general was unable to produce a formula that would either overcome Washington's obsession with his removal or stabilize his dictatorial regime for day-to-day rule. It is tempting in hindsight to view the eventual invasion as the inevitable consequence of successive developments. We consider this question at the end of our review of events during 1988 and 1989.

From June to December 1988, the governments of Panama and the United States engaged in a war of words that did little to resolve the situation. The diplomatic highlight of this period was the negotiating that lasted several months between Noriega and representatives of the Reagan administration over his "voluntary" retirement from the Panamanian scene. These discussions served only to make the Reagan administration appear hypocritical and foolish: apparently negotiating the graceful and well-funded exit of the man it had served with an indictment for trafficking in drugs.[50]

Meanwhile, and somewhat unnoticed amid the confusion, Delvalle still claimed the presidency of Panama with U.S. blessing. To improve this claim as legitimate president of Panama, Delvalle in November announced that along with five opposition parties he would form a provisional government, with the purpose of holding elections once Noriega was removed from his position as head of the Defense Forces. Perhaps to undermine this tactic by Delvalle, at the end of the year the sitting government of Panama announced that the presidential election scheduled for 1989 would be held on May 7. Initial speculation that Noriega himself would be the official candidate ended with the announcement that Carlos Duque, a Noriega business associate, would stand as the presidential hopeful of the pro-Noriega COLINA coalition.

In anticipation of the election, the opposition sought to forge a unified front. After some conflict, particularly over the position of Ricardo Arias Calderón of the Christian Democratic party on the electoral ticket, a new umbrella organization was formed—the Democratic Opposition Civil Alliance (Alianza Democrática de la Oposición Civil, ADOC). ADOC elements managed to reach agreement on Guillermo Endara, a wealthy lawyer and businessman,[51] to head the electoral ticket, with Ricardo Arias Calderón and Guillermo Ford as the vice-presidental candidates. Endara represented a compromise after the Authentic Panamanian party (PPA) had refused to accept Arias Calderón. Endara had served as a functionary in his party very much in the shadow of Arnulfo Arias, whose death in August 1988 had left the party in disarray.

As the election date approached, apparent divisions in the opposition manifested themselves. Although the major demand of the ADOC had been the removal of Noriega as head of the army, in February Endara announced that if elected he would move cautiously with respect to the military and would take no steps resulting in a "high political cost." This apparent softening on the Noriega question provoked Arias Calderón to reaffirm the nonnegotiable intention to remove Noriega if ADOC won the election. As the economic platforms of the two coalitions were strikingly similar, the election took on the character of a plebiscite on Noriega's rule.[52]

No doubt Noriega intended for the election to be a vehicle to stabilize his control over Panama, perhaps anticipating a close vote (as in 1984) that could be presented as a victory for Duque. This proved a poor strategy in retrospect, for the opposition won overwhelmingly. Soon after the polls closed, the government suspended vote counting and declared the election null and void, on the grounds that the United States had aided ADOC. At this point the Noriega regime had few remaining options, and the question was not whether but for how long it would survive. Particularly important for the external relations of the regime, the Organization of American States (OAS) abandoned its earlier sympathy and overwhelmingly passed a resolution condemning the election fraud. In light of the subsequent invasion of Panama, it is important to note that the resolution, which the U.S. representative supported, included a passage against foreign intervention: "Reaffirming: That no state or group of states has the right to intervene, directly or indirectly, no matter what the motive, in the internal or external affairs of any other."[53]

On the basis of this resolution, the OAS sent a delegation to Panama to seek to negotiate an end to the political impasse between the Noriega regime and its opponents. After a second visit by the OAS, the Noriega government agreed to talks with the opposition, which began in July 1989. The Bush administration officially supported the OAS initiative, but it was doubtful that the administration treated it seriously; it preferred more forceful and unilateral means to remove the dictator. On October 3, 1989, about 200 members of the Defense Forces attacked the Panamanian military headquarters, briefly seizing it and reportedly holding Noriega captive for an extended period. However, troops loyal to the general overwhelmed the rebels before the end of the day, in yet another abortive attempt to end the tenure of the Noriega regime. If the Bush administration's efforts to remove the general had seemed poorly calculated and badly planned before, they now appeared merely incompetent. Bush's first public comment on the coup while its fate lay in balance included the assertion that the United States was not involved. Yet it is now part of the public record that with prior knowledge of the coup attempt, the U.S. Southern Command intervened and moved to block roads by which troops loyal to Noriega could come to his aid; however, this was not done until hours after the coup began. Furthermore, a crucial roadway was left unattended, which allowed the loyalist forces to rescue their commander. Curiously, the Bush administration had chosen the previous week to remove the chief of the Southern Command and the previous month to replace the second-in-command. The U.S. press offered its consensus interpretation: the Bush administration had bungled its chance to remove the general, and in consequence Noriega was more solidly in power than ever.

While certainly the Bush administration mismanaged the October coup, given that the policy was to force Noriega's removal, there would seem little to recommend the position that the general emerged from it in a strong position. A comparison of the situation in mid-1988 and late 1989 suggests that Noriega may have finally achieved the status of "hanging by his fingertips" (as Abrams had put it so hopefully in March 1988). While the economy was feeling the initial pressures of the sanctions in mid-1988, eighteen months later it was in collapse. Early estimates for the first ten months of 1989 suggest that the economy had contracted by an additional 3 or 4 percent; the final figures for the year will undoubtedly be much worse. Prior to the aborted elections of May 1989 Panama had enjoyed considerable sympathy from other countries, but by the end of 1989 Noriega's regime was diplomatically isolated, and the OAS had condemned the government and the general by name. Furthermore, the Defense Forces had shown themselves to be splintered by the October coup attempt, and Noriega, reportedly, had grown distrustful of most of his subordinate officers. These comparisons suggest that Manuel

Noriega's days in power would not have lasted long into the next decade, perhaps not far into the new year. While this could not be proved, one would have thought that the burden of proof would have fallen upon those who removed him by violence.

Marx commented that history always repeats itself, first as tragedy, then as farce. In the case of U.S. military intervention in Panama, this sequence reversed itself: the U.S.-supported "uprising" of 1903 was in many ways farcical, a relatively bloodless parody of a struggle for independence involving the imposition of a subordinate government; the invasion of 1989 was tragic, the bloodiest and most violent week in Panamanian history to impose another, probably subordinate, government.[54] It is beyond the scope of this book to treat in detail this extraordinary reversion to the diplomacy of violence. The total cost of the invasion for Panamanians exceeded monetary calculation. Wholesale looting in retail outlets alone produced uninsured losses in excess of $400 million. At least two thousand family homes were destroyed. The national unemployment rate by mid-April 1990 had risen to between 30 and 35 percent, with higher rates in Panama City and Colon.[55] Most estimates of total deaths surpassed 700, with some estimates rising above 5,000.[56] Initial estimates of the total economic loss from the invasion ranged from $1 billion to more than $2 billion.[57] The combination of the economic sanctions and the invasion resulted in a disaster without parallel in the history of the country. Indeed, President Endara himself acknowledged as much, calling his country's predicament in March 1990 "the worst crisis in its [Panama's] history, worse even than under Noriega."[58]

The much-publicized Bush administration's proposed aid figure of $1 billion does not begin to address the formidable task of reconstruction. First, the actual cash transfer is well below the total request. Roughly $400 million represents U.S. Export-Import Bank financing of imports from the United States. Another $130 million was earmarked for payment of arrears to multilateral agencies, thus money that would never reach Panama. Other parts of the $1 billion assistance package do not fall into the "aid" category: reducing U.S. corporate taxes for companies holding conventions in Panama, restoring Defense Department purchases from Panamanian firms (which had been suspended), and reopening the U.S. sugar quota. The first of two Panama aid packages approved by Congress, nominally $500 million, provided only $42 million in directly disbursable aid.

Second, the Endara government discovered that the funds frozen during the sanctions would prove slow in returning. For reasons not made clear by the Bush administration, the release of approximately $200 million of frozen Panamanian funds had still not occurred three months after the invasion. On March 20, 1990, Senator Patrick Leahy issued a cogent indictment of Bush's aid proposal before the Subcommittee on Foreign Relations:

Panama owes the multilateral development banks (MDBs) $540 million in arrears. It owes $265 million in new payments this year, for a total due to the MDBs in 1990 of $805 million. To pay off the arrears, Panama is to use $130 million of the $200 million in its assets we are still holding. Plus, you want Congress to appropriate $130 million to give to Panama to pay to the international development banks. And, Uncle Sam has to go to Japan and Western Europe and beg them to contribute another $130 million. Then, Nick Brady (U.S. Secretary of the Treasury) has to loan Panama $150 million to pay to the World Bank, which then loans Panama back $150 million to repay Nick Brady. After paying out over $800 million this year, Panama would get less than $400 million in loans from the banks. Panama would pay out $400 million *more* than it would get.

This is scarcely the nature or magnitude of economic assistance required by Panama to initiate the process of reconstruction.

On the political front, the invasion left Panama a country on the verge of anarchy, with U.S. troops providing standard police functions. For basic functions of law and order, the Southern Command ruled the country on a day-to-day basis, which provoked fears of a resurgence of Panamanian nationalism. With no functioning legislature, with a civil service demoralized by both the purge of alleged Noriega supporters and the threat of extensive lay-offs, and with a government of the country's white and wealthy elite installed on a U.S. military base, Panama embarked on an uncertain journey into the new decade.

Chapter Eight

Conclusion

A basic purpose of this book has been to analyze what went wrong in Panama. By the mid-1980s it was clear to even the casual observer that something was fundamentally amiss in the country; the problems manifested themselves in growing political instability that culminated in a repressive regime that finally fell to the first intervention in Spanish America by U.S. troops since the invasion of the Dominican Republic in 1965. With this political instability came a disastrous deterioration of the economy, which during the previous decades had displayed one of the better growth performances in the hemisphere.[1] Observers tended to attribute the decline of the economy to the country's political instability; they implied that a return to normality, with generous infusions of foreign aid, would bring growth and prosperity. We have shown that this view was erroneous. Certainly the collapse of the economy had political causes, namely U.S. sanctions and the destruction caused by the invasion itself. However, the politically generated collapse was a veil over economic deterioration of a more fundamental nature.

For decades Panama thrived on the basis of a trade- and service-based economy, to the detriment of the sectors that dominate the accumulation of wealth in virtually all countries: agriculture and manufacturing (and mining, though Panama has virtually none). International services and commerce fueled the engine of growth: transport (the Canal and the pipeline), storage and inventory (the Colon Free Trade Zone), finance (the International Financial Center), and a miscellaneous collection of other activities (e.g., flags of convenience shipping). The combination of these activities made for growth and a strong balance of payments situation.

First, and perhaps most fundamental, this emphasis upon tertiary economic activities, which characterized the economy since Europeans first landed on the isthmus, made for an unstable political system, as argued in chapter 1. It created a weak elite largely separated from the masses of Panamanians in terms of class, ethnicity, and ties to production. Before 1903 the Panamanian elite lacked the means to dominate the populace and establish an effective political system. This weakness became more pronounced with formal independence. The massive U.S. military and political presence created by building the Canal resulted virtually in colonial status for Panama into the 1930s. While the ensuing governments were not pure clients of Washington (for certainly neither Harmodio Arias nor his more famous brother were), the weakness of the Panamanian armed forces meant that maintaining civil order fundamentally rested with the U.S. embassy and military command.[2] In this sense, the invasion of December 1989 that destroyed the Panamanian Defense Forces and left U.S. troops to patrol the streets as policemen was not a new turn of events, but a return to the early days of the republic. The basis of this political weakness of Panama's elite was the nation's economic structure: the Canal, the pipeline, the free trade zone, and the financial center, all dependent upon the vicissitudes of the international economy, the goodwill of foreigners, and particularly of the United States government. The fact that the pivotal event in Panamanian history before 1977—the framing and signing of the Canal treaty of 1903—involved no Panamanian in any important role epitomized the country's existence in the twilight zone between colony and sovereign state.

As symbolic as the Canal was, after World War II it played a supporting, not a leading, role in the dominance of services over production in the economy, as demonstrated in detail in chapter 2. In 1950, manufacturing contributed less than 9 percent of GDP and agriculture almost 28 percent, for a total share of 36 percent. In 1955, the two together reached 39 percent, and though amid fluctuations this share would be regained in the mid-1960s, it would not be exceeded. In 1970, the two commodity-producing sectors declined to 27 percent of GDP, then 24 percent in 1975, 19 percent in 1980, and 18 percent in 1985. In no other country of the world (with the possible exception of island ministates and tourist-states such as Monaco) do agriculture and manufacturing contribute such a small share to national income.

This profound distortion of the economy away from production, pursued with particular vigor by the government in the 1970s, narrowly distributed the gains from growth. Presiding over this service-led development was the towering figure of Panamanian politics in the 1970s, Omar Torrijos, one of the most complex politicians of modern Latin America. On the one hand, Torrijos embarked upon a development strategy with a politically conservative emphasis upon attracting foreign capital. On the other hand, his government not only implemented more populist reforms than any other in the history of Panama but also fundamentally revised the Canal treaties. The former brought a veneer of prosperity to Panama, and the latter generated broad popular support that would make him a legendary figure after his death.

What is sometimes called the "Torrijos project," a basically conservative development strategy and populist reform, could not be sustained. At the immediate level, the problem was one of funding a populist social policy and sustaining unprofitable public enterprises while simultaneously pursuing a capitalist economic strategy that resulted in large fiscal deficits and mounting foreign debts by the end of the 1970s. As early as 1976, the Torrijos regime began to draw back from its populist program, most obviously by revising the labor code and instituting a wage freeze. And by the end of the decade, a clear shift was made toward business interests with the adoption of measures pressed by the IMF and the World Bank. Although respectable growth rates were regained during the last of the Torrijos years, the economy remained fundamentally weak. The boom associated with the financial sector was over. Initial success had been achieved in the context of a burgeoning supply of petrodollars and raiding the market shares of other offshore banking centers. In the process, the international service sectors had generated wage levels and a wage structure that made Panama a relatively unattractive site for foreign investment in manufacturing. Central to Torrijos's social contract was aggregate prosperity based on international services that benefited few Panamanians directly and a populist social program that promised wider distribution of those benefits. By the early 1980s, the distribution mechanisms were dormant, and the prosperity had reached its limit.

In chapters 3 and 4 we analyzed the incipient weakness of the international service sector. The problem with the service activities was not that individually or collectively they were inherently flawed as contributors to growth but rather that they could not sustain the burden of serving as the engine of growth. This lesson of the 1980s—international services were ill-suited to play the leading role in the long run—had been demonstrated repeatedly in Panama in the five hundred years after the Europeans discovered the isthmus. Again and again Panama passed through periods of boom and decline resulting from the caprices of international commerce and politics. In the cases of the Canal and the pipeline, decline was the result of technical changes in world transport and the shifting pattern of international trade. On purely economic calculations Panama benefited greatly from both the Canal and the pipeline, but by the 1980s their heyday had past.

The Colon Free Trade Zone is essentially a great warehouse, and its rapid growth in the 1970s represented its filling of a market niche in hemispheric transport. Further growth could not run significantly ahead of the expansion of transisthmian transport, itself limited by the increase in interoceanic trade. In any case, the Colon Free Trade Zone produces little value added in relation to the commodities stored and moved. Whatever the advantages of the International Financial Center, its operation reinforced Panama's use of the dollar as its domestic currency. In practice, then, the government had no independent monetary policy, no exchange rate devaluation option to promote trade balance, and a particular vulnerability to U.S. economic pressure. Taken together, the many direct and indirect benefits of the IFC were quite substantial, but not without cost. Not least among the costs was the laundering of ill-gotten money, an unavoidable development given the secrecy laws that were to a great extent the raison d'être of the IFC. Perhaps more basic, dependence upon highly liquid capital inflows continuously and closely constrains the policies of any government. Domestic policies perceived as threatening to depositors can set off quick and massive capital outflow, particularly because the IFC had many competitors in the Caribbean and around the world for international deposits. By the early 1980s, before domestic political instability became acute, the IFC began to stagnate, owing in part to the international debt crisis, the contraction of the Latin American economies, and new offshore banking legislation in the United States.

By the 1980s the international service sectors had run their course as sources of dynamism. Panama required a new development strategy, a need emphasized in the World Bank report of 1985. The Bank's answer was (and is) to promote new manufacturing and agricultural exports through deregulating and further eviscerating social programs and the labor code. As demonstrated in earlier chapters, the Bank's approach is tantamount to saying that because government intervention in Panama during the 1970s and 1980s was inefficient then all government intervention is inefficient. It is also tantamount to ignoring the important role of the government in the East Asian success stories during the twentieth century or the U.S. and German successes during the nineteenth century.

The development approach of the Endara government echoes the Bank's obsession with laissez-faire economics and export promotion. Endara's second vice-president, Guillermo Ford, has been stumping for private enterprise, promising to sell off all the government's productive assets.[3] The chief economist of the Christian Democratic party and a leading adviser to the present government, Guillermo Chapman, holds out the prospect of turning Panama into another Hong Kong. The problems with Chapman's Hong Kong vision are manifold.

First, any serious historical look at Hong Kong's development experience would reveal that the conditions under which it transformed itself from a strictly entrepot economy into a major industrial exporter cannot be reproduced in Panama. Among other things, Hong Kong's industrialization was predicated upon, as succinctly put by Lawrence Krause, "massive inflows of resources of labor, capital and entrepreneurial skill (especially from Shanghai) between 1948 and 1951."[4] The other Asian entrepot turned tiger, Singapore, is anything but a model of a laissez-faire, private enterprise development strategy. After Singapore's expulsion from Malaysia in 1965, the government actively intervened in the economy by manipulating market incentives and playing a major role in capital formation. For instance, in 1984, 64 percent of all Singapore's gross national saving originated in the public sector.[5] When one considers not the city-states, but the two Asian tigers with appreciable agricultural sectors as well (hence, more appropriate for comparison to the case of Panama), both South Korea and Taiwan have relied upon extensive government roles in economic affairs. Alice Amsden, for one, has described the South Korean government's development policy as purposefully "getting the prices wrong."[6] It is also noteworthy that income distribution in both South Korea and Taiwan is markedly more equal than in Panama or the other market economies of the developing world. This feature has promoted the development of their internal markets and, as observed by Ranis,[7] allowed a more organic evolution from import-substituting to export-substituting industrialization.

Second, the success of East Asian exports was based in the initial period on low-wage, labor-intensive industries. As suggested by the Krueger model,[8] after early success and capital accumulation, labor shortages and wage increases lead progressively to the emergence of more capital-intensive industries. As we argued in both chapters 2 and 6, Panama's wage structure has been distorted by the widespread presence of capital-intensive international services, which made an export strategy based on low wages problematic. Coupled with the reality that practically all of the Caribbean Basin and most of Latin America are also being exhorted to expand labor-intensive exports, it seems more prudent for Panama in the 1990s to promote a range of products with intermedite capital intensity.

Because international competitiveness is unlikely to be attained in the short run, production for the domestic market would be important during an initial period. Although more capital-intensive production is more difficult to justify with a small domestic market, flexible manufacturing technology is loosening this constraint. Nonetheless, top priority should be placed on fashioning a regional common market that would allow greater scope for scale economies and more efficient production. There is no reason why import substitution and export promotion cannot be pursued simultaneously, in either manufacturing or agriculture.[9]

The World Bank's 1985 study on Panama also stresses the importance of promoting agricultural exports. Although correct in identifying agriculture as central to Panama's future growth, the World Bank's overwhelming, even exclusive, emphasis upon the export role, as argued in chapter 5, is highly questionable. In all countries with a substantial rural population, a successful agricultural sector performs four roles: it generates export revenue; it provides a market for industrial goods; it supplies the domestic market with food and raw materials; and it frees labor for urban employment. While the four functions need not be in conflict, the World Bank approach would make this the case and explicitly treated the first two as such.

The distribution of land in Panama became more unequal after World War II. This increased inequality was associated with a substantial expansion of the agricultural frontier: the area in farms almost doubled from 1950 to 1980. Perhaps no better example can be found of the principle that land is rarely scarce in the aggregate, only scarce for the poor. Probably the agrarian policy of the Torrijos period, particularly in the early years, slowed the process of land concentration; however, to provide the great majority of rural Panamanians with adequate farm incomes requires a much more substantial effort.

Evidence presented in chapter 5 showed that agricultural production is highly correlated with size of farm. In general, small farmers grow crops, rather than graze cattle; and within the crop sector small farmers produce basic staples rather than the principal export commodities—bananas and sugar. Under certain conditions small producers might abandon their preference for basic staple production and take quickly to the "nontraditional" exports in vogue with World Bank programs—for example, luxury vegetables and fruits and ornamental flowers. But in Panama there was no evidence of this pattern; and, in any event, it would not be achieved through market incentives alone. Over the period from 1950 to 1980 trends suggest that expanding export production relative to producing basic staples would go hand in hand with an increased concentration of land.

There would be three likely consequences of shifting to a more market-oriented and export-oriented agricultural sector in Panama, a tendency that began to take hold in the mid-1980s. First, the elimination of protection, subsidies, and price supports for basic staples would force domestic producers to face international prices,[10] which themselves are distorted by the myriad market interventions employed in developed countries.[11] As a result, small farmers would be driven from the market in Panama; greater landlessness and urban migration would occur. Second, more market-oriented agriculture would result in the concentration of landholdings, which in turn has been associated with more inefficient use of land.[12] Large farms and ranches in Panama hold considerable land idle, while on small farms this luxury cannot be afforded. Third, greater export orientation would be employment reducing. The export commodity stressed for the future by the World Bank was beef, a land-extensive activity with low value added from labor. Furthermore, for any given product, less labor is used to produce it on large farms than on small.

A policy for Panama based on smallholdings would potentially achieve all the goals previously mentioned for the agricultural sector: improve distribution, increase employment, and reduce urban migration. Because small farms tend to produce basic staples, it would likewise increase food self-sufficiency. And because it would result in more extensive cultivation through less idle land and less grazing, it might eventually generate more crop exports, particularly in the presence of adequate financial, technical, and marketing support. Such a policy would provide a viable agricultural strategy, based on considerable market interventions by the state. To an extent, this was the spirit of agricultural policy of the Torrijos period, though the distributional aspect was pursued too timidly and the support aspect too partially.

Economic policy as such was overwhelmed in Panama in the 1980s by a gathering storm of political instability, as detailed in chapter 6. In the economic sphere the government, presided over by a succession of presidents who achieved their office under dubious mandate, moved toward policies urged by the IMF and the World Bank. In the context of considerable income and wealth inequality, real wages stagnant at the level of early 1970s, high incidence of poverty, and extensive urban unemployment, this policy shift accentuated the tensions between both classes and the beneficiaries and nonbeneficiaries of Torrijos's outward-oriented growth strategy. Although the populist aspect of the strategy had been on the wane since the middle 1970s, the probusiness, World Bank–inspired policy "reforms" of the Barletta period can be seen as delivering the coup de grace to the mass base of the military regime.

From the struggle for succession after the death of Torrijos emerged Manuel Noriega, who proved brilliant at staying in power but incapable of maintaining the Torrijos political coalition that had allowed for stable rule. Chapter 7, placing this extraordinary Panamanian in his historical context, followed his rise and fall. Despite all the power he amassed under his personal control, he should be seen primarily as the symptom rather than the cause of Panama's political instability. As economic conditions worsened and mass support evaporated, it was necessary to rule Panama by raw force, and history produced Manuel Noriega to play this role.

Elliot Abrams's arrogant predictions to the contrary, the U.S. sanctions did not succeed in toppling the Noriega government. The sanctions did, however, throw Panama's economy into an acute 1930s-style depression. With George Bush in office, the United States began to express more impatience with Noriega. Bush let it be known that he would welcome the overthrow of the general. Noriega threatened back that he had the goods on Bush: evidence that Bush had supported his rise in the Panamanian Defense Forces, that Bush—despite public denials—had collaborated in the undercover contra supply operation, and that Bush had received large campaign contributions from his business associate and choice for president in the aborted 1989 elections, Carlos Duque.[13] Bush must have reasoned that Noriega's evidence would come to light eventually, with or without a U.S. invasion, and that U.S. interests demanded action.

What were those U.S. interests? It is a simple matter to dispel the official Grenada-style justification for the U.S. invasion of Panama—the protection of U.S. lives. After months of provocation, one U.S. citizen fleeing a security zone was killed; the invasion left at least twenty-seven U.S. citizens dead. In chapter 7 we argued that the 1987 decision to move against Noriega was a function of Noriega's increasingly independent foreign policy posture, his dismissal of leftist second-in-command Díaz Herrera, and the growing embarrassment from public revelations of supporting a nefarious, venal drug dealer. The decision to invade, however, required a greater motive or, at least, a strong catalyst. Three candidates present themselves.

First, after exhorting the Panamanian military to stage a coup, the United States failed to effectively support the nearly successful putsch on October 3. After arguing on the day of the coup that the United States was not involved in the attempt, Bush later changed his line and acknowledged the participation of troops from the Southern Command. Yet Bush said the United States was willing to block two supply routes and not a third, which proved the crucial one, to the Defense Forces Headquarters because he did not trust the putschists; were this so, it is hard to explain why the United States was involved at all. It seems the real reason was the Southern Command's utter confusion that resulted from the replacement of its chief commander the previous week and the second-in-command the previous month as well as a breakdown of communications with Washington. Bush was accused by Democrats and Republicans alike of wimplike behavior in the affair, although the facts suggest bungling rather than cowering was the problem. Whatever the problem, this explanation maintains that Bush needed to undo the image damage from the affair.

Second, some have argued that the United States decided that, while it was acceptable to turn over the Canal and the Zone to Panama, the military bases were too important to give up in 1999.[14] They adduce significant investment in modernizing U.S. military installations over the last year. Indeed, Ramsey Clark's Independent Commission of Inquiry reported that the Bush administration offered in early 1989 to drop charges against Noriega in exchange for extending the lease on the bases.[15] According to this position, a friendlier government, such as that of Endara, would be more likely to alter the treaties and extend the lease on some bases into the next century. To be sure, Endara, even if he foresaw such a possibility, could not openly admit it at this point.

Third, others believe that the Pentagon and the war on drugs needed a shot in the arm. The Pentagon, after all, with the Soviet menace disappearing needs a new enemy to rationalize the $300 billion defense budget. Bush has been arguing for militarizing the war on drugs, and the invasion could be a rallying point for public opinion. Noriega was a convenient target for the largest U.S. foreign military operation in over twenty years. In this regard, the invasion also served as a proving ground for some new weapons (e.g., re-exploding bullets) and an intended showcase for others (e.g., the F-117A stealth bomber).[16]

Which of these explanations (or combination thereof) is most accurate matters little to Panama. The combined effect of the 1987–1989 economic sanctions and the invasion cost the country somewhere between $3 and $10 billion and between seven hundred and several thousand lives.[17] The Endara government is confronted with an awesome task of reconstruction that lies well beyond the proposed U.S. aid package of several hundred million dollars. Even when financial normalcy returns and production recovers to its predepression levels, Panama will face the question of its long-run development. In this regard, it will encounter the development dilemma of all Latin America, and then some. Not only will a radical restructuring of its foreign debt be imperative, but a major reorientation of its economy away from its unidimensional dependence on services and low-wage exports will also be necessary. The extent to which the Endara and successive governments are able to join these challenges will determine Panama's success in its struggle for sovereignty and economic development.

Notes

Chapter One

1. The evolution of forced labor systems in Central America is treated inter alia in Hector Pérez Brignoli, *A Brief History of Central America* (Berkeley: University of California Press); Ciro Cardoso, "Sobre los modos de producción coloniales de América," *Estudios Sociales Centroamericanos,* no. 10 (1975): 87–105; Elizabeth Dove and J. Gould, "El café en la historia de Nicaragua," in *El café en la historia de Centroamérica,* ed. Hector Pérez Brignoli and M Samper K. (San José: FLASCO, 1990); and John Weeks, "Panama: The Roots of Current Political Instability," *Third World Quarterly* 9, no. 3 (1986): 763–87.

2. There were, of course, some large estates in Panama, particularly in coffee and cattle production, and the number and size of private estates seem to have grown following independence. Yet the generalization still holds: the *hacendados* did not depend on a captive labor force, the number of important landed families was diminutive, and government policy was not primarily oriented toward preserving or expanding agricultural interests. It was not until foreign capital's development of large-scale banana production at the turn of the century that the creation of a rural labor force became an important political issue. See, among others, Humberto Ricord et al., *Panamá y la frutera* (Panama: Editorial Universitaria, 1974); Stephen Gudeman, *The Demise of a Rural Economy* (London: Routledge, 1988), chap. 2; S. Gudeman, *Relationship, Residence and the Individual: A Rural Panamanian Community* (London: Routledge & Kegan Paul, 1976); Marco Gandásegui, "La concentración del poder económico en Panamá," and Ricaurte Soler, "La independencia de Panamá de Colombia," both in *Panamá: Dependencia y liberación,* ed. R. Soler (Panama: Ediciones Tareas, 1986); and Marco Gandásegui, *Las empresas públicas en Panamá* (Panama: CELA, 1982).

3. The subsequent discussion of class relations in Panama benefited from the suggestions of Lowell Gudmundson. We particularly thank him for pointing out the similarity between Panama and some other countries of the isthmus and the Caribbean.

4. From 1739 to 1849, what is Panama today actually comprised two provinces of Colombia. Thereafter, in its eternal bargaining for political influence within Colombia, Panama oscillated between one and four provinces, until its independence from Colombia in 1903. See Ernesto Castillero, *Historia de Panamá* (Panama: Editora Renovación, 1986), chaps. 10–14.

5. Merchants did, however, play a major role in most of colonial Spanish America. On Mexico, see David Brading, *Miners and Merchants in Bourbon Mexico, 1763–1810* (Cambridge: Cambridge University Press, 1971).

6. Class relations in Nicaragua in the context of the development of coffee are treated in Dore and Gould, "El café en la historia de Nicaragua." On the Caribbean, see Wells, "Terrible Green Monster." On Costa Rica, see Gudmundson, *Costa Rica before Coffee*, esp. the introduction, chap. 1, and appendix E.

7. Gold was mined in the sixteenth century, but the project was soon abandoned.

8. Cf. Gudeman, *Demise of a Rural Economy*, 14–21; Jan Knippers Black, "Historical Setting," in *Panama: A Country Study*, ed. Richard Nyrop (Washington, D.C.: USGPO, 1981); Alaka Wali, *Kilowatts and Crisis: Hydroelectric Power and Social Dislocation in Eastern Panama* (Boulder: Westview, 1989), chap. 2; Ropp, *Panamanian Politics: From Guarded Nation to National Guard.* (Stanford: Hoover Institution Press, 1982), 3; Omar Jaen Suárez, *La población del istmo de Panamá del siglo XVI al siglo XX* (Panama: Impresora de la Nación, 1978), 50.

9. Walter LaFeber, *The Panama Canal: The Crisis in Historical Perspective* (New York: Oxford University Press, 1989), 4.

10. By 1630, the largest had thirty laborers, and the average ten. See Gudeman, *Demise of a Rural Economy*, 16.

11. Not without its charm for its unabashed self-aggrandizement is the account by a principal engineer of the de Lesseps venture, Phillipe Bunau-Varilla, who would later claim to be the architect of Panamanian separation from Colombia; see Bunau-Varilla, *Panama: The Creation, Destruction and Resurrection* (New York: Robert McBride, 1920).

12. However, it may not be correct to say that the venture was finally a financial failure, as many suggest. In 1902 the United States government purchased the rights to the de Lesseps concession (and what assets remained in Panama) for $40 million (U.S.); this was considerably more, it might be noted, than the $10 million (U.S.) paid to the new government of Panama for de facto U.S. sovereignty over the Canal Zone.

13. Ropp, *Panamanian Politics*, chap. 1, has a good discussion of the relationship between the urban commercial class and the rural cattle ranchers; he stresses the latter's lack of political influence in the political process. This pattern was to be gradually altered following independence; see e.g., Gandásegui, "La concentración."

14. A similar point is made by Ropp, though we cannot attribute our more general interpretation of Panamanian class relations to him. In *Panamanian Politics* he refers to the urban merchant class: "Because the urban elite had developed as a secondary echelon within the Spanish and Colombian bureaucracies, it did not possess a high degree of self-assurance or autonomy. Its economic base was weak from the absence of a major internal source of self-capitalization" (p. 9). Our conclusion of a weak economic base is the same, but we derived it from the argument that the merchant class did not directly control a significant portion of the population at the level of production.

15. For example, the Chiari family, nineteenth-century immigrants to Panama, had sugar plantations and cattle ranches. Rodolfo E. Chiari became president in 1924 and dominated a faction of the Liberal party.

16. In his insightful review of Panamanian history, Ropp comments that the urban upper class was deterred from independence because "they realized that their political control over the predominantly black and mulatto masses was extremely tenuous"; see Ropp, *Panamanian Politics*, 9.

17. In April 1885 General Aizpuru seized Panama in defiance of the central government, and his revolt was suppressed by the landing of U.S. troops, acting under the Bidlack-Mallarin Treaty of 1846 in which the American government pledged to maintain the isthmus under Colombian rule. Bunau-Varilla, who subsequently helped engineer the separation of Panama, observed the repression of this insurrection and comments with characteristic self-congratulation: "I was witnessing the application of the diplomatic theory which, almost twenty years later, was to permit me to establish the Republic of Panama and to rescue the canal undertaking from annihilation"; see Bunau-Varilla, *Panama*, 12.

18. On January 22, 1903, the Hay-Herran Treaty, actually signed by U.S. and Colombian representatives, granted a 100-year lease to construct a canal across Panama and fortify it, renewable unilaterally by the government of the United States. The treaty was ratified by the U.S. Senate in March, but unanimously rejected by the Colombian Senate in August. The Roosevelt administration at that point ceased negotiations with Colombia, and ten weeks later a provisional government of the Panamanian elite declared independence (November 3, 1903). For a complete account, see Congressional Research Service, *A Chronology of Events relating to the Panama Canal* (Washington, D.C.: USGPO, 1977).

On the rejection by the Colombian Senate, LaFeber writes (*The Panama Canal*, 18): "Bogota wanted more money. A leading Colombian historian later wrote that his nation feared the loss of sovereignty in Panama to the powerful North Americans, and believed itself entitled to a larger sum, particularly since the U.S.-owned isthmian railroad had earned millions in profits of which the Colombians received nothing. Left unsaid was that the Colombians hoped to stall until October 1904 when the Canal Company's rights would expire. Colombia could then collect all of the $40 million ticketed for Bunau-Varilla's and Cromwell's organization."

19. The Zone was a strip of land along the Canal, ten miles wide by fifty miles long. The entire Zone was placed under U.S. jurisdiction by the 1903 treaty.

20. On the other extreme, there is little basis for LaFeber's argument that immediately after formal independence, the U.S. government imposed a humiliating victor's peace upon an independently minded and objecting Panamanian regime (LaFeber, *The Panama Canal*, chap. 1).

21. The U.S. government had demanded that the army be disbanded. This demand may not have been contrary to the interests of the commercial ruling class because army leader General Esteban Huertas's subservience to the elite was open to doubt.

22. LaFeber, *The Panama Canal*, 30.

23. In January 1923, the Liberal government presented a list of grievances associated with the 1903 treaty to Washington and requested negotiation of a new accord. By this time there was significant nationalist agitation within the middle class. Later in 1923, the people formed Acción Comunal, which became the political vehicle of the Arias brothers. In any case, the most important objections to the 1903 treaty did not seem to deal with the basic issue of sovereignty, but rather with the Canal operation's share of gains to be enjoyed by the Panamanian elite.

24. "When Arias reached the presidency in 1940 . . . he held a plebiscite to consider a new constitution, which was ratified January 2, 1941. This new constitution and subsequent government decrees were aimed at disenfranchising large segments of the urban working class." Ropp, *Panamanian Politics*, 23. Paricularly noteworthy was Article 12 of the constitution, which defined citizenship partly in terms of ethnic origin.

25. Remón not only played an important role in these first two overthrows of Arnulfo Arias (1941 and 1951), but he also managed to have himself elected president in 1952. He is usually credited with introducing the military into the economy and establishing the system of patronage and corruption that later defined Panama's Defense Forces. Remón failed to serve out his term when he was assassinated at a race track in 1955. See Dorindo Jayán Cortéz, *FFAA y poder político en Panamá* (Panama, 1986).

26. From this point on, the use of "Arias" without a given name always refers to Arnulfo Arias.

27. The boom of Canal activity during the Second World War promoted the beginnings of a fledgling, indigenous manufacturing class. This class was to have a growing influence in setting government policy in the 1950s and 1960s.

28. There is little doubt that Arias won the disputed election of 1984 and was robbed of victory by electoral fraud; see the discussion in chapter 6. According to most observers, the 1964 election was also stolen from Arias.

29. Explaining why the military played a passive role after the coups of 1941 and 1951 and then aggressively seized power for itself in 1968 lies beyond the scope of our inquiry. The answer would require a case study of the Panamanian military itself, particularly the rise of nationalism within the institution.

30. This period of high turnover included Domingo Díaz Arosemena (October 1, 1948, to July 28, 1949), Daniel Chanis, Jr. (July 28 to November 20, 1949), Roberto F. Chiari Remón (November 20 to 24, 1949), and then Arias by election. When Chiari returned to the presidency in 1960, he served four years rather than four days.

31. These were Ernesto de la Guardia (1956–1960), Roberto Chiari (1960–1964), and Marco Robles (1964–1968).

32. Ropp has a good summary of political deal making during the 1951–1968 period (*Panamanian Politics,* chaps. 2 and 3).

33. There is also evidence that David Rockefeller and the United States came to Torrijos's aid at this point. See discussion of Torrijos in chapter 2.

34. Ropp writes, "One major problem was that the commercial elite had exercised direct influence over government economic policy since the foundation of the Republic. No matter how favorable General Torrijos' policies might be, the business community had lost the ability to directly govern"; see Ropp, *Panamanian Politics,* 65.

35. An excellent discussion of the role of the Canal in Panamanian politics during the twentieth century can be found in LaFeber, *The Panama Canal.*

36. Jimmy Carter reported that Torrijos broke into tears when signing the final accords.

Chapter Two

1. In his history of the Panama Canal, LaFeber writes: "For thirty years Spanish officials pondered the idea of a waterway until finally deciding against it, in part because the King concluded, after much consultation with

his religious advisers, that if God wanted the oceans to meet He would have built the canal himself" (p. 5).

2. Arguably, Panama's commercial fortunes began to revive earlier than this during the trading spurt with the wars of independence and the subsequent establishment of the British steamship line. Still, the railroad brought a major discrete advance to economic activity in Panama unlike the gradual improvement earlier in the century.

3. LaFeber, *The Panama Canal*, 12.

4. In *The Panama Canal* LaFeber reports that as many as twenty thousand Antillean workers died before de Lesseps gave up in 1889 (p. 14). The largest number of workers employed by de Lesseps in any given year was 17,436 in 1884; see Jorge Castillo, *Formación social panameña: un análisis económico del período, 1850–1960* (Panama: Universidad de Panamá, n.d.), 50.

5. An annual average of 42,593 people worked on the Canal construction project between 1905 and 1914. The largest number of imported workers came from Barbados, which supplied 19,900 during this period. Charlotte Elton et al., *Canal: desafío para los panameños* (Panama: CEASPA, 1987), 98, 126.

6. The total number of Canal workers peaked in 1913 at 56,654. The need to repair landslides and other damages required a substantial maintenance work force during the early years of operation. Thus, the diminution of the Canal labor force was more gradual than many expected. By 1920, Canal employment was still 20,000, but it fell sharply the next year to 14,000 (Castillo, *Formación*, 51).

7. In *Panamanian Politics*, Ropp writes: "The United States in 1918 demanded and won the right to have U.S. financial advisers given control of the country's fiscal system" (p. 21).

8. See discussion in chapter 1 and, inter alia, Melida Ruth Sepulveda, *Harmodio Arias Madrid: el hombre, el estadista y el periodista* (Panama: Editorial Universitaria, 1983).

9. Soler would have been more accurate had he included Cuba along with Panama in the special group; see his *Formas ideológicas de la nación*, 35 (translation by authors). It is also true that the major study done in Panama, under the auspices of Panama's Ministry of Planning and Economic Policy, on industrialization and infant industry protection says the first government policy to support import substitution was implemented in 1950; John Panzer, *La evolución del sector industrial panameño y su relación con la protección* (Panama: Ministerio de Planificación y Política Económica, 1985).

10. The end of the war and its depressing effect on Canal employment precipitated a prolonged recession in Panama. In 1945 prices, national in-

come in Panama was 214 million balboas in 1945 and 216 million in 1950. On a per capita basis, the 1945 real income level was not recovered until 1957.

11. PREALC (Program Regional del Empleo para América Latina y el Caribe, International Labor Office), *Panamá: el patrón de desarrollo industrial, 1960–75* (Santiago: Organización Internacional de Trabajo, 1984), 17, 70. In 1971, foreign investment accounted for 70 percent of new capital formation in manufacturing; Robert Looney, *The Economic Development of Panama* (New York: Praeger, 1976), 93.

12. For some specific examples of this behavior, see Panzer, *La evolución*, 4–5. See also Daniel Wisecarver, *Panama: The Failure of State Activism* (San Francisco: International Center for Economic Growth, 1987), 28–29.

13. To be sure, Decree No. 413 of December 30, 1970, did contemplate some major alterations in tariff policy, but this decree was replaced by another in August 1971 that restored, with a few modifications, the previous tariff structure. Among other things, Decree No. 413 weakened and gradually removed tariff exemptions for imported inputs in import substitution industries while it retained full exemptions for export industries. A sharp fall in investment, a rise in unemployment, and vocal protests led to the hasty replacement of this decree.

14. See Ministerio de Planificación y Política Económica, *Estrategia para el desarrollo nacional, 1970–1980* (Panama; República de Panamá, 1978).

15. Of course, similar debt-led development proceeded throughout Latin America in the 1970s, but Panama's per capita indebtedness by 1979 was the highest in Latin America.

16. As suggested in the note to Table 2.2, the extent of the increase is exaggerated by the change in SNA (System of National Accounts) methodology in 1970.

17. The events of 1987–1989 are treated in chapter 6.

18. The manufacturing share differs from the industrial share because the latter, in addition to manufacturing, includes mining, electricity, water, and gas.

19. Unless otherwise indicated, the data in this section are from *Panamá en cifras*, various years, and the IMF, *Balance of Payments Yearbook*, various years.

20. Vilma Medica, *La población de Panamá* (Panama: Contraloría General, 1974), 7, 12.

21. Looney, *Economic Development of Panama*, 38.

22. The top 10 percent of households earned 44.2 percent of income. Among the Latin countries reported in the World Bank's *World Development Report 1989* (New York: Oxford University Press, 222–23) only Brazil had a more unequal distribution in the early 1970s.

23. See, for example, NACLA, *Panama: For Whom the Canal Tolls* 12, no 5. (September/October 1979): 24.

24. The most eulogistic account of Torrijos is provided in Graham Greene's uncritical biography *Getting to Know the General* (New York: Simon & Schuster, 1985).

25. Soler, *Panamá: nación y oligarquía* (Panama: Ediciones Tareas, 1987), 45.

26. Authors' interview with Barletta, Panama City, March 1989, and communication from Barletta, April 1989.

27. These institutions are analyzed in detail in chapters 3 and 4.

28. These concepts and the law are detailed in chapter 3.

29. One study finds that as of 1983 the redistributed land was less than one percent of cultivated area. From Gian Singh Sahota, *Poverty Theory and Policy: A Study of Panama* (Baltimore: Johns Hopkins University Press, 1990), 38. Agricultural policies and performance, as well as the agrarian reform are analyzed in chapter 5.

30. *Diálogo Social* 134 (May 1981): 13.

31. If other fringe benefits such as paid vacation leave and the thirteenth month are included, total contributions reached above 30 percent by the mid-1970s and near 40 percent by 1980. These figures are from the World Bank, *Panama: Structural Change and Growth Prospects* (Washington, D.C.: World Bank, 1985), 15–17; they are below the estimates presented in Wisecarver, *Failure of State Activism*, 31, which are not substantiated by citation or explanation.

32. ECLA, *Economic Survey of Latin America and the Caribbean*, 1972 (New York: United Nations, 1974), 202.

33. For interesting discussions on their operation, see World Bank, *Structural Change*, 70–74, and Gandásegui, *Las empresas públicas*, 91–113.

34. Apparently, when the plans for the Felipillo mill were being finalized some high military officers bought the land and then sold it to the government at a handsome profit. Such maneuvers were reportedly common.

35. The balboa is the Panamanian currency that circulates only in coin. All bills are U.S. dollars. The balboa and the dollar have run at par since the currency agreement of 1904, made presumably to facilitate payments for work on the Canal. As in several countries, many enterprises that passed to public ownership had been inefficient private enterprises yielding losses.

36. Calculated from data presented in World Bank, *Structural Change*, 37. In its critique of Panama's public enterprises, the World Bank uses the "overall balance" concept—the current account (cash flow) minus all capital expenditures. The overall balance was in substantial deficit throughout the 1970s. This concept is misleading, particularly during the early years of a project. Standard enterprise accounting would deduct from the current bal-

ance a capital consumption allowance (depreciation of the capital stock). During the early years, this allowance would typically be well below capital expenditures. There are no data on capital consumption allowance so we are left with the current account to detect trends in the efficiency of operations. Although the trend appears positive, this result may have more to do with state pricing policy for its enterprises than actual improvements in management. In the end, few general claims can be systematically sustained.

37. Authors' interview with Barletta, Panama City, March 1989.

38. Since 1977 the CATs have been transferable. Despite their relative success, the impact of CATs has been weakened by unpredictable and often lengthy administrative delays as well as their concentration in certain product groups and enterprises. Through 1985 nearly half the value of all CATs had been received by six enterprises. For a careful treatment of export promotion measures and their impact in Panama and elsewhere in the Caribbean Basin, see Eva Paus, ed., *Struggle against Dependence: Nontraditional Export Growth in Central America and the Caribbean* (Boulder: Westview Press, 1988).

39. Law No. 70 lowered taxes on reinvested profits. Law No. 71 extended the provisions of the earlier CAT legislation. Law No. 90 authorized tax credits for new employment. These three laws differed from previous legislation for incentives: they applied to the whole economy, not only industry, and enterprises benefited automatically, without a Contract with the Nation. The latter change made it more possible for smaller enterprises to benefit.

40. A different position from that of the Communist party was taken by the prolabor journal *Diálogo Social,* which referred to Law 95 as "nefarious and fascist"; see *Diálogo Social* 133 (April 1981).

41. The consumer price index increased by 17.7 percent between 1976 and 1979.

42. Dismissal was always permitted for workers with less than two years of tenure, but regular workers with more than two weeks and less than two years were entitled to a progressive indemnification according to their length of stay on the job. This provision was modified by Law No. 1 of 1986, which increased the amount of time a regular worker needed to be on the job to qualify for an indemnity from two weeks to three months.

43. To participate in this drawback or *maquila* program, companies were expected to export 100 percent of their output. This requirement was made more flexible in March 1986 by applying to only those products of a company that benefited directly from the incentives. Actually, since 1957 under Contracts with the Nation for manufacturing enterprises involved in the transformation of raw materials (as opposed to assembly operations), firms exporting 100 percent of their product were exempt from profits taxes, and from 1970 this provision applied to the exported share of output.

44. The 6.4 percent growth rate is figured after adjusting GDP figures for the accounting effect of the Canal treaties. Prior to 1980, only the wages and salaries of workers in the Zone were included in Panama's GDP; thereafter, all value added in the Canal area has been included. This change by itself led accounted GDP to increase by $117.3 million in 1980. Without adjusting for this effect, real GDP grew by 15.1 percent in 1980; with the adjustment it grew by 7.4 percent. See *Panamá en cifras 1979–1983* (Panama: Contraloría de la República), 164–66. This is just one of the many conundrums in accounting GDP in Panama that has led to different estimates of economic performance over the years. Now is as good a place as any to indicate another prominent source of statistical discrepancies.

In the official accounting procedures, value added by the oil pipeline is deflated by a composite index of oil shipping rates. Because these rates have increased more slowly than Panama's GDP deflator, the use of the former makes the estimated real value added of the pipeline increase more rapidly. Similar ambiguities exist for the estimated of real value added of other international services. See Pedro Pou, *Empleo, inversión y crecimiento en Panamá durante la década de los sesenta* (Panama: Ministerio de Planificación y Política Económica, 1985), 57.

45. Arzobispo de Panamá, *Hacia una economía más humana: reflexiones cristianas para el desarrollo de Panamá con prioridad en los más pobres* (Panama: La Estrella de Panamá, 1985), 5.

46. See the extended discussion of the agricultural sector in chapter 5.

47. Pou attributes the falling participation rates to later entrance into the labor force (due to increased years of schooling) and later exit (due to earlier retirement, partly a function of pension increases); see Pou, *Empleo*, 5–9. It seems that the slow growth in the demand for labor and the expansion of the informal (and unregistered) economy during the 1970s also help account for this trend.

48. Official rates for 1980 and 1981 are not available (World Bank, *Structural Change*, 193).

49. This share first rose to 54.0 percent in 1974 before it began to decline. This pattern is consistent with the view that identifies the Declaración de Boquete as the principal shift in the ideological orientation of Torrijos's policies. The 45.7 percent share in 1980, calculated using the new 1980 methodology for GDP computation, includes all value added in the Canal area. Because the Canal Zone was considered foreign territory in national income accounting until October 1, 1979, prior to 1980 only the wages and salaries paid out in the Canal Zone were included in Panama's GDP. Were the pre-1980 methodology used, the share would be 48.6 percent.

50. Arzobispo de Panamá, *Hacia una economía,* 5. We return to a more in-depth look at poverty and distribution in Panama in chapter 6.

51. John Harbon, "Yankee Dollars Wanted: The Canal Aside, Panama Welcomes American Investment," *Barron's* 58 (July 31, 1978): 21. Similar views are expressed in *Foreign Affairs* (October 1975) and *Business Latin America* (August 10, 1975) as well as in statements by various business leaders, including David Rockefeller, as cited in NACLA (Sept./Oct. 1979).

52. Import substitution, an internally oriented development strategy, seeks to produce goods domestically that were previously imported. For excellent discussions of this strategy, see Albert Hirschman, "The Political Economy of Import Substitution," *Quarterly Journal of Economics* 82 (1968): 2–32, and Henry Bruton, "Import Substitution" (Paper delivered to the Northeast Development Consortium Conference at Harvard University, April 29–30, 1988).

53. Panama did, of course, trade with the economies of Central America, often on a preferential basis. Nonetheless, during the 1970s only 1 percent of the Central American Common Market's import bill consisted of Panamanian exports; and, of this, 35 percent was refined petroleum. Andrew Zimbalist, "Problems and Prospects of Export Diversification: The Case of Panama," in *Struggle against Dependence,* ed. Paus, 87.

54. In fact, there is astonishingly little consensus on both the levels of this protection and the extent to which it was below levels prevailing elsewhere in Latin America. The most careful estimates we have seen come from PREALC, which find effective levels of protection in 1975 at an average of 27 percent for the manufacturing sector, ranging from 6 percent for the nonmetallic minerals branch up to 70 percent for wood products and furniture (PREALC, *El patrón,* 114). The World Bank found effective rates of protection in the early 1980s to average 80 percent and in the case of some individual products to go as high as 1,000 percent; see *Structural Change,* 88. While the latter figure seems plausible for particular goods, the former appears too high because rates were scarcely altered between 1975 and the early 1980s.

It should be recalled that much of Panama's protection prior to 1984 was from quotas. This makes it difficult to compare Panama's level of protectionism with that of other countries, but several authoritative sources have argued that Panama was less protectionist than the Latin American norm. For instance, in its 1969 *Economic Survey of Latin America,* ECLA concludes: "Panama is one of the few Latin American countries where a definitively protectionist strategy has not been put in effect. Tariff instruments have been little used and quotas have been granted on the merits of each individual case, and have not been used as a means of restricting imports in general" (p. 224).

55. High prices were also a major justification for the government's growing involvement in price regulation during the 1970s as well as an important cause of increasing contraband.

56. Another factor, according to surveys reported by PREALC, *Panamá: el patrón*, 86, appears to be high rates of capitalization and productivity in Panama relative to the rest of Central America. These surveys, however, were too incomplete and uneven to endow their estimates with much confidence.

57. U.S. workers are paid the same as Panamanian workers for the same job with the exception that their salaries are augmented by an overseas pay differential and various perquisites.

58. For the period 1971–1976, 6.2 percent of domestic loans went to agriculture and 8.4 percent to industry (calculated from PREALC, *Panamá: el patrón*, 63.

59. Pou, *Empleo*, 3, 69.

60. Arzobispo de Panamá, *Hacia una economía*, 12. It is noteworthy that the principal economists collaborating on this report were Guillermo Chapman and José Galán, now the chief economic advisers to the Christian Democratic party.

60. Hirschman, in "The Political Economy of Import Substitution," also emphasizes the role of exchange rates, geographical dispersion of industry, and government policy in sustaining import substitution. Overvalued exchange rates, of course, in Panama's case do not deter "higher" stages of industrialization because the balboa and dollar are fixed at parity. The concentration of industry in Panama City, however, may serve as a deterrent as Hirschman suggests because industrialists' children have greater access to employment not only in government but also in the international services. These opportunities, Hirschman suggests, may make entrepreneurs less likely to invest in backwardly linked industries and, hence, more prone to resist new policies restricting the availability of or raising the prices of imported inputs.

62. World Bank, *World Development Report 1989*, 175.

63. Despite the higher profit rates available to import-substituting industries, manufacturing exports from a small initial base did experience some growth between 1961 and 1975. Such exports increased from 9.5 percent to 22.2 percent of manufacturing gross output over this period (PREALC, *Panamá: el patrón*, 8). Although the share of foreign exchange spent importing inputs that was recovered by manufacturing exports increased from 65 percent in 1961 to 83 percent in 1975, the manufacturing sector was still obviously a net user of foreign exchange following the typical pattern of dependent import substitution (ibid., 45). Manufacturing exports continued to grow from $8.1 million in 1975 to $38.5 million in 1982 (World Bank, *Structural Change*, 284). The long-term, good growth record of manufacturing exports suggests that the World Bank/IMF argument of strong disincentives toward export development may be misleading. We shall return to this point in chapter 8's discussion of options for the future of Panama's economy.

Chapter Three

1. Hayakawa's comment, made while campaigning for the U.S. Senate in 1976, is cited in Paul B. Ryan, *The Panama Canal Controversy* (Stanford: Hoover Institution Press, 1977), ix. Buckley's comment came during a January 13, 1978, debate with Ronald Reagan on his program "Firing Line."

2. This refers to a voyage between New York and San Francisco. The Canal saves 5,459 miles between New York and Yokohama versus the alternative route around the Cape of Good Hope. Mileage figures are from Kenneth Jones, ed., *Panamá hoy* (Panama City: Focus Publications, 1986), 82.

3. Another study prepared for the Panama Canal Company in 1973, however, estimated annual savings at only $80 million. International Research Associates, *The Economic Value of the Panama Canal* (Palo Alto, 1973), 5.

4. Charlotte Elton et al., *Canal: desafío para los panameños* (Panama City: CEASPA, 1987), 102.

5. Some analysts have also pointed to the reopening of the Suez Canal in 1975 as contributing to the 1980s tonnage drop. However, competition between the canals is generally not direct, and, in any event, most of the effect is likely to have been felt by 1978.

6. We made this estimate using the U.S. consumer price index.

7. The 1936 and 1955 increases were intended to compensate for intervening inflation. We were not able to confirm from anyone at the Canal Commission in Panama or Washington why the annuity payment rose during the 1970s. The move to flexible exchange rates and the fall in the dollar's value relative to OECD currencies was the only possible explanation offered to us.

8. In *The Panama Canal*, LaFeber provides an excellent, detailed discussion of the treaty negotiations and the ratification debates; see chaps. 7 and 8. Among other things, LaFeber reports that a pretreaty signing poll in the United States found 44 percent of Americans said they did not know who owned the Canal and another 22 percent said they did know but were wrong (guessing Israel, Arabs, Cuba).

9. A treaty condition is not binding on both parties; it merely gives one party's interpretation of the treaty. Senator Dennis DeConcini was a freshman Democrat from Arizona. His brother Dino was running for attorney general in Arizona, and polls in that state indicated strong opposition to the Canal treaties. See LaFeber, *The Panama Canal*, 177–81.

10. This implementing legislation passed by the U.S. Senate (Public Law 96–70) has never been accepted by the Panamanians; it has provided a continual thorn in the commission's side. These difficulties are described by the former chairman of the commission's board of directors, William Gianelli, in his article, "The Panama Canal and the Canal Zone: Status and Prospects," in *Panama: An Assessment*, V. H. Krulak, ed. (Washington, D.C.: U.S. Strategic Institute, 1990).

11. It does not appear, however, that any were fired. That is, they were transferred to other agencies, retired, or moved to another job within the Canal Commission.

12. Panamanian entry into the most skilled jobs was gradual. The share (in percentages) of Panamanians in the top posts increased as follows:

	Oct. 1979	*Sept. 1989*
Professionals and managers	14	43
Skilled crafts	59	85
Floating equipment handlers	20	71
Pilots (ship captains through Canal)	2	27

The overall percent of Panamanians in the Canal's work force increased from 69.5 percent in October 1979 to 85.7 percent in October 1989; their share in the key skilled occupations increased from 38.1 percent to 67.9 percent over this ten-year period. These data are taken from Panama Canal Commission, *A Decade of Progress in Canal Operations and Treaty Implementaion* (Panama: Panama Canal Commission, 1989), 27–28.

13. Roberto Méndez, "Los 'beneficios' de los tratados Torrijos-Carter," *Diálogo Social* 132 (March 1981): 19. Méndez himself actually picked up the issue from a progovernment Panamanian journalist, Luis Restrepo.

14. On the free rent issue, the United States maintains that the troops provide Canal defense at U.S. taxpayer expense. Of course, many Panamanians see a major political liability in having U.S. bases on their soil, and yet others have suggested that the bases have allowed for extensive smuggling.

15. There is considerable sloppiness in the various estimates of this contribution. We have seen estimates ranging from $70 million up to $500 million. The U.S. Senate Staff Report on their November 1987 trip to Panama stated that the U.S. bases are estimated to contribute "upwards of $500 million annually to the economy of Panama." U.S. Senate, Committee on Foreign Relations, *Hearings Before the Subcommittee on Terrorism, Narcotics, and International Communications* Part 2, 351; hereafter, this document is cited Senate *Hearings*. Estimates above $100 million seem to include the indirect multiplier effects as well.

16. The French consulting firm's report on the state of the railroad in March 1979 concluded: "The main line track is of sturdy construction but shows signs of considerable fatigue, as 86% of the rails are 40 to 50 years old and axle loads are very high. The number of rail breaks is a source of concern: 12 to 15 per year, chiefly near the joints, which are not welded. The ballast is insufficient to hold the ties in place, and in some parts is very polluted. Tide quality is poor. . . . The drainage structures, very numerous due

to the climate, are in unsatisfactory condition: most culverts are blocked, crushed, or undermined; ditches are frequently filled up. . . . The railway has been allowed to deteriorate somewhat, physically and financially, over the last five years." SOFERAIL, *Panama Railway: Condition, Prospects and Transition Issues* (Panama: Republic of Panama, 1979), 2, 15. See also Elton et al., *Canal,* 168.

17. For a more detailed discussion of the problems with the ports, see Zimbalist, "Problems and Prospects," and the World Bank, *Structural Change,* 1985, 101–6.

18. Although the Canal is a nonprofit agency by law, it does experience unbudgeted surpluses. The real issue raised here is what is done with the potential surplus.

19. *El Boletín* 8, no. 8 (March 20, 1989): 4.

20 Many perquisites were extended as part of an "equity package" in October 1984 that was intended to replace some of the expiring benefits (e.g., U.S. military postal, commissary, and exchange privileges) stipulated in the 1977 treaties.

21. The 1988 figure was reduced by the U.S. sanctions. In 1987, the Canal spent $56 million in local purchases. The remuneration figures for 1988 include the money escrowed in the United States.

22. This figure was also reduced by U.S. policy and the political environment in Panama in 1988. The estimate for 1987 was $11 million.

23. Of course, the trade in some bulk items, such as grains, is increasing, but not as rapidly as trade in manufactured goods.

24. No commercial ship that has a beam longer than 106 feet can transit the Canal. Until 1988, the only ships with larger beams carried three commodities—iron, coal, and oil. Since 1988, however, American President Lines has purchased six container ships with beams of 129 feet. Other companies may follow suit; such a trend may be ominous for the Canal if it does not undertake widening and other investments. Ships with beams longer than 95 feet are restricted to one-way passage in some segments, lengthening Canal transit time.

25. Several lengthy studies attempting such an analysis have been carried out for the Canal Commission in recent years. Although there is some general agreement among them, there are also important differences. See TBS, *A Review of the Manalytics Forecasts of Panama Canal Commodity Traffic, Vessel Transits, and Revenue, 1985–2010* (Panama: Panama Canal Commission, 1985), and TBS, *A Sensitivity Analysis of Panama Canal Trade, 1984–2010* (Panama: Panama Canal Commission, 1986); see also Manalytics, *Forecasts of Panama Canal Commodity Traffic, Vessel Transits, and Revenue, 1985–2010* [Report to the Panama Canal Commission] (San Francisco: Manalytics, 1985).

26. Calculated from Panama Canal Commission, *Annual Report, 1988,* 56.

27. To be sure, recent unpublished projections appear to have been lowered to the 20 to 25 percent range.

28. David Grier et al., *Competitive Routing: Minibridge and the Panama Canal* (Fort Belvoir, Va.: U.S. Army Corps of Engineers, Institute for Water Resources, July 1988), 7.

29. Ibid., 25.

30. Grain and lumber are occasional exceptions to this generalization.

31. Quote from Executive Intelligence Review, *White Paper on the Crisis in Panama* (Washington, D.C.: EIR News Service, December 1987), 65.

32. These projections refer to studies carried out for the Canal Commission in 1985 and 1986. See TBS, *Manalytics Forecasts* and *Sensitivity Analysis,* and Manalytics, *Forecasts.*

33. TBS, *Sensitivity Analysis,* 1-5.

34. Speech to the American Chamber of Commerce, Panama City, August 16, 1988, 3.

35. See Elton et al., *Canal,* 50, and Elton, "Studies of Alternatives to the Panama Canal," *Maritime Policy Management* 14, no. 4 (1987): 289–99.

36. TBS, *Sensitivity Analysis,* 1-13.

37. Richard Wainio estimates that the costs of the project could be financed by a toll surcharge of less than 10 percent.

38. A more detailed discussion of this and other aspects of the centerport projects is provided in *Carta Económica* 2, no. 1 (December 1988): 1–3.

39. The 1989 loss was primarily attributable to falling grain and automobile shipments.

40. Actually, COFINA (Corporación Financiera Nacional, the government-owned development corporation) was the partner.

41. Milton Martínez, "Economía y formas de dominación en Panamá, *Revista Económica,* no. 5 (1987): 44.

42. Ibid., 47.

43. Sergina Solano Frías, "El Oleoducto Transístmico," *Diálogo Social* 135 (June 1981): 21; C. Elton, "Serving Foreigners," *NACLA Report on the Americas* 22, no. 4 (July/August 1988): 27–31.

44. Jones, *Panamá hoy,* 80.

45. Martínez, "Economía," 54.

46. *Carta Económica* 2, no. 3 (February 1989): 1.

47. *Carta Económica* 2, no. 10 (September 1989): 4. *Carta Económica* projected throughput for all of 1989 to be 30 percent below that of 1988.

48. Until now, apparently no major ecological damages have been associated with the pipeline's construction or operation. Reportedly, the few oil spills have been contained and effectively treated (Jones, *Panamá hoy,* 80.)

49. Ropp, *Panamanian Politics,* 106.

50. The exact number of Panamanian registered ships in 1986 was 11,959. This figure rose to 12,088 in 1987, fell slightly to 12, 064 in 1988, and rose to 12,163 in 1989. *Carta Económica* 2, no. 12 (December 1989): 2.

51. Between 1985 and 1988 the direct revenue from this source averaged $43.7 million, roughly 7 percent of total government revenues.

52. U.S. Congress, Committee on Foreign Relations, Subcommittee on Terrorism, Narcotics and International Operations, *Drugs, Law Enforcement and Foreign Policy: Report* 100th Cong., 2nd sess. (Washington, D.C.: USGPO, 1989), 85; hereafter this document cited Senate Subcommittee *Report.* See also José de Córdoba, "The Free Ride Has Ended for Noriega's Cronies," *Wall Street Journal,* March 6, 1990, A16.

53. Authors' interview with a former member of the Panamanian diplomatic corps in Europe, May 1989.

54. Panama's ship registry business would have suffered additional damage by President Bush's decision not to allow ships using the Panamanian flag to use U.S. ports after February 1, 1990. This policy, naturally, was revoked after the U.S. invasion.

55. Estimates on the amount of income generated for Panama's lawyers from this source vary between $4 and $40 million. Lawyers charge about $750 for handling ship registration and an annual retainer fee of roughly $150. They also charge for a variety of legal paperwork related to name changes, status modifications, formation of new companies, and so on. *Carta Económica* 2, no. 12 (December 1989): 2.

Chapter Four

1. For a more detailed discussion, see Milton Martínez, "Economía y formas de dominación en Panama," *Revista Económica,* no. 5 (1987): 28–60.

2. Asociación de Usuarios, *F.O.B.: Zona Libre de Colón* (Users Directory) (Panama City: Focus Publications, 1988), 115.

3. Approximately six hundred of these companies operate their own warehouse; the rest are tied to a "representative" company that conducts warehousing and sales for several companies.

4. This observation was made to us by Eduardo Jaén, president of IBM, Panama, during an interview in Panama City, March 1989.

5. In his prepared statement on April 4, 1988, before the U.S. Senate Subcommittee on Terrorism, Narcotics and International Operations, former U.S. intelligence officer and ambassador to Costa Rica, Francis J. McNeil stated: "Panama was long a smugglers haven, exemplified by the Free Port

in Colon, a mecca for duty free items which nationals of many Latin American countries, with the blessing of Panamanian officials, would use in schemes to get in free of duty, in countries with prohibitive tariffs, all manner of durables and electronic goods." Senate *Hearings,* Part 3, 319. Roberto Méndez cites a study done by the Panamanian business association (Sindicato de industriales de Panamá) estimating that tens of millions of dollars of goods were smuggled out of the free zone each year. Méndez, "Ajuste estructural" (unpublished manuscript).

6. The lion's share of reexports from the CFZ are destined to Latin America. In 1985, the share of reexports to the leading Latin American countries was: Aruba, 11.8 percent; Colombia, 11.4 percent; Ecuador, 11.3 percent; Panama, 8.6 percent; Venezuela, 7.8 percent; United States, 6 percent; Bolivia, 3.6 percent; Mexico, 2.7 percent; and Costa Rica, 2.6 percent. Calculated from the CFZ Directory; see *F.O.B.: Zona Libre de Colón* (Panama City: Focus Publications, 1988), 131.

7. The share of imports by country was: Japan, 23.5 percent; Taiwan, 15.5 percent; United States, 11 percent; Hong Kong, 8.9 percent; Italy, 7.7 percent; and South Korea, 6.6 percent. Ibid.

8. Luis Moreno points out that the 1988 drop was connected to small companies' difficulties in obtaining loans from the international banking center; the center was in a state of disarray from the economic and political crisis since March 1988. Moreno, *Panamá: centro bancario internacional* (Panama City: Asociación Bancaria de Panamá, 1988), 80. See also *Carta Económica* 2, no. 3 (February 1989): 1, and 2, no. 10 (September 1989): 3.

9. J. Conte-Porras, *El crédito, la banca y la moneda panameña* (Panama City: Banco Nacional de Panamá, 1983), 129.

10. Alejandro Cordero, "Crecimiento y agresión económica," *Tareas* 69 (May/August 1988); 6 (translation ours). Also on disadvantages of the dollar system, see Inter-American Committee on the Alliance for Progress, "Creation of a National Monetary System in Panama," Document prepared by the Secretariat (OEA/Ser.H/XIV/CIAP/31) (Washington, D.C.: CIAP, September 1966). Panama, however, is not alone in using the U.S. dollar as currency; it is also the case in Liberia.

11. The qualifier "real" is used because there were also several dozen paper banks that operated in Panama until mid-1970. Figures on employment and banks are from Moreno, *Panamá: centro bancario internacional.* Our discussion in this section draws heavily from the excellent analysis of this book. Its author was general manager of Chase Manhattan in Panama, a longtime president of Panama's Banking Association (formed in 1962) and member of the banking commission (formed in 1970). We also benefited from an interview with Moreno in Panama City, March 1989.

12. One critical weakness in Panama's financial system—the absence of a central bank and, hence, a lender of last resort—remained. Decree No. 238 attempted to deal with this by establishing the "Contingency Credit" plan that obligated banks to contract with a foreign bank (usually the home office) to have available at all times a credit line equal to 10 percent of local loans. The banking commission, in turn, could at its discretion direct the banks to access this credit, in theory providing the needed safety valve for liquidity problems. The plan turned out to be inoperable in practice for a number of reasons, among them the fact that the banking law did not obligate the banks to loan out the funds from the credit. The inoperability of the contingency credit became painfully apparent during the liquidity crisis following the freeze of NBP accounts in the United States in March 1988.

13. Comisión Bancaria Nacional, *Banking Law of Panama* (Panama City: Republic of Panama, 1986), 28.

14. Ingo Walter, *Secret Money: The Shadowy World of Tax Evasion, Capital Flight and Fraud* (London: George Allen & Unwin, 1986), 92.

15. Moreno, *Panamá: centro bancario internacional*, 320 (our translation).

16. This discussion is based in part on Harry Johnson, "Panama as a Regional Financial Center: A Preliminary Analysis of Development Contribution," *Economic Development and Cultural Change* 24, no. 2 (January 1976): 261–86.

17. Moreno, *Panamá: centro bancario internacional*, 106–9.

18. Ibid., 288.

19. Ibid., 196.

20. Cordero, "Crecimiento," 7.

21. See Zimbalist, "Problems and Prospects."

22. Moreno, *Panamá: centro bancario internacional*, 196.

23. Because of a change in national income accounting methodology in 1970, it is not possible to compare pre-1970 with post-1970. The ratio of national savings to GDP in 1970 was 17.9 percent while this ratio averaged 14.7 percent during 1978–1982. Calculated from CEPAL, *Anuario estadístico de América Latina y el Caribe, 1985* (Santiago: United Nations, 1986), 380–81.

24. Keith Griffin, *Underdevelopment in Spanish America* (Cambridge: M.I.T. Press, 1971).

25. Four of the seven members of the commission are appointed by the government; the other three are appointed by the banking association and represent the private banks.

26. Senate *Hearings*, Part 3, 66.

27. Ibid., 318.

28. Senate Subcommittee *Report,* 89.

29. Ibid., 90.

30. Ibid., 97. An excellent article summarizing the ties between Noriega and the U.S. government, dating back to 1960, is Frederick Kempe, "Ties That Blind," *Wall Street Journal,* October 18, 1989, 1, 20. Kempe quotes Vermont Senator Patrick Leahy, former member of the Senate Intelligence Committee, as saying: "Noriega played U.S. intelligence agencies and the U.S. government like a violin." See also Kempe, *Divorcing the Dictator: America's Bungled Affair with Noriega* (New York: G. P. Putman's Sons, 1990), and John Dinges, *Our Man in Panama* (New York: Random House, 1990).

31. Senate *Hearings,* Part 2, 38.

32. Ibid., 82.

33. Transit S.A. collected a fee of 1 percent on all merchandise entering and exiting the Colon Free Zone, plus $1.50 per package. Although the last tax report of Transit shows annual revenue of $4 million, estimates range upward of $40 million in actual revenue. See de Córdoba, "Free Ride," A16.

34. For more details, see Larry Rohter, "Trafficking in People: Was It One More Racket?" *New York Times,* April 10, 1990.

35. Senate *Hearings,* Part 2, 238.

36. Senate Subcommittee *Report,* 112.

37. Senate *Hearings,* Part 2, 243.

38. Ibid., 251.

39. Senate Subcommittee *Report,* 116.

40. Ibid., 116.

41. Of course, personnel considerations, the presence of domestic banking activities in Panama, or interest in laundering business led many U.S. banks to stay in Panama.

42. Communication from Blake Friscia, vice-president for Latin American operations, Chase Manhattan Bank, New York, November 1988.

43. Moreno, *Panamá: centro bancario internacional,* 108.

44. Ibid., 97.

45. Delvalle was elected first vice-president in the fraudulent 1984 elections and became president when Noriega forced the resignation of President Nicolás Barletta. In fact, fraud was involved in this resignation as well because Barletta only handed in a letter of temporary separation from the presidency, not resignation. Noriega, however, had the letter read to Congress as a resignation, and that is what Congress supposedly approved.

46. Moreno, *Panamá: centro bancario internacional,* 97, 102. Total assets are to be distinguished from offshore (international) deposits, a subset of total assets, as reported in Table 4.2.

47. Other exchange innovations are reported by Moreno; ibid., 49–53.

48. Panama's goals for the reinsurance center are discussed in "Panama: Much More than a Canal," special advertising section of *Business Week*, June 26, 1978.

Chapter Five

1. An interesting discussion on the deleterious effects of cattle promotion on Central America's economies can be found in Robert Williams, *Export Agriculture and the Crisis in Central America* (Chapel Hill: University of North Carolina Press, 1986).

2. The omission of farms smaller than one hectare makes little difference because these accounted for only 0.2 percent of total land in 1970 and 0.5 percent in 1980. Unless otherwise noted, the numbers given for land distribution here and in the text for the 1950–1980 period all come from República de Panamá, Dirección de Estadística y Censo, *Censos nacionales de 1980, cuarto censo nacional agropecuario, volumen IV, compendio general* (Panama: Contraloría General de la República, 1981), cuadros 4, 5, 7, and 8.

3. Food and Agricultural Organization (FAO), Economic and Social Policy Department, *1989 Country Tables* (Rome: FAO, 1989), 216–17.

4. CADESCA/CEE, *Apoyo a la caracterización de los productores de granos básicos del istmo centroamericano: Panamá* (Panama: CADESCA, Octubre de 1987), 25.

5. *Censo nacional agropecuario,* 55.

6. Table 5.3 covers farms down to 0.5 hectares, but it omits those smaller even though data are available. We omitted the range 0 to 0.5 because the numbers for 1970 and 1980 seem inconsistent. For 1970, slightly over 20,000 farms smaller than 0.5 hectare were enumerated, and over 48,000 for 1980. Although it is possible that the number of microfarms increased by 140 percent, more likely the enumeration in 1970 was not complete. Figures also suggest inconsistencies in definition or enumeration: the number of farms in Panama province of less than 0.1 hectares increased from 3,682 in 1970 to 12,350 in 1980; even if this increase had occurred, these units were probably urban and semiurban garden plots, falling into a separate analytical category from rural minifundia. *Censo nacional agropecuario,* cuadro 5.

7. William Merrill, *An Analysis of the Agricultural Sector of Panama.* Prepared for the government of Panama (1973), 122.

8. FAO, *Informe de la misión interagencial sobre el seguimiento de la conferencia mundial sobre reforma agraria y desarrollo rural* (Panama: FAO, 1986), 36.

9. The price per hectare was six balboas for the first 20 hectares, fifteen balboas for the 21–50 range, thrity for the 51–100 range, and sixty for the

101–200 range, which marked the upper limit. Except in rare cases, the prices for the upper ranges were well below market value. FAO, *Informe de la misión,* 37.

10. World Bank, *Structural Change,* 58.

11. Land held by farms over 1,000 hectares increased from 12.6 percent of the total in 1950 to 16.3 percent in 1970. And although the size categories are arbitrary, it is still striking that the proportion for all ranges above 50 hectares increased, while for all ranges below 50 hectares the proportions declined and the number of farms increased.

12. The exceptions tended to be concentrated in the showcase *asentamientos* (producer or credit and service cooperatives) formed under the agrarian reform, particularly in sugar cane, where sustained income and property gains accrued to the poor rural population. By the end of 1972, only 5,323 families had been resettled on asentamientos; today, the number is much smaller as most asentamientos have broken up. A useful discussion of the early agrarian reform can be found in Stanley Heckaden, *Los asentamientos campesinos: una experiencia en reforma agraria* (Guatemala City: UNICEF, 1973); the sugar cooperatives are treated in Stephen Gudeman, *The Demise of a Rural Economy* (London: Routledge & Kegan Paul, 1978); other interesting studies are William Merrill et al., *Panama's Economic Development: The Role of Agriculture* (Ames: Iowa State University Press, 1975), Marco Gandásegui, *La fuerza de trabajo en el agro* (Panama: CELA, 1985), and Gian Singh Sahota, *Poverty Theory and Policy: A Study of Panama* (Baltimore: Johns Hopkins University Press, 1990).

13. Merrill et al., *Analysis of the Agricultural Sector,* 110.

14. The average size of farms over 500 hectares was also little changed over the decade: 1,471 hectares in 1970 and 1,387 in 1980.

15. "Large farms frequently are held for capital appreciation and use only a small proportion of their land for crop production, devoting most of their land to extensive livestock production." See Merrill et al., *Analysis of the Agricultural Sector,* 104–5.

16. FAO, *Informe sobre el Instituto de Investigación Agropecuria (IDAP) de Panamá* (Panama: FAO, n.d. [circa 1985]), 18, citing a 1982 Inter-American Development Bank report. See also CADESCA/CEE, *La caracterización de los productores,* 22–25.

17. Many large tracts are inefficiently farmed and would still make a sensible target for redistribution. Our point here, however, is that the amount of land represented by large estates is generally less in Panama than elsewhere in Latin America and that sufficient arable and idle land is available for colonization to provide an initial basis for agricultural development.

18. This was Keynes's point in *The General Theory:* except in the special case of full employment, relative prices are in part the result, not the cause,

of the allocation of resources. This point was further developed by Clower and Liejonhufvud at a level of theoretical generality that makes it equally valid for developed and underdeveloped economies. For a relatively nontechnical explanation, see John Weeks, *A Critique of Neoclassical Macroeconomics* (London: Macmillan, 1989), chap. 9.

19. Merrill et al., *Analysis of the Agricultural Sector*, 104–5. The argument that large farms use land inefficiently is also made in FAO, *Informe sobre el IDAP*, 18.

20. Large farmers use relative prices as a guide to the relative profitability of alternative crops, with the limitation that some farmers' output decisions may also affect relative prices and thereby mediate their response to a priori prices.

21. *Censo nacional agropecuario*, cuadro 19.

22. That is, to argue that the unequal distribution of land in Panama has not depressed wages because wage levels are higher in Panama than elsewhere in the region is to miss the theoretical point: whatever might the wage level be at any moment (determined by the action of market and nonmarket forces) it would be higher were the distribution of land more equal and peasant incomes correspondingly higher.

23. *Censo nacional agropecurario*, Table 43.

24. CADESCA/CEE, *La caracterización de los productores*.

25. The calculations in the table use the economically active agricultural labor force, so some inaccuracy is involved due to unemployment. This problem is probably rather small because most unemployment in Panama was urban during these years. The table also ignores any change in the degree of underemployment in agriculture.

26. Perhaps indirect evidence of the relative scarcity of labor in agriculture is indicated by the fact that workers on the banana estates did better in terms of real wages than private-sector employees as a whole. World Bank, *Structural Change*, 302.

27. "Factor and product prices are closely regulated, there is considerable intervention in marketing and the Government participates heavily in the provision of credit, the supply of inputs and machinery and in direct agricultural production." Ibid., 58.

28. This conclusion is reinforced when one considers that Panama's population growth rate was 3.3 percent per year during the 1960s and 2.8 percent during the 1970s. Although performance was relatively better in the 1970s, it scarcely kept up with population growth. Indeed, Panama was required to more than double its cereal imports during the 1970s.

29. With regard to corn, the bank was inaccurate in its assessment that "far from redistributing income to the rural poor, current pricing policy hence effectively subsidizes relatively efficient farms . . . [who] are likely to be relatively wealthy." World Bank, *Structural Change*, 63. As shown below,

one-third of marketed corn was grown on holdings of less than ten hectares in 1981. See MIDA, *El plan alimentario de emergencia* (Panama City: Government of Panama, 1989), chap. 2, for a detailed assessment of the price support program with respect to corn, which deals with production and sales by size of farm.

30. "Ceterius paribus, price controls can be justified only to mitigate the social effects of an actual or impending scarcity of a mass consumption good or when monopoly or oligopoly exist." World Bank, *Structural Change*, 82. Note the definitiveness of the statement.

31. Ibid., 81.

32. Keith Schneider, "The Farm Economy Is Fine and Can Expect More Aid," *New York Times*, February 4, 1990, sect. 4, p. 4.

33. MIDA, *El plan*, 2.

34. It is surprising that the composite index shows an increase over the period so much greater than for rice and corn because these two products account for a large proportion of the price-supported commodities in terms of total marketed value. The likely explanation for this pattern is that market prices for the other products rose more rapidly. This, in turn, could either have resulted from natural market forces or market control exerted by the producers.

35. World market prices for both commodities were quite unstable in the 1970s and 1980s with a declining trend. See FAO, *Production Yearbook, 1979* (Rome: FAO, 1979), 293, and *Production Yearbook, 1987* (Rome: FAO, 1987), 335.

36. Some of this may be accounted for by declines in farms somewhat larger than ten hectares.

37. In the case of artificially sustained prices, there is also the question of effective demand. That is, land use could fall because yields were rising more rapidly than demand was growing. It is unlikely, however, in this instance (i.e., rice and corn between 1960 and 1980) that effective demand was a binding constraint on land use since Panama's net cereal imports grew from 39,000 metric tons in 1965, to 44,000 in 1970, and to 108,000 in 1980.

38. In the Panamanian statistics this is referred to as *a chuzo*, literally "by stick." The term comes from the very primitive planting technique of making a hole in the ground with a pointed stick and dropping in the seed.

39. Evidence consistent with this assumption is found in the Merrill report, which for 1971–1972 gives rice yields per hectare for the 0.5–5 hectare range to be 20 quintals, and 51 quintals for farms greater than 50 hectares. Merrill et al., *Analysis of the Agricultural Sector*, 111.

40. This term from neoclassical economics, named after Italian economist Vilfredo Pareto, refers to an equilibrium allocation of resources from which it is impossible to make someone better off without making someone

else worse off. More generally, the term "pareto optimal" is often used to refer to a situation of perfect efficiency that maximizes society's welfare.

41. This variability is measured in a quite dubious manner in the report. The "degrees of incentives" are measured as the ratio of Panamanian producer prices to U.S. agricultural prices. Because the U.S. prices are also support prices, the ratios may reflect nothing more than the variation in "degrees of incentives" in the United States. World Bank, *Structural Change*, 61–62.

42. Ibid., 62.

43. Ibid., 58.

44. Hecksher and Olin were Swedish economists who wrote during the first half of this century. Their theory views each country as possessing certain "endowments" of land, labor, and capital. The ratio of each country's endowments determines the relative prices of the factors: if there is a lot of land compared to labor, for example, then land should be relatively cheap and labor relatively expensive. If land is cheap, then producers will be prompted to use a lot of it relative to labor. As a consequence, the average output per unit of land will be low, and the average output per unit of labor high.

45. "At the normal free market world prices, the Panamanian sugar industry would not be profitable." Merrill et al., *An Analysis of the Agricultural Sector*, 184. It should be pointed out, however, that less than 20 percent of world sugar trade is on the spot market. For a discussion of the world sugar market and its prospects, see A. Zimbalist and C. Brundenius, *The Cuban Economy: Measurement and Analysis of Socialist Performance* (Baltimore: Johns Hopkins University Press, 1989), chaps. 7 and 9.

46. The report concluded that commercially viable coffee production would be impossible for the smallholder and require massive investments for large-scale production. Merrill et al., *An Analysis of the Agricultural Sector*, 190.

47. World Bank, *Structural Change*, 77.

48. "Although grass fed beef production is where Panama's greatest comparative advantage lies in agriculture, misguided price and marketing policies have stunted growth for several decades." Ibid., 77.

49. There are other, more purely economic problems on the supply side. Most serious, successful beef exports require quite careful quality control, which is difficult to achieve with production based upon land-extensive grazing. Major investment would be required by both the state and the private sector to achieve this quality control both on ranches and in the slaughter houses.

50. There is some potential for growth in citrus fruit exports, but it is not likely to be substantial. In this quality-demanding market, Panama would be

competing against not only other Caribbean Basin economies but also against Brazil, Israel, and Spain. If considered part of agriculture, fish exports could be added to the promising category, but here too it is not clear how quantitatively important growth in fishing exports can become.

51. Merrill et al., *An Analysis of the Agricultural Sector,* 35.

52. Ibid., 36.

53. "Most of the marketing channels for the major food products are controlled at some point by a small number of firms. The oligopolistic structure of the marketing channels cannot be altered to any great extent without reducing the operational efficiency of the markets." Ibid., 259.

Chapter Six

1. There is a full discussion of the 1972 constitution and its 1978 amendments in chapter 4 of Richard Nyrop, ed., *Panama: A Country Study* (Washington, D.C.: USGPO, 1980).

2. Moreno, *Panamá: centro bancario internacional,* 102, 111.

3. Elizabeth Milne, "Panama Successfully Blends Program of Fiscal Adjustment with Strongly Revived Growth," *IMF Survey,* March 23, 1981, 84.

4. World Bank, *Structural Change,* 299. Details on this IMF standby can be found in *IMF Survey,* April 9, 1979.

5. Official figures on unemployment are not available for 1980 and 1981. The World Bank estimates an adjusted unemployment rate (based on labor force participation rates during 1963–1971) for 1982 at 17 percent; World Bank, *Strucutral Change,* 193.

6. For an interesting discussion of the characteristics of the poor in Panama, see Gian Singh Sahota, *Poverty Theory and Policy* (Baltimore: Johns Hopkins University Press, 1990).

7. A. Cordero et al., *Distribución del ingreso en Panamá* (Panama, 1980); and Roberto Pinnock and Charlotte Elton, "Rural Poverty in Panama: Trends and Structural Cases," World Employment Programme Research Working Paper, 10–6/WP 60 (Geneva: ILO, 1983), 32–33.

8. This well-known and widely accepted proposition was orignated by Ernst Engel, a nineteenth-century Prussian statistician (not to be confused with Karl Marx's collaborator Friedrich Engels).

9. As pointed out in chapter 3: Canal net tonnage (upon which payments to the government are made) peaked in 1982; the Colon Free Zone net exports also peaked in 1982 at $441 million and then fell precipitously to $194 million in 1984 and $122 million in 1987; assets in the international banking center peaked in 1982 at $49 billion, fell to $33 billion in 1984, and then to $14 billion in July 1988.

10. To be sure, aided by the buoyant service sector and the inauguration of the transisthmian oil pipeline in late 1982, the economic crisis for Panama came a year or two later for Panama than for the rest of Latin America. Whereas real GDP began to fall in Latin America as a whole in 1982, it did not fall in Panama until 1984. Nevertheless, growth was minimal from 1982 to 1984. Indeed, the World Bank estimates that in 1983 "without a very large increase in value added associated with the Transisthmian Oil Pipeline operation, real per capita GDP would have declined by 6.5 percent"; see World Bank, *Structural Change*, 4.

11. At the end of 1982, Panama's foreign debt as a share of its GDP was 72.2 percent, compared to 32.7 percent in Mexico, 25.9 percent in Argentina, and 25.1 percent in Brazil. See Wisecarver, *Failure of State Activism*, 8. The Panama figure uses only public debt. Because the dollar is used internally, the government does not typically guarantee private-sector debt as elsewhere in Latin America.

12. Dr. César Quintero, the head of the electoral tribunal, resigned due to fraud. Fraud was also denounced by the Panamanian Bishops' Conference and a team of international election observers. When the U.S. recognized Barletta, a dispute erupted within the U.S. embassy in Panama, resulting in the resignation of at least one senior officer. The evidence of electoral fraud in 1984 is detailed in Raul Arias de Para's *Asi fue el fraude* (Panama, 1984). See also Richard Millet, "Looking beyond Noriega," *Foreign Policy* 71 (Summer 1988), and Ricardo Arias Calderón, "Panama: Disaster or Democracy," *Foreign Affairs* 62, no. 2 (Winter 1987/88).

13. Senate *Hearings*, Part 2, 308.

14. The claim is usually made that Barletta submitted his resignation to the National Legislature. In fact, he submitted under duress a letter of separation (lasting for thirty days), but Noriega's henchmen in the legislature conducted a forced vote on a supposed resignation request by Barletta at a special 5 A.M. session. This version was related to us by Congressman Guillermo Cóchez and later corroborated by Barletta.

15. The other mill is owned by the long-standing oligarchic Chiari family. Of the twelve, preindependence families of the Panamanian oligarchy identified in the Gandásegui study (1976), the Chiari family was the only one whose wealth was based on landed enterprise. According to Roberto Méndez, editor of *Carta Económica*, the Chiari family was allied to Noriega up to his overthrow.

16. These figures are calculated from *Panamá en cifras, 1982–1986*, 188–211.

17. New international loans exceeded debt-service payments for Panama until 1984. The negative capital flow in 1984 equalled $72.4 million, in 1985 $301.6 million, in 1986 $93.7 million, in 1987 $346.1 million, and in

1988, after the U.S. sanctions and suspension of most payments, $4.3 million. CEPAL, *Panamá: la situación económica a principios de 1989,* LC/ MEX/L.98 (Mexico: CEPAL, March 1989), 49.

18. The IMF program was successful in one crucial area for debt repayment: with respect to the international payments, current account went from a negative $51 million in 1982, to a positive $416 million in 1983, and to a positive $302 million and $455 million in 1984 and 1985. *Panamá en cifras, 1982–1986,* 162–63.

19. This issue is treated in detail in Zimbalist, "Problems and Prospects."

20. In the jargon of merchant business, companies that operate ocean vessels are usually referred to as "steamship lines." "Shipping companies" is used generally to refer to overland operations, though here we use the term colloquially to refer to companies with ocean ships engaged in international commerce.

21. *IMF Survey,* July 29, 1985, 237.

22. World Bank, *Structural Change,* 88.

Chapter Seven

1. Although Noriega continued to play an intelligence role during the late 1970s, it appears that he was dropped from the CIA payroll in 1977 and then rehired in 1981. At the time he was dropped from the CIA payroll Noriega was actually being paid off by both the CIA and the U.S. Defense Intelligence Agency. Reportedly, while George Bush headed the CIA in 1976, Noriega's annual retainer with that agency was $110,000; he was rehired in 1981 at the rate of $185,000, with funds paid directly into his account in the Bank for Credit and Commerce International. See Frederick Kempe, "The Noriega Files," *Newsweek,* January 15, 1990, 19–28, and Kempe's *Divorcing the Dictator* (New York: G.P. Putnam & Sons, 1990). See also Dinges, *Our Man in Panama.*

2. For example, Larry Rohter writes, "there is strong evidence that the Panamanian military began dealing in drugs almost as soon as it seized power in 1968 and that the United States knew of that involvement much sooner than is supposed." *New York Times Magazine,* May 19, 1988, 26. Apparently John E. Ingersoll, director of the Bureau of Narcotics and Dangerous Drugs of the State Department under Richard Nixon, in 1986 told Seymour Hersh (then with the *New York Times*) that his agency had "hard information" in the early 1970s that Noriega was in the drug trade. See also Senate *Hearings;* Senate Subcommittee *Report,* and the discussion and references in chapter 4.

3. For example, Millet, "Looking beyond Noriega," 46–63, treats this issue not at all.

4. We shall not deal with this allegation in any detail. Cuba may or may not have obtained items of sophisticated and military-related technology through Panama; however, Panama did serve an important function in allowing Cuba to circumvent the U.S. trade blockade. Panama played a similar role for Nicaragua when trade sanctions were imposed on that country by the Reagan administration.

5. Many writers maintain that soon after the polling the United States had clear evidence that the 1984 election was less than honest. See Millet, "Looking beyond Noriega," and Arias Calderón, "Panama: Disaster or Democracy." Also see the discussions of the elections in chapter 6.

6. *Central American Report,* January 31, 1986.

7. *U.S. Congressional Record,* April 25, 1988, S4687. Also see Senate *Hearings* and Senate Subcommittee *Report.*

8. Kempe, "The Noriega Files," 22.

9. Nancy Cooper et al., "Drugs, Money and Death," *Newsweek,* February 15, 1988; reprinted in the *Congressional Record,* February 9, 1988, E219.

10. *Congressional Record,* February 26, 1988, S1583.

11. Cooper, "Drugs, Money and Death."

12. *Central Amrican Report,* April 27, 1987, and May 22, 1987.

13. *Central American Report,* June 6, 1987, and *Latin American Monitor,* June 1987.

14. Ricardo Arias Calderón, president of the Christian Democratic party, wrote in *Foreign Affairs,* "Ambassador Davis clearly related the future of the canal to democratizaion." See Arias Calderón, "Panama: Disaster or Democracy," 342.

15. Two articles in the *Miami Herald,* November 14 and 27, 1986, reported that the speech by Davis was part of a conscious U.S. campaign to link the transfer of the Canal to political changes within Panama.

16. Cf. John Weeks and Andrew Zimbalist, "The Failure of Intervention in Panama: Humiliation in the Backyard," *Third World Quarterly* 11, no. 1 (January 1989): 11.

17. As required by the Torrijos-Carter Treaties, the school was removed from Panama to the United States. The alumni of the School of the Americas include Anastascio Somoza, Argentina's dictator Videla, and, interestingly enough, Manuel Noriega. This institution has been scrutinized in a number of studies. For example, see Jenny Pearce, *Under the Eagle* (Nottingham: Russell Press, 1981).

18. "[E]ven the most dire possible event, closing of the Canal, doesn't seem to overly [sic!] worry too many people, including the US Navy." Article by John Walcott in the *Wall Street Journal,* March 24, 1988.

19. A useful survey of the Canal's importance written from a military perspective is found in John Major, "Wasting Asset: The U.S. Re-Assessment

of the Panama Canal, 1945–1979," *Journal of Strategic Studies* 3, no. 2 (September 1980): 123–46.

20. Ironically, these exercises coincided with the anniversary of the 1964 demonstration against U.S. occupation of the Canal Zone, during which twenty-one Panamanians were killed when U.S. soldiers opened fire.

21. See, for one, Brian Becker and E. Brown, "Shocking Revelations on Panama Invasion," *Guardian*, March 28, 1990.

22. See *This Week in Central America*, no. 26 (July 14, 1986), which summarizes reports that the Reagan administration considered but rejected plans to pressure Noriega out, for fear that he would be replaced by Díaz Herrera.

23. In his book, Díaz Herrera (1988) actually places the date as May 25, 1987. According to Díaz Herrera, he had been summoned to Noriega's headquarters in order to be dismissed, but he successfully manipulated the discussion to arrange for a (face-saving and tactically convenient) thirty-day vacation first and then a dismissal.

24. "Informed sources said U.S. contingency planning has begun for facilitating the departure of Noriega, including the question of where he might go into exile." *Washington Post*, July 23, 1987.

25. Millet, "Looking beyond Noriega," 52.

26. "Strong suspicions that the main motive for the Reagan administration's [attack on Noriega] . . . had to do with the Nicaraguan counterrevolutionaries have been fully confirmed by Alfonso Chardy of the Miami Herald." *Central American Report*, June 12, 1987, referring to an article in that newspaper of May 10, 1987, which had related the criticisms of Noriega to U.S. pressure on several Latin American countries to weaken the Contadora peace process.

27. See discussion in Guillermo Sánchez Bourbon, "Panama Fallen among Thieves," *Harper's* (December 1987).

28. *New York Times*, March 3, 1988.

29. *New York Times*, March 12, 1988; emphasis added. In the same vein and more specific, Charles Redman, State Department spokesman said, "We did not suggest the removal of other officers [than Noriega]." *New York Times*, March 22, 1988.

30. "It is odd to hear Administration officials sing the military's praises when it is layered with General Noriega's cronies who have shared in the profits from drug-trafficking and other criminal activities." *New York Times*, March 27, 1988.

31. The opposition leaders presented a list of high-ranking officers whose removal they saw as essential to reforming and depoliticizing the Defense Forces, but the Reagan administration refused to accept this demand as part of its negotiations with Noriega. *New York Times*, March 22, 1988.

32. *New York Times Magazine,* May 19, 1988.

33. Noriega became only the second foreign leader ever to be indicted in the United States (the first was Norman Saunders, the chief minister of Turks and Caicos Islands in March 1985, also on drug dealing). The indictment of Noriega was one of many events in the process of his removal that seems in retrospect particularly ill-advised and bumbling. Because Panama and the United States had no extradition treaty, the indictment had no practical impact as long as Noriega remained in Panama; however, the United States wanted him out of Panama. The indictment was a barrier to achieving this, for it prevented Noriega from seeking exile in a country with which the United States did have such a treaty. As hard as it is to believe, the *Boston Globe* reported that there had been little or no coordination between the Justice Department and the State Department on serving the indictment and that the foreign policy implications of the indictment had not been seriously considered. See *Boston Globe,* December 30, 1989.

34. The chronology of this period and the relation between the freeze on deposits and the bank run in Panama are treated in detail in chapter 4.

35. *Central American Report,* April 7, 1989. It is also true that an inquiry into the sanctions and the escrowed monies by the U.S. General Accounting Office found unexplained disbursements out of the sequestered accounts. See U.S. General Accounting Office, *GAO Review of Economic Sanctions Imposed against Panama,* Testimony of Frank C. Conahan, assistant comptroller for National Security and International Affairs (Washington: GAO, July 26, 1989), 11.

36. In 1987, 60 percent of Panama's commodity exports went to the United States, so the preferences covered just less than 20 percent of the total.

37. *Central American Update,* March 16, 1988.

38. A U.S. reporter interviewed a dock worker who said, "Any moment they come up with the money, I'll go back. . . . There's no politics here. Noriega is not the issue . . . it's feeding my kids. No pay, no work, simple as that." *New York Times,* March 16, 1988.

39. For one account of Mr. Abrams's bravado, see *New York Times,* March 28, 1988.

40. U.S. GAO, *Review of Economic Sanctions,* 7.

41. For an excellent, detailed account of the liquidity crisis, the gradual reopening of banks and the devising of alternative payment schemes, see Moreno, *Panamá: centro bancario internacional.*

42. *Central American Report,* July 8, 1988.

43. Excellent journalistic coverage of this aborted coup was provided by Carla Anne Robbins in *U.S. News and World Report.*

44. The effect of the sanctions on the banking center was discussed in chapter 4. The decline in deposits was precipitous during 1987–1988. In

July 1987, deposits stood at $40.8 billion (U.S.); they were $33.2 billion at the end of that year and $10.1 billion in September 1988. U.S. embassy in Panama, *Panama International Center Still in Business despite Traumatic Developments in 1988* (Panama: U.S. Embassy, n.d.), 5.

45. The sanctions also engendered a management crisis at the Canal, eventually leading to the resignation of the Reagan-appointed chairman of the board of directors, William Gianelli, in May 1989. Gianelli complained that complications from the sanctions were making it impossible to run the Canal efficiently. Briefly, nonpayment of payroll taxes of Panamanian employees to the Noriega government provoked Noriega, among other things, to prevent Canal employees from obtaining license plates. Unable to drive in their personal cars, the Canal Commission had to devise alternative ways to transport their employees to work, including emergency bus and taxi shuttle service on both sides of the isthmus, high-speed launches, emergency lodging, and rations. The direct cost to the Canal Commission of these emergency measures came to $3 million between March and September 1989. Panama Canal Commission, *A Decade of Progress in Canal Operations and Treaty Implementation* (Panama: Panama Canal Commission, 1989), 30, and authors' interview with William Gianelli, January 22, 1990. Separately, Gianelli commented on the effect of U.S. sanctions on the Canal: "Moreover, the operation of the Panama Canal has been placed in jeopardy. . . . A consequence of this economic warfare is that the morale of Commission employees is at an all-time low. The conviction is strong among them that they have been made pawns in the disputes between the two countries and they are beginning to blame the United States for placing them in such a helpless situation." Gianelli in *Panama: An Assessment*, ed. Victor Krulak, 11.

46. Robert White, former U.S. ambassador to El Salvador, estimated while on his trip to the country in late April, that half the labor force was without work. *Christian Science Monitor*, May 2, 1988.

47. *Central American Update*, June 10, 1988. The litany of miseries resulting from the U.S. sanctions goes on and on. According to Panamanian Minister of Agriculture Darisnel Espino, sanctions caused a loss of agricultural output of $300 million (U.S.). Luis Moreno estimated that $7 billion (U.S.) had moved out of the International Financial Center to the Cayman Islands and the Bahamas. Senator D'Amato stated that more than 25,000 middle-class Panamanians had fled to Costa Rica by mid-April. And the relief agency of the Roman Catholic Church, CARITAS, reported that the poor in Panama were growing desperately short of food.

48. The official figure is cited in the Inter-American Development Bank's *Economic and Social Progress in Latin America, 1989 Report* (Washington, D.C.: IDB, 1989), 463. Indesa, run by two economists who advise the Chris-

tian Democratic party, published its estimates in *Resultados del desempeño de la economía panameña en 1988,* January-February 1989.

49. Reported in GAO, *Review of Economic Sanctions,* 20.

50. The government of Spain apparently agreed to grant Noriega sanctuary. Press reports indicated that U.S. negotiators conceded him the liberty of taking all or considerable part of his personal fortune with him.

51. In their book ¿*Quienes son los dueños de Panamá?* (Panama: Ceaspa, 1987), WIlliam Hughes and Iván Quintero list seven companies on which Endara serves on the board of directors or management committee (p. 187). One such company, Banco Interoceánico, where Endara has served as secretary of the board of directors since 1972, was linked to money-laundering operations for the Colombian drug cartels by an article in the *New York Times,* February 6, 1990.

52. The economic and social programs of the two coalitions and their similarity are analyzed in detail in *Carta Económica* 2, no. 4 (March 1989). Neither coalition called for structural economic reform.

53. *Central American Report,* May 19, 1989.

54. The legitimacy of the Endara government is at best dubious. First and foremost, whether or not Endara was legitimately elected in May 1989, he came to power on the basis of a U.S. military action that violated both the U.N. Charter and the Canal Treaties. It is true that the Endara slate had nearly a three-to-one margin with roughly 80 percent of the votes counted in the May elections, but it is also true that this vote was more of a plebiscite against Noriega than it was a presidential election.

55. Michael Massing, "New Trouble in Panama," *New York Review of Books,* May 17, 1990, 47, reports that the unemployment rate in Colon hit 60 percent!

56. Although official U.S. estimates are not surprisingly lower than this, it is notable that some Panamanian sources cite up to 12,000 dead and 27,000 homeless. After some delay, the U.S. Southern Command announced a death count that included 23 U.S. soldiers, 314 members of the Panamanian Defense Forces, and 202 Panamanian civilians. However, on March 26, 1990, the U.S. Defense Department revised that distribution to 50 Panamanian soldiers without altering the total. This recount, hardly noticed in the U.S. press, suggested that the invasion had hardly been the "surgical" operation claimed by the Southern Command and certainly not limited to military targets. The highest published estimate for deaths we have seen is 5,000, based on sources at the University of Panama; see *Latinamerica Press,* January 18, 1990. Deaths of U.S. citizens apparently came to 27—a rather high price to pay for an invasion that purportedly was staged, like that in Grenada in 1983, to protect U.S. lives. James Ottley, Episcopal bishop of

Panama, attests to having seen 17 mass graves and estimates 3,000 dead, a figure also accepted by Bishop Ariz of Colon. Ramsey Clark's Independent Commission of Inquiry places 3,000 as the lower bound of possible deaths. See Larry Rohter, "Panama and U.S. Strive to Settle on Death Toll," *New York Times,* April 1, 1990, and Becker and Brown, "Shocking Revelations."

57. The initial losses will have a multiplier effect on economic activity as job loss and vacant buildings reduce labor income, rent, and tax revenues. For a detailed discussion of estimated losses and their multiplier effects, see the review of a survey by the Center for Economic Studies of Panama's Chamber of Commerce in *Carta Económica* (January 1989). Roberto Henríquez, director of Panama's Chamber of Commerce, put estimated losses from the invasion itself at $2.2 billion (*Latin America Weekly Report,* January 18, 1990, 1).

58. Massing, "New Trouble in Panama," 43.

Chapter Eight

1. For instance, between 1970 and 1985, of the twenty-five countries reported by the Inter-American Development Bank (IDB) in the hemisphere, Panama's growth record was surpassed by only five—Brazil, Costa Rica, Dominican Republic, Ecuador, and Mexico; see IDB, *Social and Economic Progress in Latin America,* 463.

2. One expert, for instance, characterized the relationship: "The oligarchy ruled at the pleasure of the U.S. authorities and relied on the might of the U.S. military to maintain the peace." Tom Barry, *Panama: A Country Guide* (Albuquerque: Inter-Hemispheric Education Resource Center, 1990), 8.

3. See, for instance, David Asman, "Panama's Hong Kong Vision," *Wall Street Journal,* February 15, 1990, A14, and *La Prensa,* January 11, 1990.

4. Krause writes: "Capital and entrepreneurs also came to Hong Kong from the West and Southeast Asia. . . . The many trading companies doing business in Hong Kong provided their manufacturers with easy access to export markets." Lawrence B. Krause, "Hong Kong and Singapore: Twins or Kissing Cousins," *Economic Development and Cultural Change* 36, no. 3 (April 1988): s49.

5. Ibid., s60.

6. Alice Amsden, *Asia's Next Giant* (New York: Oxford University Press, 1989). See also Paul W. Kuznets, "An East Asian Model of Economic Development: Japan, Taiwan and South Korea," *Economic Development and Cultural Change* 36, no. 3 (April 1988); Zimbalist and Brundenius, *Cuban Economy,* chap. 10; Peter Evans et al., eds., *Bringing the State Back In* (New York: Cambridge University Press, 1976).

7. Gustav Ranis, "Challenges and Opportunities Posed by Asia's Superexporters: Implications for Manufactured Exports from Latin America," in *Latin America's Economic Development: Institutionalist and Structuralist Perspectives*, ed. J. Dietz and J. Street (Boulder: Lynne Rienner Publishers, 1987).

8. Anne Krueger, *Growth, Distortions, and Patterns of Trade among Many Countries* (Princeton: Princeton University Press, 1977).

9. Naturally, as discussed in chapter 2, certain incentive distortions engendered by faulty policy, such as low or no protection for intermediate good production, will have to be eliminated. Again, simply because a certain set of government price interventions is misguided, it does not logically follow that all government interventions are undesirable. It is one thing to infer caution from difficult experience, and it is quite another to fall prey to teleological logic and ideology.

10. This assumes that the common practice of Noriega's government of granting monopoly import licenses will end under Endara.

11. For example, U.S. government subsidies to grain producers in the 1980s averaged $8.1 billion a year, considerably in excess of Panama's GDP. Schneider, "The Farm Economy," E4.

12. Whereas some modernization and mechanization has occurred on large farms, the same could be accomplished on medium or even smaller farms in the context of credit and service or production cooperatives. The generalization that land on large farms in Panama is inefficiently used still holds.

13. See Kempe, *Divorcing the Dictator*, or, for a more circumspect and analytical treatment, see Dinges, *Our Man in Panama*.

14. See, for instance, *Central American Report*, January 12, 1990, 1.

15. Becker and Brown, "Shocking Revelations."

16. Of course, in the case of the F-117A at least the intention was not realized, having missed its target by several hundred yards. The missed target was discovered by accident several weeks after the Pentagon had declared bull's eye accuracy in carrying out its mission. See ibid. and Michael Gordon, "Stealth Jet's First Mission Was Marred, Pentagon Says," *New York Times*, April 4, 1990.

17. One source claims the combined damage may run as high as $10 billion; see *Central American Report*, January 12, 1990, 2.

References

Amsden, Alice. *Asia's Next Giant.* New York: Oxford University Press, 1989.

Arias Calderón, Ricardo. "Panama: Disaster or Democracy." *Foreign Affairs* 62, no. 2 (Winter 1987/88): 328–47.

Arzobispo de Panamá. *Hacia una economía más humana: reflexiones cristianas para el desarrollo de Panamá con prioridad en los más pobres.* Panama: La Estrella de Panamá, 1985.

Asman, David. "Panama's Hong Kong Vision." *Wall Street Journal,* February 15, 1990.

Asociación de Usuarios. *F.O.B.: Zona Libre de Colón.* Panama City: Focus Publications, 1988.

Barletta, Nicolás. *Memoria.* Panama: Republic of Panama, 1976.

Barry, Tom. *Panama: A Country Guide.* Albuquerque: Inter-Hemispheric Education Resource Center, 1990.

Becker, Brian, and E. Brown. "Shocking Revelations on Panama Invasion." *Guardian,* March 28, 1990.

Black, Jan Knippers. "Historical Setting." In *Panama: A Country Study,* ed. Richard Nyrop, 1–50. Washington, D.C.: USGPO, 1981.

Bourbon, Guillermo Sánchez. "Panama Fallen among Thieves." *Harper's,* December 1987.

Brading, David. *Miners and Merchants in Bourbon Mexico, 1763–1810.* Cambridge: Cambridge University Press, 1971.

Bruton, Henry. "Import Substitution." Paper delivered to the Northeast Development Consortium Conference at Harvard University, April 29–30, 1988.

Bunau-Varilla, Phillipe. *Panama: The Creation, Destruction and Resurrection.* New York: Robert McBride, 1920.

CADESCA/CEE. *Apoyo a la caracterización de los productores de granos básicos del istmo centroamericano: Panamá.* Panama: CADESCA, 1987.

Cardoso, Ciro F. S. "Sobre los modos de producción coloniales de América." *Estudios Sociales Centroamericanos,* no. 10 (1975): 87–105.

Castillero, Ernesto. *Historia de Panamá.* Panama: Editora Renovación, 1986.

Castillo, Jorge. *Formación social panameña: un análisis económico del período 1850–1960.* Panama: Universidad de Panamá, n.d.

Castro, Guillermo. *Panamá: Recuentro y Perspectivas.* Panama: CELA, 1986.

CEPAL. *Anuario estadístico de américa latina y el caribe, 1985.* Santiago: United Nations, 1986.

————. *Notas sobre la evolución social del istmo centroamericano hasta 1980.* Mexico: CEPAL, 1982.

————. *Panamá: La situación económica a principios de 1989.* LC/MEX/L.98. Mexico: CEPAL, March 1989.

————. *Statistical Bulletin for Latin America* 9, nos. 1–2. New York: United Nations, 1972.

Comisión Bancaria Nacional. *Banking Law of Panama.* Panama City: Republic of Panama, 1986.

Congressional Research Service, Library of Congress. *A Chronology of Events relating to the Panama Canal.* Washington, D.C.: USGPO, 1977.

Conte-Porras, J. *El crédito, la banca y la moneda panameña.* Panama City: Banco Nacional de Panamá, 1983.

Cooper, Nancy, et al. "Drugs, Money and Death." *Newsweek,* February 15, 1988.

Cordero, Alejandro. "Crecimiento y agresión económica." *Tareas* 69 (May/August 1988).

Cordero, Alejandro, et al. *Distribución del ingreso en Panamá.* Panama, 1980.

Correa Vásquez, Virgilio. *Centelleo de la Industria Panameña.* Panama, 1986.

Cortez, Dorindo Jayán. *FFAA y poder político en Panamá.* Panama, 1986.

de Para, Raul Arias. *Así fue el fraude.* Panama, 1984.

de Córdoba, Jośe. "The Free Ride Has Ended for Noriega's Cronies." *Wall Street Journal,* March 6, 1990.

Dinges, John. *Our Man in Panama.* New York: Random House, 1990.

Dore, Elizabeth, and J. Gould. "El café en la historia de Nicaragua." In *El café en la historia de Centroamérica,* ed. Hector Pérez Brignoli and M. Samper K. San José: FLASCO, 1990.

Economic Commission for Latin America and the Caribbean (ELLA). *Economic Survey of Latin America and the Caribbean.* Various years.

────── . *Statistical Yearbook of Latin America and the Caribbean*. Santiago: United Nations, various years.

Elton, Charlotte. *Este país més a més*. Panama: CEASPA, 1988.

────── . "Studies of Alternatives to the Panama Canal." *Maritime Policy Management* 14, no. 4 (1987): 33–50.

Elton, Charlotte, et al. *El canal: desafío para los panameños*. Panama: CEASPA, 1987.

Evans, Peter, et al., eds. *Bringing the State Back In*. New York: Cambridge University Press, 1976.

Executive Intelligence Review. *White Paper on the Crisis in Panama*. Washington, D.C.: EIR News Service, 1987.

Food and Agriculture Organization (FAO), Economic and Social Policy Department. *Informe de la misión interagencial sobre el seguimiento de la conferencia mundial sobre reforma agraria y desarrollo rural*. Panama: FAO, 1986.

────── . *Informe sobre el Instituto de Investigación Agropecuaria (IDAP) de Panamá*. Panama: FAO, n.d. [circa 1985].

────── . *1989 Country Tables*. Rome: FAO, 1989.

────── . *Production Yearbook*. Rome: FAO, 1975, 1979, 1987.

────── . *World Crop and Livestock Statistics, 1948–85*. Rome: FAO, 1987.

────── . *World-wide Estimates and Projections of the Agricultural and Non-agricultural Population Segments, 1950–2025*. Rome: FAO, 1986.

Frías, Sergina Solano. "El oleoducto transístmico." *Diálogo Social* 135 (June 1981).

Gallardo, María Eugenia, and Jośe Roberto López. *Centroamérica en cifras: la crisis*. San Jośe: Facultad Latinoamericana de Ciencias Sociales (FLACSO), 1986.

Gandásegui, Marco. "La concentración del poder económico en Panamá." In *Panamá: dependencia y liberación*, ed. R. Soler, 99–184. Panama: Ediciones Tareas, 1986.

────── . *La fuerza del trabajo en el agro*. Panama: CELA, 1985.

────── . *Las empresas públicas en Panamá*. Panama: CELA, 1982.

Gianelli, William. "The Panama Canal and the Canal Zone: Status and Prospects." In *Panama: An Assessment*, ed. V. H. Krulak, 1–17. Washington, D.C.: United States Strategic Institute, 1990.

Gordon, Michael. "Stealth Jet's First Mission Was Marred, Pentagon Says." *New York Times*, April 4, 1990.

Greene, Graham. *Getting to Know the General*. New York: Simon & Schuster, 1985.

Grier, David, et al. *Competitive Routing: Minibridge and the Panama Canal*. Fort Belvoir, Va.: U.S. Army Corps of Engineers, Institute for Water Resources, 1988.

Griffin, Keith. *Underdevelopment in Spanish America.* Cambridge: M.I.T. Pess, 1971.

Gudeman, Stephen. *The Demise of a Rural Economy.* London: Routledge, 1988.

———. *Relationship, Residence and the Individual: A Rural Panamanian Community.* London: Routledge & Kegan Paul, 1976.

Gudmundson, Lowell. *Costa Rica before Coffee.* Baton Rouge: Louisiana State University Press, 1986.

Harbon, John. "Yankee Dollars Wanted: The Canal Aside, Panama Welcomes American Investment." *Barron's* 58 (July 31, 1978).

Heckaden, Stanley. *Los asentamientos campesinos: una experiencia en reforma agraria.* Guatemala City: UNICEF, 1973.

Hirschman, Albert. "The Political Economy of Import Substitution." *Quarterly Journal of Economics* 82 (1968): 112–32.

Hogan, Michael. *The Panama Canal in American Politics.* Carbondale: Southern Illinois University Press, 1986.

Hughes, William, and Iván Quintero. *¿Quienes son los dueños de Panamá?* Panama: CEASPA, 1987.

Indesa. *Resultados del desempeño de la economía panameña en 1988.* January/February 1989.

Intenational Labour Office. *Year Book of Labour Statistics.* Geneva, various years.

Inter-American Committee on the Alliance for Progress. "Creation of a National Monetary System in Panama." Document prepared by the Secretariat (OEA/Ser.H/XIV/CIAP/31). Washington, D.C., September 1966.

Inter-American Development Bank. *Social and Economic Progress in Latin America.* Washington, D.C.: IDB, 1989.

International Monetary Fund. *Balance of Payments Yearbook.* Various years.

International Research Associates. *The Economic Value of the Panama Canal.* Palo Alto, 1973.

Johnson, Harry. "Panama as a Regional Financial Center: A Preliminary Analysis of Development Contribution." *Economic Development and Cultural Change* 24, no. 2 (January 1976): 261–86.

Jones, Kenneth, ed. *Panamá hoy.* Panama City: Focus Publications, 1986.

Kempe, Frederick. *Divorcing the Dictator.* New York: G. P. Putnam & Sons, 1990.

———. "The Noriega Files." *Newsweek,* January 15, 1990.

———. "Ties That Blind." *Wall Street Journal,* October 18, 1989.

Krause, Lawrence B. "Hong Kong and Singapore: Twins or Kissing Cousins." *Economic Development and Cultural Change* 36, no. 3 (April 1988): 545–66.

Krueger, Anne. *Growth, Distortions, and Patterns of Trade among Many Countries.* Princeton: Princeton University Press, 1977.

Krulak, Victor. *Panama: An Assessment.* Washington, D.C.: United States Strategic Institute, 1990.

Kuznets, Paul W. "An East Asian Model of Economic Development: Japan, Taiwan and South Korea." *Economic Development and Cultural Change* 36, no. 3 (April 1988): s11–43.

LaFeber, Walter. *The Panama Canal: The Crisis in Historical Perspective.* New York: Oxford University Press, 1989.

Looney, Robert. *The Economic Development of Panama.* New York: Praeger, 1976.

Major, John. "Wasting Asset: The U.S. Re-Assessment of the Panama Canal, 1945–1979. *Journal of Strategic Studies* 3, no. 2 (September 1980): 123–46.

Manalytics. *Forecasts of Panama Canal Commodity Traffic, Vessel Transits, and Revenue, 1985–2010.* Report to the Panama Canal Commission. San Francisco: Manalytics, 1985.

Martínez, Milton. "Economía y formas de dominación en Panamá." *Revista Económica,* no. 5 (1987): 28–60.

Massing, Michael. "New Trouble in Panama." *New York Review of Books,* May 17, 1990.

Méndez, Roberto. "Ajuste estructural." Unpublished manuscript.

———. "Los 'beneficios' de los tratados Torrijos-Carter." *Diálogo Social* 132 (March 1981).

Merrill, William, et al. *An Analysis of the Agricultural Sector of Panama.* Prepared for the government of Panama, 1973.

———. *Panama's Economic Development: The Role of Agriculture.* Ames: Iowa State University Press, 1975.

Millet, Richard. "Looking beyond Noriega." *Foreign Policy* 71 (Summer 1988): 46–63.

Milne, Elizabeth. "Panama Successfully Blends Program of Fiscal Adjustment with Strongly Received Growth." *IMF Survey,* March 23, 1981, 82–86.

Ministerio de Agricutura (MIDA). *El plan alimentario de emergencia.* Panama City: Government of Panama, 1989.

———. *Resumen anual de la situación agropecuaria.* Panama City: Government of Panama, 1988.

Ministerio de Planificación y Política Económica. *El desarrollo nacional y la recuperación de la zona del canal de Panamá.* Panama: República de Panamá, June 1978.

———. *Estrategia para el desarrollo nacional, 1970–1980.* Panama: República de Panamá, June 1978.

——— . *Informe Económico*. Panama, various years.

Moreno, Luis. *Panamá: centro bancario internacional*. Panama City: Asociación Bancaria de Panamá, 1988.

NACLA. *Panama: For Whom the Canal Tolls* 12, no. 5 (September/October 1979).

——— . *Panama: Reagan's Last Stand* 22, no. 4 (July/August 1988).

Nyrop, Richard, ed. *Panama: A Country Study*. Washington, D.C.: USGPO, 1980.

Organización de las Naciones Unidas para la Agricultura y la Alimentación. *Informe sobre el Instituto de Investigación Agropecuaria (IDAP) de Panamá*. Rome: FAO, n.d.

Panama Canal Commission. *Annual Report*. Washington, D.C.: USGPO, 1988.

——— . *A Decade of Progress in Canal Operations and Treaty Implementation*. Panama: Panama Canal Commission, 1989.

Panama Canal Company. *Annual Report*. Washington, D.C.: USGPO, various years.

Panamá en cifras. Panama: Contraloría de la República, various years.

Panzer, John. *La evolución del sector industrial panameño y su relación con la protección*. Panama: Ministerio de Planificación y Política Económica, 1985.

Paus, Eva, ed. *Struggle against Dependence: Nontraditional Export Growth in Central America and the Caribbean*. Boulder: Westview Press, 1988.

Pearce, Jenny. *Under the Eagle*. Nottingham, U.K.: Russell Press, 1981.

Pérez Brignoli, Hector. *A Brief History of Central America*. Berkeley and Los Angeles: University of California Press, 1989.

Pinnock, Roberto, and Charlotte Elton. "Rural Poverty in Panama: Trends and Structural Cases." World Employment Programme Research Working Paper, 10–6/WP 60. Geneva: ILO, September 1983.

Pou, Pedro. *Empleo, inversión y crecimiento en Panamá durante la década de los sesenta*. Panama: Ministerio de Planificación y Política Económica, 1985.

Programa Regional del Empleo para América Latina y el Caribe (PREALC). *Panamá: el patrón de desarrollo industrial, 1960–1975*. Santiago: Organización Internacional del Trabajo, 1984.

——— . *Panamá: Evolución y estructura de los salarios*. Santiago: Organización Internacional del Trabajo, 1985.

——— . *Panamá: Segmentación del mercado de trabajo*. Santiago: Organización Internacional del Trabajo, 1982.

Ranis, Gustav. "Challenges and Opportunities Posed by Asia's Superexporters: Implications for Manufactured Exports from Latin America." In

Latin America's Economic Development: Institutionalist and Structuralist Perspectives, ed. J. Dietz and J. Street, 128–46. Boulder: Lynne Rienner Publishers, 1987.

República de Panamá, Dirección de Estadística y Censo. *Censos nacionales de 1980, cuarto censo nacional agropecuario, volúmen IV, compendio general.* Panamá: Contraloría General de la República, 1981.

—————. *Estadística panameña, situación económica, hoja de balance de alimentos; años 1984–1985.* Panama: Contraloría General de la República, 1988.

Ricord, Humberto, et al. *Panamá y la frutera.* Panama: Editorial Universitaria, 1974.

Robbins, Carla Anne. "General Noriega's Freeze-Frame Fall." *U.S. News and World Report,* April 25, 1988.

—————. "Waiting for the Next Coup to Topple Noriega." *U.S. News and World Report,* March 28, 1988.

Rohter, Larry. "America's Blind Eye: The U.S. for Years Has Ignored Corruption in Panama." *New York Times Magazine,* May 29, 1988.

—————. "Panama and U.S. Strive to Settle on Death Toll." *New York Times,* April 1, 1990.

—————. "Trafficking in People: Was It One More Racket?" *New York Times,* April 10, 1990.

Ropp, Steve C. "Military Retrenchment and Decay in Panama." *Current History* 89, no. 543 (January 1990): 7–20.

—————. *Panamanian Politics: From Guarded Nation to National Guard.* Stanford: Hoover Institution Press, 1982.

Ryan, Paul B. *The Panama Canal Controversy.* Stanford: Hoover Institution Press, 1977.

Sahota, Gian Singh. *Poverty Theory and Policy: A Study of Panama.* Baltimore: John Hopkins University Press, 1990.

Schneider, Keith. "The Farm Economy Is Fine and Can Expect More Aid." *New York Times,* February 4, 1990.

Sepulveda, Melida Ruth. *Harmodio Arias Madrid: el hombre, el estadista y el periodista.* Panama: Editorial Universitaria, 1983.

Secretaría de Integración Económica de Centroamérica (SIECA). *Compendio estadístico centroamericano.* Guatemala: SIECA, 1981.

SOFRERAIL. *Panama Railway: Condition, Prospects and Transition Issues.* Panama: Repúblic of Panamá, 1979.

Soler, Ricaurte. *Formas ideológicas de la nación panameña.* Panama: Ediciones Tareas, 1985.

—————. "La independencia de Panamá de Colombia." In *Panamá: dependencia y liberación,* 9–30. Panama: Ediciones Tareas, 1986.

———. *Panamá: nación y oligarquiá.* Panama: Ediciones Tareas, 1987.

Suárez, Omar Jaen. *La población del istmo de Panamá del siglo XVI al siglo XX.* Panama: Impresora de la Nación, 1978.

TBS (Temple, Barker & Sloane). *A Review of the Manalytics Forecasts of Panama Canal Commodity Traffic, Vessel Transits, and Revenue, 1985–2010.* Panama: Panama Canal Commission, 1985.

———. *A Sensitivity Analysis of Panama Canal Trade, 1984–2010.* Panama: Panama Canal Commission, 1986.

Torrijos, Omar. *Ideario.* San Jośe: Editorial Universitaria Centroamericana, 1982.

Trudeau, Garry. "A Philatelist's Panama." *New York Times,* May 4, 1990.

U.S. Embassy in Panama. *Panama International Center Still in Business despite Traumatic Developments in 1988.* Panama: U.S. Embassy, n.d.

U.S. General Accounting Office. *GAO Review of Economic Sanctions Imposed against Panama.* Testimony of Frank C. Conahan, assistant comptroller for National Security and International Affairs. Washington, D.C.: GAO, 1989.

U.S. Congress. Senate. Committee on Foreign Relations. *Hearings Before the Subcommittee on Terrorism, Narcotics and International Communications.* 100th Cong. 2nd sess., 1988, pts. 2 and 3.

———. Subcommittee on Terrorism, Narcotics and International Operations. *Report of Drugs, Law Enforcement and Foreign Policy.* Washington, D.C.: USGPO, 1989.

Vilma Médica. *La población de Panamá.* Panama: Contraloría General, 1974.

Walcott, John. "Reagan Sets Summit Meeting in Moscow as Officials Fail to Resolve Difficulties." *Wall Street Journal,* March 24, 1988.

Wainio, Richard. Speech given to the American Chamber of Commerce, Panama City, August 16, 1988.

Wali, Alaka. *Kilowatts and Crisis: Hydroelectric Power and Social Dislocation in Eastern Panama.* Boulder: Westview Press, 1989.

Walter, Ingo. *Secret Money: The Shadowy World of Tax Evasion, Capital Flight and Fraud.* London: George Allen & Unwin, 1986.

Weeks, John. *A Critique of Neoclassical Macroeconomics.* London: Macmillan, 1989.

———. "Panama: The Roots of Current Political Instability." *Third World Quarterly* 9, no. 3 (1986).

Weeks, John, and Andrew Zimbalist. "The Failure of Intervention in Panama: Humiliation in the Backyard." *Third World Quarterly* 11, no. 1 (1989): 1–27.

Wells, Allen. "The Terrible Green Monster: Recent Literature on Sugar, Coffee and Coerced Labor in the Caribbean." *Latin American Research Review* 23, no. 2 (1988): 189–206.

Williams, Robert. *Export Agriculture and the Crisis in Central America.* Chapel Hill: University of North Carolina Press, 1986.

Wisecarver, Daniel. *Panama: The Failure of State Activism.* San Francisco: International Center for Economic Growth, 1987.

World Bank. *Panama: Structural Change and Growth Prospects.* Washington, D.C.: World Bank, 1985.

———. *World Development Report.* New York: Oxford University Press, 1989.

Yau, Julio. *El Canal de Panamá.* Madrid: Editorial Mediterráneo, 1972.

Zimbalist, Andrew. "Problems and Prospects of Export Diversification: The Case of Panama." In *Struggle against Dependence: Nontraditional Export Growth in Central America and the Caribbean,* ed. Eva Paus. Boulder: Westview Press, 1988.

Zimbalist, Andrew, and C. Brundenius. *The Cuban Economy: Measurement and Analysis of Socialist Performance.* Baltimore: John Hopkins University Press, 1989.

Index

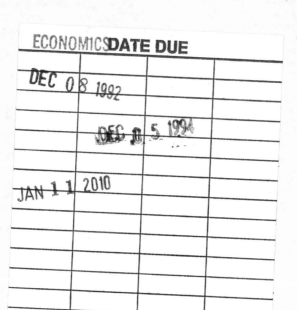

Compositor: BookMasters, Inc.
Text: 10.5/13 Sabon
Display: Sabon
Printer: Edwards Bros.
Binder: Edwards Bros.

BM